After the Revolution

After the Revolution

Twenty Years
of Portuguese Literature,
1974–1994

Edited by
Helena Kaufman
and Anna Klobucka

Lewisburg
Bucknell University Press
London: Associated University Presses

Associated University Presses
440 Forsgate Drive
Cranbury, N.J. 08512

Associated University Presses
16 Barter Street
London WC1A 2AH, England

Associated University Presses
P.O. Box 338, Port Credit
Mississauga, Ontario
Canada L5G 4L8

The paper used in this publication meets the requirements of the American National Standard for Permanence of Paper for Printed Library Materials Z39.48–1984.

Library of Congress Cataloging-in-Publication Data

After the Revolution : twenty years of Portuguese literature,
    1974–1994 / edited by Helena Kaufman and Anna Klobucka.
        p.   cm.
    Includes bibliographical references and index.
    ISBN 0-8387-5336-1 (alk. paper)
    1. Portuguese literature—20th century—History and criticism.
I. Kaufman, Helena, 1962– . II. Klobucka, Anna, 1961– .
PQ9054.A38   1997
869.09'0042—dc21   96-46875
                                                                              CIP

PRINTED IN THE UNITED STATES OF AMERICA

Contents

6 CONTENTS

Acknowledgments

Books such as this one have a surprising tendency to turn from an overwhelming and rather frustrating task into a rich and rewarding enterprise. This transition is due, for the most part, to the experience of working and sharing ideas as well as a vision of the final project with a number of wonderful people. We would like to preface this study by acknowledging various contributions that were so generously presented to us during the course of our work.

Special thanks go to the volume's contributing authors, who dedicated their time and skill to write essays solicited by two unknown assistant professors at the starting points of their careers. We would like to express our gratitude to all the institutions and people, in the United States and in Portugal, who supported this project. First and foremost, we thank the Department of Spanish and Portuguese at the Ohio State University and its former chair, Stephen Summerhill. We also thank the Tinker Foundation, which provided financial support that aided greatly in the writing of our introductory essay. We thank all those interviewed: Lídia Jorge, Ana Vicente, Joana Varela, Francisco Belard, and Maria Isabel Barreno. We would also like to express our gratitude to the editors, research assistants, and work-study students: Kevin Kaufman, Müge Galin, Hanna Götz, Elsa Reverendo, and Rachel Haring. We hope that this book will mean as much to all of you as it does to us. We gratefully acknowledge the permissions to use materials published by Contexto, Presença, Assírio e Alvim, Caminho, and Sociedade Portuguesa de Autores.

After the Revolution

1
Introduction

Politics and Culture in
Postrevolutionary Portugal

HELENA KAUFMAN and
ANNA KLOBUCKA

Looking at the last twenty years of Portuguese history, one can define three periods along socioeconomic, cultural, and intellectual lines. The late 1970s, the years immediately following the revolution of 25 April 1974, can be characterized as a period of adjustment in which there was an emotionally charged, difficult journey toward a democratic society. The second period, which roughly corresponds to the 1980s, has been defined economically and politically by the preparation for and then actual joining of the European Community. In cultural terms, it was the time of active reassessment of revolutionary victories and losses as well as an attempt to define and interpret the "new," post-1974 Portugal. The 1990s, still in progress and therefore lacking a definitive closure, have brought a mixture of political stability (the first five years) and political change in the form of the most recent parliamentary and presidential elections in which the Portuguese Social Democrats were defeated.

The catalyst for the events on 25 April 1974 was a deep frustration in the military with the prolonged colonial war. However, the need for political and social reform was so widely felt throughout Portuguese society that when the Movimento das Forças Armadas (Movement of Armed Forces, or MFA) staged a coup, it received the overwhelming support of the general population, leading to a bloodless, pacific overthrow of the regime. The "revolution"—understood as the aftermath of the coup—was a lingering and, at times, tortuous political process that extended over the next six years, precisely when the new social order was to be determined.

13

The Late 1970s

The late 1970s were profoundly marked by political struggle between radical elements within the military MFA that were ideologically influenced by the Portuguese Communist Party (PCP). The late seventies were also radicalized by former soldiers returning from service in Africa, and by the more moderate, traditionally liberal forces representing a relatively wide spectrum of political parties, among which the most influential were the Portuguese Socialist Party (PSP) and the Portuguese Social Democrats (PSD). The first provisory government, formed by General António de Spínola with Adelino da Palma Carlos as prime minister, survived only until July 1974, and the general himself was forced to resign in September. After a failed coup attempt organized by Spínola in March 1975 with the support of some conservative military officers, the government, headed by the prime minister Vasco Gonçalves and the new president, Costa Gomes, took a turn toward a left-wing authoritarian rule, threatening the transformation of Portugal into a "socialist democracy" modeled on Eastern European regimes. These political developments signaled significant economic changes to come: the nationalization of banks, breweries (including the famous Sagres brewery), and the steel, cement, and shipbuilding industries, as well as the implementation of a cooperative system in agriculture. Scared by this unstable political situation and the sudden radicalization of the revolution, foreign capital withdrew its investments, causing a big drop in economic growth. Loss of the African markets and their cheap raw materials, coupled with the return of many Portuguese from the former colonies *(os retornados),*[1] completed the picture of economic troubles. Nevertheless, the leftist government remained bound to the schedule of national elections established in the immediate wake of 25 April—only to be resoundingly defeated by the Socialists and Social Democrats who jointly received almost 70 percent of the vote in the April 1975 electoral contest.

Prime Minister Vasco Gonçalves resigned in August and the new government of Admiral Pinheiro de Azevedo changed yet again the course of national politics. The radical Left within the military made a coup attempt to control the situation but was defeated by moderate forces in November 1975. In the parliamentary elections of April 1976, the Socialists won a clear majority and Mário Soares formed a new government in July of the same year. Following the presidential elections in June, Ramalho Eanes became president. It is important to observe, however, that even though the leftist forces did not receive enough popular support to establish a postrevolutionary regime, they strongly influenced the shape of the new constitution of 1976. An eighteen-member Council of the Revolution was formed to protect one of the most important articles of the constitution concerning Portugal's commitment to socialism and to safeguard the nationalization processes.[2]

The year 1976 marked the end of the very intense period of political struggle that followed the coup of 1974. In the words of the writer Lídia Jorge, that struggle "replaced the blood which was absent" in the overthrow of the dictatorship.[3] And this was followed by more political instability, caused now in part by the difficulties of forming a coalition among the moderate-liberal parties. The Socialist government of Mário Soares fell in December 1977 and was followed by a Social-Center Democratic coalition (until July 1978), a centrist minority government of Carlos Alberto de Mota Pinto (until January 1979), and finally, until the elections of December 1979, a cabinet led by an independent, Maria de Lourdes Pintasilgo.

In the 1970s political and social reality engulfed other aspects of cultural life, allowing neither critical distance nor intellectual detachment. The literary production of the period is assessed in terms of "silence," maintained by some authors despite the abolition of censorship, or as *a escrita da revolução* (writing about the revolution), borrowing Eduardo Lourenço's term (1984, 7–17). What characterized this type of writing was its conscious response to the urgency of the moment and its untroubled attitude toward how the period's literary legacy would be judged in time. Writers marched, organized, debated, and traveled abroad as the cultural spokesmen and women of the revolution: there seemed to be little time left for writing, or at least writing that would not betray the shape of a political speech hastily set in verse. One of the surprises of that period was that very few manuscripts emerged from the proverbial "desk drawers" that were supposed to shelter unpublished masterpieces unacceptable to the former regime. Nevertheless, publishing flourished: in 1975, there were in Portugal no fewer than 1337 independent publishers (Dionísio 1993, 481), a truly astonishing figure for a country of ten million people. A singular insight into the intellectual climate of the period is provided by a look at bestseller lists from 1974 and '75, when sociology and political science greatly outsold literature—with one significant exception: that of erotic and pornographic fiction. *Das Kapital* remained the most consistently best-selling book, along with various works by Lenin, Engels, Portugal's own Álvaro Cunhal, and leaders of liberation movements in former African colonies, such as Angola's Luandino Vieira, Cape Verde's Amílcar Cabral, and Mozambique's Samora Machel. One (borderline) literary work that made the best-seller lists for a couple of weeks was the feminist manifesto collectively authored by "the three Marias," the *Novas Cartas Portuguesas*, first published two years earlier only to be confiscated by the censors. It was not the only best-selling book dealing with the rights of women—the remaining ones, however, were well-seasoned takes on the subject by Marxist-Leninist masters: Lenin's *Emancipation of Women* and *Party Work Among Women*, and Samora Machel's *Liberation of Women* (Dionísio 1993, 501–9).

    This extreme politicization of best-seller lists was closely mirrored by what was happening at the same time in culture at large. One of the most visibly and dynamically present art forms was mural paintings, whether spontaneously executed as a highly developed form of political graffiti or undertaken by artist collectives, such as the huge Belém mural publicly painted by forty-eight artists during the celebrations of Portugal's first national holiday following the coup. The other dominant art form was large-scale musical performances in the genre called in Portuguese revolutionary lingo *música de intervenção*—politically charged folk song, often following very closely on the heels of current events. The new regime's preoccupation with making cultural activity widely accessible to "the people" in a manner as democratic and, at the same time, as spectacular as possible was satisfied by promoting large gatherings that assumed the appearance of political rallies as much as concerts, where singers of all sorts and kinds, both recognized and unknown, some never before identified with the genre, followed one another on stage in a sort of musical parade largely unconcerned with individual recognition and compensation (or, for that matter, with the overall consistency and quality of the show). To quote some more of that time's privileged public discourse, such events were supposed to allow their protagonists—which meant both performers and audiences—to "celebrate freedom," "solidify the collective," and "generate energies" for further struggle (168).

    Political commitment, collective participation and immediacy of impact may thus be considered defining features of Portuguese cultural life during the early revolutionary period. The seventies should still be viewed, regardless of the political turmoil, as a time when the leftist ideals of a new civil society, shared by a majority of those who made the revolution, were very much alive. The vision of popular participation in every aspect of public life—from politics to culture—was still uncorrupted by the frustrating confrontation with practical reality. A serious debate and assessment of the period would take place only in the 1980s, one decade after the overthrow of the Salazar-Caetano regime.

The 1980s

That second period, the 1980s, began with a half decade of parliamentary politics dominated by two coalitions: the center-right Aliança Democrática (Democratic Alliance), which defeated the Socialists in 1979 and established the government of António Sá Carneiro,[4] and a central block formed by the PSD and the Socialist parties. The central block won the elections in April 1983 and its government, led by Carlos Alberto da Mota Pinto, survived until 1985. Because of internal disputes, Mota Pinto resigned and left Mário Soares with the function of caretaker until the new parliamentary elections in October of that year.

In spite of the continuing political instability, the first five years of the 1980s are considered a time of painful yet long awaited economic reforms. In fact, Portugal experienced a miniboom, with the economy growing 3 percent between the years 1980 and 1982.[5] By then, Portugal was getting ready for the membership in the European Economic Community (EEC)— which it was scheduled to join, along with Spain, on 1 January 1986—and striving to meet goals established by the International Monetary Fund (IMF). In 1982, in a crucial revision to the constitution, all references to Socialism, especially those regarding the means of production, were removed from the document, thus paving the way for large-scale free-market reforms. Even though there were still formal indicators of the crisis—in both economic and social terms—they were in fact, as Boaventura de Sousa Santos points out, moderated by compensatory mechanisms operating within the social structure, such as small-holding agriculture, an underground economy, and the state's practice of neutralizing its own policies through unofficial channels (Maxwell 1986, 167–97).

Intellectually and culturally, these five years were a crucial first attempt at a comprehensive interpretation and assessment of, and a response to, the post-Salazarian, postrevolutionary Portugal. The tenth anniversary of the revolution certainly precipitated the appearance of publications concerning the topic. Two representative examples are the February 1986 edition of *Revista Crítica de Ciências Sociais* and the series of articles about literature in the March 1984 edition of *Colóquio/Letras*, both of which provide a good summary of the debate's main points.

Before 1974, intellectuals—writers, academics, artists—formed a group that had been, to one degree or another, actively opposed to the dictatorship. Some had been exiled, some jailed, and others been part of the political and cultural underground. They therefore had an important role to play in the revolutionary changes that took place afterward. They shared with leftist politicians the image of the revolution as an event brought about by and for the people (o povo). And it is precisely that aspect of the revolutionary ideological heritage that, placed at the core of the debate in the 1980s, generated most of the disappointment and bitterness.

It is problematic whether popular participation in governance would have been significant had the radical military retained power in 1975. The fact remains that the only politician to make populist appeals to grassroot organizations was Sá Carneiro, whose government was short-lived. Tom Gallagher interprets the failure to fulfill the revolutionary promise in the exercise of power as a result of "oligarchical features ingrained in the [Portuguese] political culture" (1985, 207). Another failure was the failure to decentralize the political system in order to shrink the gap separating Lisbon from the provinces, a gap plaguing Portuguese political, economic, and cultural life since the nineteenth century. Recognition of this fiasco can be clearly heard in Lídia Jorge's regional novel, O Dia dos Prodígios (1980), in the dialogue between the soldiers of the revolution and the people of the Algarve, Portugal's southern province: "Oh friends. It was the hour of the oppressed and humiliated. 'And who are they?' asked Manuel Gertrudes. 'Who are they?' The soldier's heart swelled with pride. 'You. You. It is you'" (1989, 154).

The question of culture seems even more complex. It requires a discussion of such concrete manifestations of cultural politics as the educational system and, at the same time, a more subjective and abstract assessment of popular participation in what we call "art." Moreover, culture in all its various embodiments, constitutes an expression of the dominant ideology. What seems to have happened in Portugal, at the outset of the 1980s, was the realization that culture, which was then in the hands of politicians and intellectuals who defeated the dictatorship, did not express the ideals originated by the revolutionary change of 1974. The simple fact that culture was in the hands of these traditional agents of cultural politics indicates that, for once, change could not be radical and totally break down more traditional prerevolutionary structures. Portuguese society was about to favor, as A. Sousa Ribeiro affirms, "an institutional and instrumental vision of culture" (1986, 14).

The institutionalization of cultural politics as such should not be viewed only in negative terms. In fact, it allowed for many cultural developments that helped in turn to create conditions vital to the existence of a new civil society. Among these developments should be mentioned the establishment of the Ministério da Cultura (Ministry of Culture), which evolved from the MFA's revolutionary Acção Cultural (Cultural Action). The latter transformed itself into the Secretaria do Estado da Cultura (Secretary of

State for Culture). Another development was the foundation of the Instituto do Livro (Book Institute) to regulate editorial politics in the 1980s. The debates of the time did not refer directly to the activities and raison d'être of these institutions, but did address the fact that the people *(o povo)* remained in the position of object and not subject of culture.[6]

This same inability to transform mechanisms at the very base of the sociocultural structure is reflected, according to some intellectuals (Pedro 1986, 41–56), by the attempt to reform the educational system. The ideological core of the intended reform paralleled that proposed for culture in general: the elimination of social discrimination based on the separation between intellectual and manual labor. However, a number of measures taken to achieve that goal failed, as Emília Pedro proves in her analysis, because "contradictions between theoretical and practical discourse [as well as] the goals made explicit by the new ideology were, from the beginning, in education and other domains of social, political and economic life, passively blocked by the silenced ideology which, gradually and stubbornly, kept putting things 'in its place'" (49).

It is probably clear by now that when the 1980s began, there was a rather disenchanted mix of opinions, voiced by intellectuals. Based on the honest analysis of different social realities, they were concerned mostly with the unfulfilled promise for revolutionary change. Contrary to the pessimistic tone of their remarks, the literary production of the period is generally regarded with well-deserved enthusiasm. Freedom of expression, artistic experimentation, change, plurality of discourses, all found ample expression in the literature of the period.

What made the 1980s so dramatically different from the 1970s was the realization that, as Lídia Jorge observes, "a literature committed to history and to politics [was possible] but without renouncing the poetic formulation of the narrative." Describing that literature, she further remarks: "[I]t was something like a transfiguration . . . of the reality; the reality is present with all its fundamentals but the poetic transfiguration surfaces very strongly, violently; it is a violent writing."[7]

Indeed, that "violence" can be felt in both the molding of a new narrative language and structure—the very matter of literary expression—and the originality, sometimes even boldness (most commonly present in the works of parodic intent), with which the thematic concerns were met. A major theme that found its way into literature during the 1980s was history: the silenced years of the Salazar regime and the so-called remote past, the source of national myths and symbols; the African experience and colonial war; the "provincial condition" characterizing a majority of Portugal's population; and the concept of national identity. The predominant genre of the period was fiction, written by three groups of authors: those already nationally recognized, like Agustina Bessa Luís or Vergílio Ferreira; those who published before the revolution but who were now reemerging with an interesting new "face," like José Cardoso Pires, or especially, José Saramago, the symbol of this literary boom; and, finally, the new authors who made their literary debut in the 1980s, like António Lobo Antunes, and many women writers, such as Lídia Jorge, Clara Pinto Correia, and Teolinda Gersão. There were other important developments in Portuguese literary life, first and foremost the study and organization of the work of Fernando Pessoa (1888–1935), Portugal's greatest twentieth-century poet.

While at the end of the first postrevolutionary decade Portuguese literature was enjoying a truly spectacular boom, the political and socioeconomic reality of the country appeared much less encouraging. By the mid 1980s, international commentators were noting with concern Portugal's continuing lack of political stability and the disappointing performance of its economy, as well as expressing doubts over the country's ability to compete successfully within the European Community, which it was scheduled to join on 1 January 1986 (Maxwell 1986, 3–17). It was amid such a climate that parliamentary elections took place in 1985, followed by presidential elections early the next year. In the first contest, the centrist Social Democratic Party headed by Aníbal Cavaco Silva won 34 percent of the vote and was able to form a minority government, with Cavaco Silva as prime minister. In January 1986, the Socialist Soares won the presidential vote.

The 1990s

It would surely come as a surprise to the observers of Portugal's troubled political waters in the late seventies and early eighties that, almost a decade later, both Cavaco Silva and Soares would still be holding their respective offices. In fact, their standing has only improved over the years: the 1991 presidential elections brought Soares, now almost uniformly considered Portugal's most popular politician, a landslide reelection victory in his bid for a second five-year term. As for the Social Democrats, it took them just two years to secure a clear parliamentary majority in 1987 elections. The Cavaco Silva government went on to complete a four-year term (for the first time in post-Salazar Portugal's history), which led to another victory for the PSD in the 1991 elections when the party captured 50.4 percent of the vote and a majority of 130 of 230 seats in the National Assembly.

The fact that this period of political stability coincided with Portugal's entrance into the EEC stimulated and provided solid ground for sweeping economic changes, with modernization, widespread privatization, and a reduction in state controls as the main defining factors. In a full-scale reversal of the mid-seventies nationalization campaign, the liberalization of the economy has accelerated steadily since the late eighties, culminating in 1990 legislative changes that allowed 100 percent privatization of state companies (MacDonald 1993, 48). The reforms proved largely successful: in the second half of the eighties, the Portuguese economy grew faster than those of all other European Community members for several consecutive years. A 1992 article in the *Wall Street Journal* would hail Portugal's "post-authoritarian boom" as an exemplary transition from "dirt-poor dictatorship to stable and increasingly prosperous democracy" that the newly emerging economies of post-Communist Eastern Europe might do well to emulate (Gumbel 1992, A11).

Such enthusiastic assessments have not, however, been uniformly shared by all, particularly since the global recession in recent years has contributed to the slowdown of Portugal's economic growth. Some of the dissenting voices could be heard during the 1991 electoral campaigns: Soares, dubbed "Socialist only in name," was criticized by the Left for "turning his back on the country's many poor people and for neglecting its lamentable social services."[8] For his part, Soares took to expressing doubts publicly about the social impact of Cavaco Silva's economic policies, while the Socialist Party leader Jorge Sampaio claimed that the country's new prosperity was making the rich richer and the poor poorer. In addition, many professional groups were increasingly at odds with the government, complaining about expanding red tape and administrative rules changed on a whim.

Not least among the critics of Portugal's contemporary realities have been the country's intellectuals, continuing their time-honored tradition of political commitment and social responsibility. Their most immediate concern has been the gradual but growing impact that the political changes and economic reforms of Social Democrats have started to have on Portuguese culture. The government's free-market approach to the management of culture, as well as of the economy, manifested itself most visibly in the privatization of mass-media outlets: in 1991, with the sale of the prestigious Lisbon newspaper *Diário de Notícias*, all of Portugal's newspapers returned to private hands, and in October 1992 the country's first private television station went on the air, ending a twenty-seven-year monopoly by the two state-run networks.

During the decade of Social Democratic rule, culture at large has been refashioned as a specialized branch of the market economy, a branch to be managed by properly trained professionals. This is reflected by changing terminology: what used to be referred to, in the seventies, as "cultural animation," an educational activity meant to foster widespread cultural production and collective participation, has become now "cultural management," a professional discipline in which courses are offered by several Portuguese colleges. As for the steadily increasing importance of corporate sponsorship, its implications are not always as dreary as when a theatrical company wishing to stage a play by Ibsen had to satisfy its sponsor's demands by placing a gigantic bottle of shampoo in the middle of its foyer (Dionísio 1993, 359). Nevertheless, it does profoundly affect cultural activity: events most likely to attract sponsorship are those capable of attracting large audiences and, at the same time, incapable of generating controversy that might prove damaging to the sponsor's image. Controversy is also absent from the discourse promoting the supposedly blissful marriage of the market economy and cultural production, which can sometimes reach rather ingenious heights: that was the case, for example, when French carmaker Renault wished to stage the Portuguese unveiling of its latest model in the Belém Cultural Center, a newly constructed compound of exhibition and performance halls. According to Renault's arguments, the unveiling was, in effect, "an artistic and cultural event, given the innovative aspects" of the car (Dionísio 1993, 105).

Concurrent with the government's policy of forcing cultural activity to confront on its own the workings of a free-market economy has been the official insistence on the undesirability of any sort of political involvement in the area of culture, an attitude articulated in contrast to, and as a reaction against, the politics of cultural interventionism favored both by Salazar's New State and the revolutionary left before and after 25 April. While it is difficult to find fault with the official dogma that the role of the state is not to develop and propagate its own brand of culture, but rather to create conditions for autonomous cultural manifestations of the civil society, it is also doubtful whether mass, root-level cultural animation can indeed be identified as the direction the Portuguese society has been taking in recent years. If in 1984 António Sousa Ribeiro could complain about the attitude of cultural consumerism and apathy prevailing among *o povo* (unaffected, in this respect, by the radical ideals of the revolution), today such criticism rings truer than ever, as "mass culture" is channeled almost exclusively through television and the production and appreciation of "high culture" remains restricted to the society's elites.[9]

In spite of the PSD government's professed noninterventionist stance in the area of culture, recent years have been marked by a number of minor and major skirmishes between the office of the Secretary of State for

Culture (SEC) and leading cultural and artistic associations and individuals. In April 1992, in response to a projected broad restructuring of several institutions administered by the SEC (involving, among other goals, the merger of the National Library [Biblioteca Nacional] and the Book and Reading Institute [Instituto do Livro e da Leitura]), as well as measures such as the imposition of a value-added tax on the sale of books, more than sixty civic organizations from around the country joined in the creation of the Frente Nacional para a Defesa da Cultura (National Front for the Defense of Culture).[10] Shortly afterwards, another protest took place following the arbitrary withdrawal, ordered by a subsecretary of the SEC, of José Saramago's latest novel, *O Evangelho Segundo Jesus Cristo*, from the list of Portuguese candidates for the 1991 European Literary Prize.[11] In more general terms, many intellectuals deplore the lack of dialogue between Portugal's ruling politicians and the country's cultural elites, a situation hardly helped by the token inclusion of individual prominent figures in government institutions.[12] Jokes have circulated, with varying degrees of malice, about the cultural "ignorance" of the "technocrats" running the country, not exempting Cavaco Silva himself.[13]

While the policies of the PSD government have no doubt significantly transformed the country's economic and, to a lesser degree, cultural infrastructure, the single defining circumstance of the late eighties and early nineties has been Portugal's accession to the European Community. Aside from the economic and sociopolitical changes this event entails, the direction of many intellectual debates is influenced by the symbolic significance of the country's new geopolitical status, with discussions of national identity once again coming into prominence. Eduardo Lourenço's 1988 collection of essays, *Nós e a Europa*, may be considered emblematic in this respect; in a recent interview its author claimed that Portugal is going through a period of "cultural nationalism exceeding that of the former regime."[14] In more practical terms, what matters is perhaps less Portugal's changed position with regard to the European "center" than its relationship to its nearest geographic and/or cultural counterparts, particularly Spain and Brazil. Due to the internal workings of the EEC, the two Iberian neighbors have become more tightly bound, altering their historically uneasy (mis)alliance. To cite but one example, in 1991 Spain and Portugal were chosen to inaugurate the EEC's Interreg program, designed to boost regional development across national borders, and became the site of a three-year effort to develop and integrate regional economies in both countries. By 1987 Spain had emerged as a close second to Britain among foreign investors and ahead of Portugal's traditional leader, France.[15] In the area of culture, it is worth noting that literary works by Portuguese authors have achieved a far more prominent status on the Spanish publishing scene than had been their usual due. In April 1990, for example, the Spanish translation of Saramago's *História do Cerco de Lisboa* led the list of novels recommended by the Madrid daily *El País*.[16]

As for Brazil, this former Portuguese colony has also been growing closer to its erstwhile *metrópole*, as Portugal's EEC membership makes it an attractive ground both for rich Brazilian investors and for less-affluent emigrants hoping to escape their country's economic woes. As the *New York Times* reported on 15 February 1991, "[a]lmost overnight, Brazil seems to be supplying Portugal's top soccer players, its most popular television soap operas and stars, even its best dentists. Brazilian musicians, artists, journalists and publicists are finding work here, while Brazilian tourists are discovering Portugal." While the full impact of this new cultural proximity between the two countries remains to be assessed, it seems certain to surpass the limited, if pervasive, influence long exercised on Portuguese mass culture by the enormously popular television soap operas imported from Rio de Janeiro.

Portugal's changing international status is also closely related to the one area of culture that constitutes an exception to what has been described above as modern refashioning of traditional cultural segregation, an exception that also contradicts the government's claims to the apolitical stance that it has assumed with regard to culture. The late eighties and, in particular, the nineties have seen a marked increase, both in number and in prominence, of multidisciplinary cultural megaevents of international dimensions that have an explicit political goal of conveying a positive image of the country for both internal and, in particular, external use. A string of such events stretches through the nineties, largely determining the definition of privileged cultural practices and of the dominant concept of culture: the Europália in 1991, followed by the Portuguese participation in the 1992 Expo in Seville; Lisbon becoming the official "cultural capital of Europe" in 1994; finally, the crowning event, Portugal being scheduled to host the universal Expo in 1998, on the five-hundredth anniversary of Vasco da Gama's journey to India. For a country the size of Portugal, those are truly gigantic events: the budget for the 1994 "Cultural Capital of Europe" was three times as large as that of the previous "European capital" (Antwerp). Many, if not most, cultural activities that have taken place in Portugal during the decade have been in one way or another integrated within the framework provided by those events, designed as all-inclusive grab bags that fulfill the crucial ideological function of allowing for peaceful and unproblematic coexistence—which does not mean interaction—of the elitist "high culture" and the populist "mass culture." Thus, despite the noninterventionist rhetoric of the Social Democrats, culture in the nineties depends more than ever on an important segment of the government's global policies: PSD's strategy with regard to Portuguese culture has been often characterized as *a política de grandes obras* (grand works policy), designed to promote and propagate "the national Portuguese values, Portugal's history and place in the world."[17] In fact, the memory of 25 April itself has neatly blended into the promotion of Portugal's new political and cultural image. In the course of the 1994 celebrations, for instance, its twentieth anniversary constituted just one of the items on display in the showcase entitled "Lisbon—the Cultural Capital of Europe" (where, by the way, it coexisted unproblematically—if ironically—with such resuscitated bulwarks of Portuguese cultural nationalism and conservatism as commemoration of the Discoveries and colonial expansion).

It would be futile to attempt any kind of concise evaluation of the literature written in Portugal since the late eighties. The essays gathered in this volume provide a rich and satisfying picture. In fact, several observers of Portuguese literary life have noted that, following the fiction boom of the eighties, the artistic spirit of recent years appears somewhat muted, less exuberant (or, to use Lídia Jorge's term, less "violent"), and certainly more difficult to assess in an unequivocal manner. There is a wider variety of interests and individual styles. While "the great theme: what it means to be Portuguese" continues to exercise an allure (naturally heightened in the wake of the European integration), one observes also a certain "thematic universalization" and a renewed appeal of "the great Pascalian themes" of life, death, and relationships between individuals.[18] It is still true, however, that Portuguese authors are more popular among the country's reading public than foreign writers, while until just a few years ago the opposite had traditionally been true. The literary boom of the eighties clearly generated what one of its main protagonists calls "a sort of self-confidence in literature" associated with the critical acclaim and international recognition of the national writers.[19] Whatever new directions might emerge from the current *período de pausa,*[20] their antecedents are likely to be found, in one way or another, amid the turmoil and excitement—and the disillusion and malaise—of the two postrevolutionary decades.

This collection of essays attempts to describe, analyze, and interpret the literary events and practices that characterize the last two postrevolutionary decades of Portuguese political and cultural life. In this era, which established so many "post-" trends and movements, it may seem less than original to choose this approach. However, it becomes clear that while the contributors to this volume employ various critical and interpretative tools to comment on a diverse and extensive body of work and the emphasis shifts from one genre or author to another, the organizing principle remains the same: the events of 25 April 1974. Signifying change and rupture, with implications still to be resolved, the 1974 revolution informs explicitly and implicitly all major themes and issues discussed in this volume, emerging as a principal agent behind what Ellen Sapega calls Portuguese "cultural renegotiation."

The narrative, which these essays constitute as a whole, is certainly not the only valid one that could be constructed, and different editors would probably tell a different story. Many essays gathered here comment on each other, discussing well-known texts and theories, and all attempt to engage the reader in a discussion of topics, such as national identity, postimperial consciousness, New Europe, and interdisciplinary approaches to literary study, which in their scope reach beyond a particular Portuguese context. The authors bring different perspectives not only as independent scholars but also as individuals experiencing and studying Portuguese cultural reality from a different locus: Portuguese and American universities.

We have chosen to preface this collection of articles dealing with Portuguese literature with an essay by Boaventura de Sousa Santos, not a literary critic but a social scientist, that outlines the characteristics of the Portuguese "transition state" and the transformation of Portuguese society over the last fifteen years as it has renegotiated its position in the world system. It is our opinion—one that the literary essays to follow seem to support—that to understand Portuguese cultural change of the post-revolutionary period, one has to engage in an interdisciplinary research encompassing the historical and synchronic, the economic and social, the political and cultural. Sousa Santos offers a new approach to long-debated issues, such as Portuguese "uniqueness" expressed through the evolving concepts of national identity and international persona. His essay provides a social scientist's descriptive and analytical expertise as an alternative to the more traditional, philosophically oriented, mythical interpretations of Portuguese national reality.[21] It is our intention to call our readers' attention to this new approach, and we refer them to other essays in the volume where the mythical/psychoanalytic discourse of national identity is also discussed.[22]

The section on the novel, although the largest one in the volume, does not exhaust the topic. Many authors and themes did not find their way into the essays presented here, as it would clearly be impossible to accommodate them all. Instead, the commentary focuses on what we consider to be the main feature of the Portuguese post-1974 narrative: its centrality in the creation of the new national consciousness altered by the postrevolutionary (and, symptomatically, postmodern) crisis of ideologies. Ellen Sapega, in her discussion of the revolution's effect on the image of national identity, carefully deconstructs discourses traditionally put into service for creating narratives of the national subject. Her insightful commentary on one of the most recent (and probably most quoted) of such discourses—Eduardo Lourenço's theory of national identity—points to fictional emplotments of spatial configurations of the nation and the novel's persistent challenge to the Salazar regime's political ideology. National identity and, especially, the question of de-problematized versions of postcolonial reality inform also the essay by Phyllis Peres. In her discussion of two novels by António Lobo Antunes, Peres interprets literary echoes of the colonial war and its impact on the Portuguese people's image of themselves—national identity recognized in relation to other(s). The essay by Helena Kaufman and José Ornelas focuses on the emergence of history and its reconstruction through fictional narration. A detailed analysis of discursive techniques in the work of such authors as José Saramago, Lídia Jorge, Augusto Abelaira, or José Cardoso Pires demonstrates not only the contemporary novel's commitment to rewrite and redefine national history but also an ontological belief that "fiction is historically conditioned and history discursively structured" (Hutcheon 1988, 120).

One of the most striking but seldom-discussed developments in the last few decades of Portuguese culture has been the unprecedented surge of literary works, particularly works of fiction, composed by women writers. In her article, Isabel Allegro de Magalhães provides a broad overview of writings by Portuguese women published since 1974. In stressing their unspoken commitment to an inclusive, all-encompassing perspective (reserved, until recently, for male authors), while at the same time arguing for their equally strong allegiance to a gender-based difference, in life as much as in writing, the critic touches upon one of the many contradictions attending the lives and works of contemporary Portuguese women.[23] Ana Paula Ferreira's account of women's fictions of the Portuguese revolution pursues this line of inquiry, zeroing in on the unresolved tensions inherent in the problematic dyad "Women and Revolution." In addition, the two articles constitute in themselves a provocative dialogic ensemble, representing, as they do, diverging (if not necessarily mutually exclusive) directions of feminist and/or woman-centered investigation.

While during the last two decades the literary genre that commanded most attention has doubtlessly been the novel, the group of articles describing recent developments in other literary genres prove that this is in no way due to any noticeable decline in artistic interest and quality of Portuguese poetry or drama. Fernando J. B. Martinho's exhaustive overview of poetry written in Portugal since 1974 clearly demonstrates that there has been no stagnation of imaginative inventiveness and discursive richness, qualities that have traditionally characterized the Portuguese lyric. On the contrary, new and fascinating directions may be discerned, not least among them the broad, carnivalesque scope of dialogic questioning of past and present texts and realities, an orientation shared in fact with other genres. In his presentation of contemporary Portuguese drama, José Oliveira Barata highlights two particularly significant aspects: its formal Brechtian connection and its substantive commitment to shaping the country's present through a reimagining of its past. In addition, his article addresses a question, also touched upon by other contributors, of the artistic and ideological implications of the audience's response to politically encoded "pre-1974" literary works in the radically altered "post-1974" social and political environment.

Finally, a fitting closure for this grouping of articles dealing primarily with literary texts is provided by Onésimo Almeida's study of the Portuguese essay of the last decades. His commentary highlights the most important authors and works of the genre while focusing on its cultural specificity, which sometimes escapes the confines of a strict definition.

Notes

1. As many as six hundred thousand, as estimated in the article, "On the Edge of Europe: A Survey of Portugal," *Economist*, 30 June 1984, 10.
2. For a more detailed account of the constitution of 1976 and its implication for the emergence of Portuguese democracy, see Gallagher 1985.
3. Quotation from the interview given to Helena Kaufman in June 1993.
4. Sá Carneiro died in a plane crash and in January 1981 Francisco Pinto Balsemão became prime minister, backed by the same Aliança Democrática party.
5. Assessment made by the *Economist*, 30 June 1984, 10.
6. The commentary on the subject is provided in Sousa Ribeiro 1986. Also see Pintasilgo 1986. Pintasilgo even more pessimistically states that "the governmental programs [in the cultural sphere] are . . . a *patchwork* " and, moreover, "there is practically no indication that culture can function [in Portuguese society in the eighties] as a totalizing/comprising space, a point of departure" (65).
7. Quoted from the interview given to Helena Kaufman, June 1993.
8. *Economist*, 12 January 1991, 42.
9. Quoted from the interview with Lídia Jorge, June 1993
10. *Jornal de Letras*, 21 April 1992, 3.
11. *Jornal de Letras*, 5 May 1992, 3. *O Evangelho Segundo Jesus Cristo* eventually

received the 1991 Grand Prize of the Associação Portuguesa de Escritores (Portuguese Writers' Association). See *Jornal de Letras*, 23 June 1992, 8–9.

12. Quoted from the interview with Lídia Jorge, June 1993.
13. Quoted from the interview with Joana Varela, June 1993.
14. "Uma certa ideia de Europa," *Expresso Revista*, 27 March 1993, 46.
15. See the *Economist*'s survey of Portugal, 28 May 1988.
16. *Economist*, 5 May 1990, 24.
17. Quoted from the interview with Lídia Jorge and Francisco Belard, June 1993.
18. Quoted from the interview with Lídia Jorge, June 1993.
19. Ibid.
20. Ibid.
21. See also Santos 1992.
22. See the essays by Sapega and Peres.
23. Ana Vicente, who currently heads the government-affiliated Commission for Equality and Women's Rights (formerly Commission on the Status of Women), informed me in an interview in June 1993 that there are several such contradictions. On the one hand, 43.6 percent of Portuguese workers are women; women constitute 62 percent of all college graduates under thirty years of age; among the member countries of the EEC, Portugal has the greatest percentage of women occupying positions of responsibility in public administration. On the other hand, only 6 percent of candidates elected to local governments are women and the issues of women's rights are consistently marginalized in the political forum.

References

Dionísio, Eduarda. 1993. *Títulos, Acções, Obrigações (Sobre a Cultura em Portugal, 1974–1994)*. Lisboa: Edições Salamandra.

Gallagher, Tom. 1985. "Democracy in Portugal since the 1974 Revolution." *Parliamentary Affairs* 38:202–18.

Gumbel, Peter. 1992. "Portugal: A Recovery that East Europe Can Emulate." *Wall Street Journal*, 1 May.

Hutcheon, Linda. 1988. *A Poetics of Postmodernism*. New York: Routledge.

Jorge, Lídia. 1989. *O Dia dos Prodígios*. Lisboa: Dom Quixote.

Lourenço, Eduardo. 1984. "Literatura e Revolução." *Colóquio/Letras* 78:16.

MacDonald, Scott B. 1993. *European Destiny, Atlantic Transformation: Portuguese Foreign Policy under the Second Republic, 1974–1992*. New Brunswick, N.J.: Transaction Publications.

Maxwell, Kenneth, ed. 1986. *Portugal in the 1980s: Dilemmas of Democratic Consolidation*. New York: Greenwood Press.

Pedro, Emília. 1986. "Para uma Análise da Complexidade das Relações entre Cultura, Educação e Processos de Mudança." *Revista Crítica de Ciências Sociais* 18/19/20 (Fevereiro): 41–56.

Pintasilgo, Maria de Lourdes. 1986. "Deambulação pelo Espaço/Tempo do 25 de Abril." *Revista Crítica de Ciências Sociais* 18/19/20 (Fevereiro): 63–70.

Santos, Boaventura de Sousa. 1992. "Onze Teses por Ocasião de Mais uma Descoberta de Portugal." *Luso-Brazilian Review* 29, no. 1: 97–115.

Sousa Ribeiro, António. 1986. "A Cultura depois de Abril." *Revista Crítica de Ciências Sociais* 18/19/20 (Fevereiro): 41–56.

Seixo, Maria Alzira. 1984. "Ficção." *Colóquio/Letras* 78:16.

State and Society in Portugal

BOAVENTURA DE
SOUSA SANTOS

Introduction

The postwar period gave birth to a world that for three decades seemed to be neatly divided between developed and underdeveloped countries. From different and often conflicting perspectives the social theories then developed—modernization, development, imperialism, and dependency theories—tried to account for this division and to establish blocked or unblocked passages, friendly or hostile linkages, between the poles of division. In the last ten or fifteen years this situation seems to have changed drastically. In the first place, countries of intermediate development emerged under very different forms. Though for the world-system theorists these intermediate entities had always been there as the semiperiphery, it is recognized that they have assumed a much greater prominence. Social theory has variously denominated them as semi-industrialized countries, newly industrializing countries, belated centers, dependence with development and, of course, semiperiphery. Secondly, internal changes in the developed countries have led to social conditions in these countries that are similar to those which used to characterize lesser-developed countries, such as underground economy, informal sector, meaninglessness of democratic mechanisms, political corruption, segmented labor markets, degradation of the general welfare, urban violence, increased inequalities, new and broader forms of social exclusion, and destitution. This is what has been called the interior third world.[1]

These changes have been so strongly perceived that some have seen in them the emergence of a new international political economy of global interdependence, a fairly disorganized and quasi-chaotic global network of

31

deterritorialized, transnational flows of capital, services, and people in a world without a center, reproducing itself through a myriad of changing, unstable, and underdetermined vertical and horizontal relations.[2]

In my view, as long as the benefits of the international division of labor are not equally distributed (as long as hunger and political oppression cannot be said to be randomly distributed throughout the world), and as long as capital accumulation on a world scale is based on the same contradiction between socialization of production and individual appropriation of surplus, recent trends should not be overemphasized or overgeneralized to make them the prolegomena of a paradigmatic change in the mode of development of industrial capitalism. This is not to say that this mode of development is not undergoing profound changes or that we don't need a new, alternative mode of development, but if this is the case other trends must be emphasized, other readings of present conditions must be proposed.

However, the above-mentioned trends do signal some important changes in the world and in the ways we see it, which comparative sociology has still to grasp. On the other hand, as the United States has been forced to share its hegemony with Europe and Japan, the world has become more polycentric, with different regions gravitating around different centers, and the proliferation of the center seems to be an ongoing process. On the other hand, the periphery of the world has become more and more fragmented, giving rise both to more cruel forms of exclusion and to an ever growing range of intermediate, semiperipheral countries that differ in national patterns of development according to the region of the world in which they are located.

Moreover, global interactions have known in recent years a new intensity from the transnationalization of production systems to the worldwide dissemination of information and images through the media and to mass translocation of people as tourists, as migrant workers, or as refugees. As a result, social reality seems to change as fast as the epistemological foundations of the knowledge or knowledges we develop about it, if not faster. A double trend is emerging that will determine the comparative research in the nineties. As global interdependence and interaction intensifies, social relations in general seem to have become increasingly deterritorialized, crossing borders that previously were policed by customs, nationalism, language, and ideology, and oftentimes by all of them together. In the process, the nation-state, whose main characteristic is probably territoriality, becomes a relatively obsolete, or at least unprivileged, unit of interaction. But on the other hand, and in apparent contradiction with this trend, there are emerging new regional and local identities built around a new prominence of rights to roots (as opposed to rights to options). This localism, both old and new, once considered premodern and today being recoded as postmodern, is often adopted by translocalized groups of people and therefore cannot be traced back to specific genius loci or sense of place, but it is nevertheless always grounded on the idea of territory, be it an imagined or symbolic, real or hyperreal territory.[3] This dialectic is thus between territorialization and deterritorialization.

The impact of this dialectic on comparative sociology is threefold. Firstly, as social reality becomes more obsolescent, more translocal, and less exotic, it becomes also more comparable if not fungible. Each empirical object becomes implicitly or explicitly comparable to the rest of the world. Furthermore, the specific characteristics of a given country are potentially paradigmatic, generalizable to other countries. Secondly, the effect of deterritorialization on a country's social features manifests itself as disjuncture or uneven development. Accordingly, different social characteristics may be paradigmatic in opposite directions. For instance, a given country may have some features paradigmatic of a third-world condition and other features paradigmatic of a first-world condition. Its specificity as a social formation lies in the specific mix of such features.

This mix—and this is the third impact of the dialectic mentioned above—however unstable, is hyperterritorialized. Therefore, more theoretical innovation and specification and more "local knowledge" are required to do justice to the unique national combinations of transnationalized features.

The new conditions for comparative sociological work I have just sketched seem to be particularly prominent in countries of intermediate development. Such countries—be they Portugal, Ireland, Spain, and Greece, or Mexico and Brazil, or South Korea and Taiwan—bring the dialectic of territorialization/deterritorialization to a specific high tension. As a consequence, their mix of paradigmatic features is particularly volatile. The intermediate countries of Western Europe are a case in point because their social mix is being doubly reconstructed as peripheral countries in one of the great regions of the world system (the European periphery) and as full members of the center of that region (the EEC). Of all these countries, Portugal is perhaps the most telling illustration of a complex mix of social features pointing in opposite paradigmatic directions, a configuration shuffled and reshuffled in the historical short circuit of the past fifteen years in which there converge and melt such different social temporalities as the five-centuries-long temporality of the European expansion, the two-centuries-long temporality of the democratic revolutions, the one-century-long temporality of the socialist movement, the forty-year-long temporality of the welfare state. In early 1974 Portugal was one of the least developed countries of Europe and at the same time the oldest European colonial empire. The longest-lasting fascist-type regime in Europe was dismantled in a bloodless revolution on 25 April 1974 and soon thereafter the greatest popular mobilization of postwar Europe put the goal of socialism on the political agenda of major political parties. Some months later, an ambiguous resolution of the revolutionary crisis opened up a long and tortuous process towards a social-democratic welfare state at a time where in Western Europe and elsewhere in the central countries the welfare state was entering a period of deep crisis.

For all these reasons, Portugal is a fascinating laboratory, though also very complex and very demanding in terms of sociological analysis. Bearing in mind the dialectic between territorialization and deterritorialization, the analytical framework I develop in the following combines the world-system theory (adequate to capture the dynamics of deterritorialization) and the regulation approach (adequate to capture the dynamics of territorialization).

In the following, I will argue that:

1. Portugal is a semiperipheral society in the European region of the world system. For many centuries this semiperipheral position was based on the Portuguese colonial empire. Since the demise of the empire in 1974, Portugal has been renegotiating its position in the world system. It seems that a semiperipheral position of some kind will be maintained, this time based on the terms of Portugal's integration in the European Economic Community and on its privileged social relations with Portuguese-speaking Africa.

2. Once the state corporatist regime of accumulation and the mode of regulation imposed by the Salazar state were dismantled, no new regime of accumulation and mode of social regulation has become stabilized and created its own routines of production and reproduction. Portugal is thus undergoing a period of transition that runs at different paces according to the different areas of social practice.

3. Such a period of transition manifests itself in significant inconsistencies, disjunctures, or discrepancies. Two of them deserve special attention: (a) the discrepancy between capitalist production and social reproduction or, in other words, between the norm of production and the norm of consumption; (b) the discrepancy between the institutional forms of the fordist mode of regulation and the predominantly nonfordist, competitive regulation of the wage relation.

4. The social and cultural differentiation and heterogeneity derived from the above-mentioned conditions have been regulated by the state. The cen-

trality of the state in the social regulation throughout the last fifteen years accounts for the priority of the political in this period. Such heterogeneities and discrepancies have, in the very process of their regulation by the state, inscribed themselves in the institutional matrix of the state, a phenomenon which I will render through two concepts: *the parallel state* and *the hetero-geneous state.*

5. Since it has not been possible to institutionalize a fordist regulation of the wage relation, it has not been possible to institutionalize a welfare state either. In this respect the Portuguese state is a *quasi- or lumpen-wel-fare state.* However, the resulting deficit in state welfare is partially covered by a strong welfare society. This welfare society, though couched in social relations and symbolic universes that could be easily labeled as premodern , bears striking similarities with the kind of welfare society that Rosanavallon (1981, 1988), Lipietz (1989), Aglietta and Brender (1984), and others have been trying to resuscitate and that some would call the postmodern welfare society.

6. The old and new equilibria of such a complex social and political structure are being destabilized, recomposed, and reinvented in the process of integration in the European Economic Community. To a substantial extent the centrality of the state in social regulation in this period has derived from the leading role of the state in the negotiations that led to the integration. The state regulates the dialectic of identity and difference between Portugal and European core countries thereby assuming a political form that I designate as the *state-as-imagination-of-the-center.* The internal autonomy of the state, which during fascism lay in an autarchic, isolationist, hypernationalist mode of development (perhaps, rather, underdevelopment), lies now in the process of integration in the EEC and, thus, in a context of ever decreasing national sovereignty.

7. The future of the European Economic Community is an open question. At the political level it is very early to even sketch the political form of the future Euro-state. At the economic level, the current priority given to the creation of the internal market is no guarantee that the internal market will also be a unified market. At the social level, the low priority of the so-called social dimension at the present time invites the suspicion that for a long time Europe will develop at two different speeds. The transitional period of Portuguese society is thus juxtaposed to the transitional period of Europe as a whole. Predictions are therefore doubly risky. With this caveat in mind, however, I would propose that, as far as Portugal is concerned, a semiperipheral mode of regulation is underway and is likely to stabilize in a few years after 1993.

The Semiperiphery in the Intersection of
the Hyperlocal and the Transnational:
Combining the World-System Theory
and the Regulation Approach

A review of the social scientific knowledge accumulated in the last forty years both about the central, developed, or first-world countries and the peripheral, less-developed or third-world countries will show that such knowledge falls short of an adequate picture of Portuguese society. While some aspects of Portuguese society approximate those usually identified with the central countries—as, for instance, regarding demographic structures, norms of consumption, political system, social stratification, cultural patterns, and social order, in other aspects it approximates third-world characteristics, as in the case of price-income formation, balance of payments, labor market, some infrastructural equipment, investment in R&D, and the presence of noncapitalist modes of production.

In terms of some social and economic indicators Portugal occupies an intermediate position in the world system. Rough as it is, the GNP per capita is one such indicator. In the study on the evolution of the GNP per capita throughout the world in the last fifty years, conducted by Arrighi and Drangel, Portugal occupies a consistent intermediate position (Arrighi and Drangel 1986). A richer indicator is the degree of homogeneity between the sectorial structure of employment. Using this indicator and comparing different countries in 1960 and 1983 Mateus (1987, 54) shows the intermediate condition of Portuguese society.[4] Some other features of Portuguese society are neither more nor less than comparable features in other countries. They are just different and call for theories that will account for them.

For the world-system theory, the existence of societies with intermediate levels of development is a structural, permanent, and relational feature of the world system. The first formulation of the semiperiphery in Wallerstein's *The Modern World System* (1974) is rather descriptive. Later on Wallerstein would stress the political content of the semiperiphery. By their very intermediate character, semiperipheral countries perform a function of intermediation between the center and periphery of the world system and, very much like the middle classes at the nation-state level, they contribute to the smoothening of the conflicts and tensions between the center and the periphery. As Wallerstein puts it, "In moments of expansion of the world-economy, [semiperipheral] states find themselves attached as satellites to one or another core power and serve to some extent as economic transmission belts and political agents of an imperial power" (1984, 7).

In recent years, much research has been done on semiperipheral countries and the concept of semiperiphery has been further refined. Drawing on the research conducted at the Fernand Braudel Center, Carlos Fortuna says that the semiperipheral states are characterized by a network of productive activities in which there is a relative equilibrium between core productions and peripheral productions, from which they derive a specific capacity of institutional and political maneuvering in the interstate system (1987, 180). But as W. Martin rightly emphasizes, "to recognize the endurance of the semiperiphery raises far more questions than it answers." The most crucial questions, according to him, are: "[I]f semiperipheral states sit astride core-peripheral networks, how is such a position attained and maintained in the face of the strongly polarizing forces of the world-economy?; if the semiperiphery is more than simply a statistical cutting point on developmental indices, how has the zone itself operated over time as part of a developing capitalist world?; how and why has the semiperiphery, at least in the twentieth century, operated as a primary locus for social, labor, nationalist, and anti-systemic movements?" (1990, 4).

This is not the place to scrutinize in detail the concept of semiperiphery, much less the world-system conception of which it is a constituent. I will limit myself to two points. The first point refers to the regionalization of the semiperipheral condition. According to the world-system theory, one of the structural features of the world capitalist economy is the competition among core countries. As a result, the world system is divided into regions, zones of influence, which constitute clusters of particularly intense economic, social, political, and cultural relations among a given group of countries, one or some of which constitute the center (the United States, Japan, Western Europe). Though the general type of intermediation accomplished by intermediate societies is defined at the level of the world system as a whole, the specific intermediation functions are established at the level of the particular region of the world system to which the particular society belongs and depend to a great extent on historical national developments within that region.

The function of intermediation implies that a given country acts in some areas as a peripheral country vis-à-vis a given central country and, in other areas, as a central country vis-à-vis the periphery. For instance, from the eighteenth century on Portugal functioned as a transmission belt in the world system, acting as a center vis-à-vis its colonies and as a periphery vis-à-vis Great Britain. The hypertrophy of tourism and of emigration in Portugal constitutes a clear sign of this peripheral function of this country vis-à-vis the norms of production and the norms of consumption prevailing in the central European countries (Mateus 1987, 55). On the other hand, the integration in the EEC will eventually enable Portugal to perform another central function vis-à-vis its former African colonies. In both cases, however, the intermediation functions are specific to the history of Europe and are an integral part of the social development of Portugal as an European country.

The second point I want to raise refers to the characterization of semiperipheral societies as both intermediate in terms of levels of development and intermediary in terms of their functions in the world system. The two characteristics are, of course, related, since the intermediation function presupposes an intermediate level of development and, conversely, the latter reproduces itself, partly at least, through the performance of the intermediation function. But they are conceptually autonomous, and it seems mistaken to assume a linear or mechanical relation between them. The intermediate nature of a given society translates itself in social characteristics that are specific of that society and, in a sense, unique. It is a product of its historical national development and of the multiple ways in which that development has intermingled with worldwide socioeconomic processes. It is thus deeply inscribed in the social structure and social praxis. In sum, the intermediate character is a quality and not just a quantity, and it represents the territorialized dimension of the global interactions in which a given country may be involved. The intermediation function may also be a long-lasting phenomenon, but it has a different logic of development. Because the capitalist world economy is politically organized in an interstate system, the intermediation function is subjected to political discontinuities that may result in shorter or longer periods of disjunctures, discrepancies, or hiatuses between intermediate structures and intermediate functions. When in 1974–75 the Portuguese empire came virtually to an end, the intermediation function Portugal performed on the basis of its colonies also came to an end. However, its intermediate structures and processes remained untouched. The materiality and the quality of such structures and processes were deeply inscribed in Portuguese society and their complex modes of social reproduction extended far beyond the possession of the colonies. Such structures and processes are autonomous and active in appropriating, reconstructing and also limiting whatever opportunities arise for the emergence of new intermediation roles. Precisely because Portugal is undergoing a transitional process of the renegotiation of its position in the world system, I think a closer attention must be given to the specific quality of its material and symbolic intermediate character.

To accomplish that, we must resort to a theoretical perspective that concentrates on the specificity of national developments and analyzes them within an encompassing framework, running from the historical to the synchronic, from the economic to the social, the political, and the cultural. The complementarity sought for between such a theory and the world-system theory will only be possible if both theories share some theoretical and even metatheoretical concerns. I think this is the case of the French regulation approach. Though this is not really a theory, but rather a general analytical orientation from which different theories have been emerging, I think that, in general, both approaches share a Marxist past as well as the need to eliminate the economistic and mechanistic biases of some Marxism. Both focus on social relations in capitalist development and most particularly on exchange relations and wage relations. Both are holistic in nature and focus on the consolidation and transformation of social cohesion through time: the regulation approach, on the social cohesion of individual nation-states, the world system on the social cohesion of the capitalist world economy.

The regulation approach is theoretically very loose. The version adopted here seems to me to be the most adequate to capture the dynamics of Portuguese social development in the last fifteen years. It is generally acknowledged that one of the weaknesses of the regulation approach is the absence of a theory of the state that will account for the multiple and decisive roles the state performs in the processes of emergence and consolidation of the modes of social regulation (Boyer 1986, 52; Jessop 1990, 196). Following the initial suggestion of Wallerstein, it has been recently emphasized that such roles are particularly decisive in semiperipheral societies (Martin 1990, 7). In this paper I address this question by focusing on the specific centrality of state regulation in a period of transition between modes of social regulation in a semiperipheral social formation in the European region of the world system. Furthermore, I will analyze the ways in which the process of transitional social regulation inscribes itself in the institutional matrix of the state by identifying the different partial political forms that together constitute the fragmented totality of the state in the transition from one mode of social regulation to the next.

The Crisis of the Mode of Social Regulation: Norms of Production and Norms of Consumption in a Period of Transition

It may have been only a coincidence, but it is interesting to note that the end of the fascist regime in Portugal took place at a moment in which the central countries were entering a period of crisis. I mean the crisis of that mode of regulation which, according to Aglietta (1976), Boyer (1986), and others, had dominated particularly since the end of World War II. This mode of social regulation was characterized by intensive capital accumulation, indexation of wages to productivity, and mass consumption. It was the fordist mode of regulation. One would expect that this crisis would reverberate in a semiperipheral society with close economic ties with the countries most hit by the crisis, the central countries of Western Europe. But the revolution of 25 April 1974 by itself started a national crisis of social regulation in Portuguese society. It was a sweeping crisis, running through all the sectors of social life and unsettling deep-rooted and long-lasting aspects of national historical development, a crisis that indeed for a short period assumed the form of revolutionary crisis. Thus the crisis occurred within a crisis and this is a crucial factor for the understanding of some features of Portuguese society in the last fifteen years.

The Revolutionary Crisis (1974–75) and the Parallel State

This is not the place to give a full account of the Portuguese revolution. It is even highly probable that the historians of the future will deny the status of a true revolution to the Portuguese events of 1974–75, just as they have with the German revolution of November 1918 (Broué 1971).

The Portuguese revolution began as a military revolt led by a sizable group of democratic and antifascist young officers who were eager to put an end to the colonial war. In relation to the political project at home the programme of the Movement of the Armed Forces (MFA) was straightforward in spite of its generalities: immediate destruction of the fascist features of the state apparatus; elections for a constitutional assembly where parliamentary democracy would be restored; political pluralism and autonomy of working-class organizations; and an antimonopolist economic policy aiming at a more equitable distribution of wealth. Concerning the colonial question, however, the programme was rather ambiguous. It called for a political settlement in a large Portuguese space. Such ambiguity was the inevitable consequence of the fact that the young officers had felt compelled to compromise with General Spinola, who, excepting Costa Gomes, was the only general who had had conflicts with the rulers in the last period of the regime. To compromise was then considered important, not only to minimize the possibility of resistance by some military units loyal to the old regime, but also to avoid any attempt at a unilateral declaration of independence by the white population in the colonies, particularly in Angola.

Spinola clearly represented the interests of monopoly capital while the young officers of the MFA were granted, from the start, tremendous popular support by the working class and large sectors of the petty bourgeoisie.

This popular mobilization (economic and political strikes broke out throughout the country) was instrumental in bringing about Spinola's total defeat, as well as the neutralization of the rightist elements inside the MFA and the political radicalization of its more leftist elements. This fact, plus the firm rejection of the leading African liberation movements of any Spinola-type solution for the colonial question, was the main precondition for what would become the most remarkable decolonization process of modern times, though much denigrated in recent years—a decolonization process almost totally free from neocolonialist features.

The qualitative changes in the political process took place after March 1975, the true beginning of the revolutionary crisis: extensive nationalization of industry; total nationalization of the banking and insurance system; land seizures in Alentejo; house occupations in large cities; workers' councils; self-management in industrial and commercial enterprises abandoned by their former owners; cooperatives in industry, commerce, and agriculture; neighborhood associations; people's clinics; and cultural dynamization in the most backward parts of the country. None of these measures, taken individually, challenged the capitalist foundations of society or the class nature of state power. However, all these measures taken together—along with the internal dynamics of working-class mobilization and of popular initiative, the generalized paralysis of the state apparatus, and the ever more serious conflict within the armed forces—did indeed bring about a revolutionary crisis. But on no occasion was there a situation of dual power conceived of as a situation of "global confrontation" between "two dictatorships" (Lenin 1960, 3:50; Trotsky 1963, 101). Although a full analysis of this fact is still to be made, it seems to me that one of the major explaining factors lies in the very nature of the events that led to the revolutionary crisis. It all started as a military revolt, that is, a revolt from above, originating within the state apparatus itself. The aim was to destroy the fascist state power, but only the most explicitly fascist features of the state were destroyed, such as the political police, the political courts and prisons, the one-party system, and paramilitary fascist militias. The state apparatus was otherwise kept intact, with its fifty-year heritage of authoritarian ideology, recruitment, training, and practice. Though under popular pressure there were some purges of personnel in public administration and industry, they were rather limited in number, often opportunistic, and, in some crucial sectors of the state apparatus such as the administration of justice, virtually nonexistent. In any case, purges were always restricted to personnel and never reached the structures of the state power. As to the two branches of the repressive state apparatus—the police (PSP and GNR) and the armed forces—the situation was even more striking. Since the police offered no resistance to the young officers of the MFA, there was no need to dismantle or even restructure the organization; only the top officers were replaced. As to the armed forces, they were shaken to their roots; but precisely because the revolt originated in their ranks and the political process was kept under military leadership, the armed forces felt globally relegitimized and postponed any profound internal restructuring. This explains, among other things, why the soldiers' committees appeared very late in the process and without internal dynamics.

In sum, the state apparatus, once cleansed of its distinctly fascist features, did not collapse. It rather suffered a generalized paralysis. Because the political events had started inside it, it was "relatively easy" to bring about the paralysis of the bourgeois state power. In this sense there was no bourgeois rule. But neither, and for similar reasons, was there a proletarian rule. In this connection the role played by the big working-class parties (the Socialist Party and the Communist Party) must be briefly mentioned. Having gained considerable influence in the state apparatus and inside the armed forces after March 1975, the Communist Party (PCP), the only political organization worth the name at the time, looked rather suspiciously on the spontaneous mobilization and creative organizations of the working class, both at the point of production and at the point of consumption. Under the mystifying argument that the enemy had already been destroyed by the nationalization of monopoly capital and that the sector of the MFA then in power would, if supported, carry out the class interests of the proletariat, the PCP always favored policies inside the state apparatus and rejected as adventuristic the idea of revolutionary legality and of popular power. The Socialist Party (PS), of recent formation and heterogeneous composition, resented the influence of the Communists in the state apparatus and rejected as authoritarian any political form but parliamentary democracy. Drawing its support from the bourgeoisie, sectors of the petite bourgeoisie, and the working class, who resented the power politics and the arrogance of the Communists, the Socialist Party soon became the opposition party par excellence. As in Germany in 1918, the Socialists became the leading party in a broad coalition of bourgeois and conservative political forces.

It may be said that the same process that had quite rapidly obtained the suspension or neutralization of bourgeois rule had at the same time prevented proletarian rule from emerging in its own name. This was less a situation of dual power than a situation of dual powerlessness, as I would characterize it. The situation was resolved in favor of bourgeois rule in November 1975 (Santos 1979).

The Portuguese revolution shows, indeed, as one of its striking features, that the capitalist state may undergo a generalized paralysis for an extended period of time without coming to an end. On the contrary, it remains intact as a kind of reserve state that will only be reactivated if the relations of forces change in its favor.

The end of the revolutionary crisis and the inauguration of the first constitutional democratic government in almost fifty years did not end the social crisis, though it did change its nature. In terms of social regulation we can say that the crisis began before 1974 and has continued from 1976 to the present day. I will now proceed to analyze this crisis, focusing on three strategic factors: capital accumulation, wage relation, and the role of the state.

Social regulation of exchange relations and wage relations is a complex process made of basically three structural elements: state law (state normalization), contract (contractual normalization) and shared values (cultural normalization) (Boyer 1986, 55; Aglietta and Brender 1984, 77). What characterizes the authoritarian regime is the hypertrophy of state normalization and its pretended tutelage over the other forms of normalization. The willingness of monopoly capital, quite evident after 1969, to enter direct negotiations with workers' representatives epitomizes the growing conflict between state normalization and contractual normalization. As to the cultural normalization, the student movements of 1962 and of 1969, the migratory flows, the colonial war, and the strikes showed that the fascist ideology of the loving, hardworking family running a simple life with scarce means and no ambition of upward mobility, an ideology soaked in rural mythology and religious mysticism, had, in fact, no normalizing power anymore.

The revolution of 1974, by dismantling the political form of the Estado Novo and its institutional base, created some of the conditions for the emergence of new institutions congruent with the changes in the regime of accumulation as it opened new, immense opportunities for social, political and cultural experimentation in all fields of social practice.

Once the political form of the Estado Novo was dismantled, the struggle for the choice of new institutions of social regulation was open. This struggle, which is typical of a crisis of social regulation, took place in Portugal, contrary to what happened in central countries, in the context of much broader social and political struggles. At stake was not just the institutionalization of a new wage relation and new exchange relations but rather the construction of a new political form, that of a modern democratic state. For this reason, the struggle was from the beginning concentrated on the control of the state. Under these circumstances there was not much room for contractual normalization. Moreover, after almost fifty years of authoritarian tutelage, neither capital nor labor had any experience of autonomous

organization and negotiation. As in central countries, a strong, socially committed and efficient democratic state would have been necessary to promote, to assist, or even to create interest groups and to establish the rules of
negotiation among them. But since it had itself become the center of the
struggle, the state could not perform such function.

Indeed, as the social conflict intensified, the state became increasingly
weak, fragmented, and paralyzed. This however did not prevent, but rather
promoted, the promulgation of important labor legislation and social legislation under the pressure of the increasingly radicalized labor movement,
amplified by the multiple forms of popular mobilization that took place
then. This legislation took the social democratic legislation of the Western
European countries as a model, and in some cases it went beyond it in
favoring the interests of the working class (autonomous labor organizations, right to strike, prohibition of lockout, social benefits or indirect salaries,
stability of employment, minimum wages, collective contracts, restrictions
on layoffs and dismissals). The impact of this legislation was soon translated into the relative weight of wage income in the national income. While
in 1973 wages and salaries were 43.7 percent of the GDP; in 1974 they
were 48.9 percent; and in 1975, 57.6 percent.

The radicalization of the labor movement put capital as a whole on the
defensive and not just its less modern or nonmonopolist fractions. Because
the control of the state was the privileged arena of struggle, capitalist forces
tried several times to get control of the state and stop the further radicalization of the popular movement. The attempts failed and each time they
failed they prompted new popular offensives that fueled power to the more
radicalized sectors inside the Movement of Armed Forces. The most dramatic movement of this process was the nationalization of monopoly capital
and the occupation of the big latifundia by farm workers and sharecroppers.
At this stage the crisis changed in quality. In terms of social regulation it
ceased being a mere crisis of the mode of regulation and became a crisis of
the regime of accumulation, if not a crisis of the mode of development
itself, that is, a crisis of the capitalist mode of production.

The nationalizations dramatized the fact that the laws and institutions
created during the revolutionary crisis, though in formal terms very similar
to those of the fordist mode of regulation in central countries, had a very
different material base—indeed, a material base that contradicted them flatly.
Instead of securing and stabilizing an intensive capitalist accumulation led
by monopoly capital, those laws and institutions were part and parcel of a
political and social movement that crushed monopoly capital, prompted
massive capital flights to Brazil, South Africa, and elsewhere, and otherwise disrupted the productive order both in the nationalized industries and

in those converted into cooperatives or self-management enterprises after they had been abandoned by their former owners. The private capital that continued production saw its profit rate fall dramatically as a consequence of the wage increase. In general little inclined to invest in technological innovation and frightened by the overall social instability, this fraction of the capital could not compensate for the increased labor costs through productivity gains. On the contrary, the rate of productivity fell abruptly during the revolutionary crisis. Thus the inconsistency between the legal and institutional framework, on the one side, and social practice, on the other, could not be more dramatic and has indeed remained to this day, under different forms and in different degrees, a structuring factor in the political and social development of Portuguese society.

When the revolutionary crisis came to an end on 25 November 1975—with the ousting of the leftist factions of the Movement of the Armed Forces, the stop imposed on the insurrectional vertigo of the Communist Party, and the general decline of popular mobilization—it was clear that the strategic political goal had switched from the construction of a socialist state to the construction of a modern, democratic European state and thus, ultimately, to the restoration of capitalist rule. But the solution of the crisis represented a complex compromise between different military factions and between them and the political parties, and the ambiguity of this political outcome was to reproduce, under different forms, the discrepancy between the institutional and legal framework and the social practice already observed during the revolutionary crisis.

In April 1976 the Constitutional Assembly promulgated the new Constitution of the Republic. This constitution was very programmatic in its style. Besides confirming all the political, civic, social, and cultural rights typical of an advanced democracy, it established the political form of the state as a representative democracy combined with some forms of direct democracy under the constitutional control of the Revolutionary Council. It also pronounced the irreversibility of the nationalizations and the agrarian reform at the same time that it declared, as the ultimate goal of national political development, the construction of socialism—not just a weak social-democratic version of socialism, but its strong version, meaning the construction of a society without classes and without the exploitation of man by man.

Under such a constitution, the gap between the institutional framework and the social and political practice was extremely wide. In fact, the constitution lacked the state backing to carry on its program. From the first constitutional government on it was clear that, in concrete political terms, the state's objective was to restore capital accumulation and to build a democratic, social-democratic European polity. This was the first, constitutional dimension of what I call the *parallel state:* a constitutional state busily constructing a modern democratic capitalist society under a constitution that pointed toward a classless socialist society. This dimension of the parallel state lasted very long, until 1989, when the second revision of the constitution eliminated its remaining socialist elements.

The restoration of the regime of accumulation and its consolidation in a new mode of social regulation was no easy task. The dramatic increase in wage incomes had a fatal impact on the balance of trade. The consumption of consumer durables, mainly domestic equipment, by the working classes, which was the trademark of the fordist wage relation in postwar central countries, was made possible to the Portuguese working class only with the 1974 revolution. In the following years Portugal had the fastest growing rate of purchase of TV sets and washing machines in Europe. The imports soared and with them the public deficit and the foreign debt. The first stabilization program with the IMF was signed in 1978 and the usual prescription was imposed: restriction on internal consumption, and promotion of exports.

Such a policy meant the devaluation of Portuguese labor, first brought about by inflation and the devaluation of Portuguese currency. But it also meant the degradation of the wage relation. The labor laws and institutions promulgated in the previous period (1974–77) were an important obstacle. Contrary to other laws and institutions of the previous period that by their nature were closely related to the exceptional social conditions of a revolutionary crisis (such as the laws on vacant house occupations), the laws and institutions regulating the wage relation were comparable to, if sometimes more advanced than, those in force in the central countries of Western Europe, which were now the political model to be emulated. To repeal such laws would discredit the dominant political discourse and the state itself. Moreover, any attempt at repealing them would invite the immediate reaction of the trade unions, for whom those laws represented a cherished victory not to be easily given away. Though on the defensive, the labor movement was still strong, with an aggressive leadership controlled by the Communist Party.

The fordist laws and institutions remained in force, but they lacked the economic material base that would be coherent with them. Confronted with this incoherence between institutional regulation and accumulation and prevented from changing the law, the state adopted two unofficial long-range policy orientations that have since conditioned social development as a whole.

The first one consisted in distancing itself from its own legislation and institutions by failing to implement the laws, or implementing them in highly selective ways, by not persecuting the violations of the laws, even if not promoting such violations, by postponing the factual setting up of the institutions created by law, by cutting the budget of the institutions already in operation, by allowing others to be co-opted by the social groups they were supposed to control, etc.

A certain measure of discrepancy between law in books and law in action is arguably an intrinsic characteristic of the modern state, as the sociology of law has shown. What is striking in the Portuguese case is the degree and the quality of that discrepancy and the way it is disseminated in the different state agencies, each one acting as a kind of microstate with its own conception of the measure of law to be applied. This is the phenomenon which I call the parallel state: the formal state running parallel to an informal state; a centralized state covering the self-contradictory actions of diffuse microstates; and the maximalist official state coexisting side by side with the minimalist, unofficial state.

As a consequence of the parallel state the private capital felt relatively relieved from strict institutional regulations of the wage relation and was able to gradually restore the conditions of accumulation. In 1976 the wage income represented 56.5 percent of the national income; in 1978 it represented 44 percent; and in 1983, 42.3 percent. The parallel state has allowed for grotesque forms of exploitation, typical of the periods of primitive accumulation, to occur in a country with fordist laws and institutions. In January 1986 around 120,000 workers of 874 factories and firms were working without being paid, sometimes for several months in a row, keeping on the job for the fear of unemployment. According to the trade unions, the employers then owed the workers 15 million dollars. Particularly in the north where the export sector is concentrated, the illegal use of child labor is still frequent, as is the practice of hiring workers (mainly women) for wages below the minimum wage. It has also been common to withhold social security payments, not only the employers' contributions but also the employees' contributions deducted from their wages.[5]

The parallel state is a very ambiguous state form because, in it, the absentism of the state is one of its most active forms of intervention. For instance, it has been argued that if the labor courts had functioned efficiently in the north during the late seventies and early eighties many firms that sustained the export boom would have gone bankrupt with all the disruptive consequences in terms of employment and balance of trade. The parallel state is thus the political form of a disjunction or discrepancy in the mode of social regulation, according to which the laws and institutions of a fordist mode of regulation are not matched by a fordist wage relation. It is also a very unstable political form. It depends on a game that cannot be reproduced in a stable way. It is the outcome of a political game in which capital has been too weak to impose the repeal of fordist legislation but strong enough to prevent its effective implementation; whereas labor has been strong enough to prevent the repeal of the laws, but it has been too weak to impose their effective implementation.

Moreover, there are autonomous state reasons against the parallel state. It resembles a third-world pattern of state action or, in any case, a non-European pattern, and for that reason its potential for delegitimation has increased as the country has entered the European Economic Community. Indeed, 1986 marks the beginning of the decline of the parallel state. Its slow decline in recent years has been sped up by the government stability, by the first major impact of the integration in the EEC (the inflow of structural funds), by the second revision of the Constitution in 1989, and finally by the type of exchange relations and wage relations that came to prevail.

The Heterogeneous State (1): The Social Construction of Social Actors

As the parallel state has declined as a long-range policy orientation, another policy orientation has become more prominent. This policy orientation I will call *the heterogeneous state.* It comprises a complex set of state actions aimed at reducing the distance and the discrepancy between the institutional framework and the socioeconomic relations, this time acting mainly on the latter and through state initiatives that presuppose an active participation of social forces and organizations. The goal is to develop some measure of coherence, of stable social regulation, among highly heterogeneous production and exchange relations and among highly segmented or discontinuous labor markets. This policy orientation invites a closer look into the social structure and the social actors in the past fifteen years.

I have argued that for very different reasons both the authoritarian Estado Novo and the revolutionary crisis were characterized by the hypertrophy of state normalization to the detriment of contractual normalization. In the first period it was labor in particular that lacked the autonomy to organize and negotiate, while in the second it was capital that lacked that autonomy. It is my contention that the past fifteen years have been dominated by a broad social and political process, which still goes on today, aiming at creating or promoting the creation of social actors that will accept and reproduce a mode of social regulation in whose terms institutional regulation and socioeconomic practice meet on a more realistic level, if a less brilliant one. This process, which involves all the social forces and actors, has been regulated by the state, and here lies the centrality of the state throughout this period.

The first substrategy refers to contractual normalization. Contractual normalization presupposes the existence of organized social actors willing to dialogue and to enter a social pact. Both in terms of political development and social structure, Portuguese modern history has not favored the emergence of such social actors. Neither capital nor labor has a tradition of autonomous organization and negotiation. As a result, the goal of contractual normalization in the postrevolutionary period had to start almost from zero. This difficulty was and still is inscribed in the social structure itself.

As to capital, the Portuguese bourgeoisie has always been highly heterogeneous. On one side is a small sector of modern entrepreneurs with a profit structure based on technological innovation, productivity gains, high wages, and links with transnational capital, a sector that was seriously affected by the nationalizations of 1975; on the other side, a myriad of small entrepreneurs with a profit structure based on low wages investing in traditional and less and less competitive sectors, addicted to state protectionism, possessing a tentist mentality and behavior typical of a contradictory class location between bourgeoisie and petite bourgeoisie. Since these two large sectors are in turn internally diversified, the organization of interests becomes very difficult and centralized capital-labor agreements become highly improbable. After the revolutionary crisis, the emerging capital organizations had very low membership participation, were dominated by sectors used to state protectionism and repression of labor, and adopted a highly political outlook of revanchism against the revolution and the "chaos" it had created, and against the new labor and social legislation, claiming the payment of damages to the former owners of the nationalized industries.

As to labor, the Portuguese social structure is even more heterogeneous. On one side is a small sector of urban proletariat, working in nationalized or foreign capital industries and services, with a high level of unionization and a proletarian class habitus. On the other side is the immense majority of the working class, working in small private enterprises in small towns and rural areas, oftentimes owning a small plot of farmland, with a family income drawing from different sources and a petite bourgeois or peasant class habitus. In the fastest growing industrial zones of Portugal almost 40 percent of the workers live in families with some agricultural activity and are, for that reason, semiproletarians, or part-time farmers. After the revolution, the labor organizations had a massive membership inherited from the revolution, but were in fact dominated by the small urban sector and their leadership was controlled by the Communist Party. The General Confederation of Workers (CGTP), though already on the defensive, kept a very aggressive discourse dominated by the resentment at the failure of the revolution and the betrayal of socialism by the Socialist Party; in such a mood they had very little inclination to negotiate with the class enemy.

The obstacles to contractual normalization were, therefore, almost cyclopic. The social deficit was not only of corporatist association but, more deeply, a deficit of actorship. In my view, the state has been playing a central role in reducing this social deficit. Indeed, one of the main dimensions of state normalization has been the promotion of contractual normalization. The objective has been to promote the emergence of new social partners (and to recycle old ones) that will be interested in social dialogue and concertation and that indeed will derive their representativity and legitimacy from their success in dialogue and concertation. Such dialogue and concertation must proceed according to rules established by the state and under its supervision, a condition that must also be accepted by the social partners.

The state has been central in socially regulating the demands of capital organizations. On the one hand, it has legitimized—and indeed subscribed and amplified—those that are politically feasible and forward-looking and that are based in economic and technological imperatives consensually accepted by both the entrepreneurs and the state bureaucrats. On the other hand, it has suppressed, trivialized, or neutralized those demands that are politically unfeasible and backward-looking, derived from resentment and revanchism against the revolution. These policies have consisted, at different times or occasions, in encouraging the emergence of new organizations or promoting those already existing, providing financial and institutional support for specific initiatives, using the mass media to diffuse capitalist messages, setting up state institutions in which capital organizations have great influence, recruiting high government officials from the ranks of capital, and so forth.

As regards labor, the strategy has been mainly oriented to isolate the Communist confederation of trade unions, the CGTP, refusing contacts with it, producing a sustained hostile discourse against the confederation's discourse and practice, minimizing its victories and amplifying its defeats, encouraging individual unions to separate from the confederation, and, above all, encouraging the emergence of a new confederation with a different, democratic style and unionist practice based on dialogue, negotiation, and concertation. In this respect the Socialist Party, which was the governing party in the immediate postrevolutionary period, played a key role. Considering themselves a working-class party and having led, during the revolutionary crisis, the struggle against the Communists' position that would make it illegal to create more than one confederation of unions, the Socialists felt that a new confederation controlled by them or at least in tune with their political program was required by the challenges of the democratic reconstruction of the economy, as had happened in other European countries (France, Italy, and Spain). In 1978 the General Union of Workers (UGT) was founded. It was constituted by a majority of unions of the service sector, with a very outspoken leadership using an aggressively anti-Communist discourse and promising a new, autonomous, and democratic labor activism. Since its creation, the state always showed its preference to deal with the UGT and always tried, whether appropriately or inappropriately, to contrast its ideology and practice with those of the CGTP.

Following some European models, the Permanent Council of Social Concertation was founded in 1984, composed of six representatives of the government, six representatives of labor (three representatives of each confederation), and six representatives of industrial, commercial and agrarian capital, with wide consultative functions covering all economic, fiscal, and monetary policies. At first the CGTP refused to join the council, having agreed to participate actively only after 1987.

The social construction of social actors and of contractual normalization has been a rather ambiguous process. At the same time that they have gained recognition as nationwide social actors, the labor organizations have lost strength and influence in the day-to-day tasks of securing the interests of the workers at the point of production. Many employers have felt strong enough to prohibit the entry of union delegates into their factories. And the real wages have been falling in spite of the growth of productivity. If we take 1972 as 100, the average productivity increased in 1982 to 145.8 while the real wage cost decreased to 75.2. The alarming decrease of union membership is the mirror image of the poor performance of trade unions throughout this period.

This phenomenon invites a closer look into the accumulation process and wage relations and therefore into the role of the state in creating the structural conditions of accumulation and the pattern of reproductive specialization (the second policy or substrategy of the heterogeneous state).

The Heterogeneous State (2): Toward a New Regime of Accumulation

One major dimension of state intervention in this field has been the emergence and consolidation of a new sector of monopoly capital, which eventually assumed the role that was performed by the monopoly sector smashed by the revolution. In this respect it is important to contrast agrarian capital with industrial and financial capital. The dismantling of the agrarian reform started earlier, in 1977, and is by now virtually accomplished. Most of the land has been returned to the former owners and their descendants. The reconstitution of the agrarian bourgeoisie has been much easier, in social and political terms, than the reconstitution of industrial and financial monopoly capital. First, the agrarian reform occupied only 18 percent of the arable land of the country. Second, the cooperatives and collective units of production set up in the aftermath of the occupation of the latifundia were strongly influenced by the Communist Party and the latter was increasingly isolated both politically and socially. Third, the rural proletariat had always been a small sector of the labor force; it had very little organizational experience and also little influence in the CGTP.

The reconstruction of the industrial and financial capital has been a much more complex economic and political process. First, contrary to what happened in the agrarian reform, the industries, the banks, and insurance companies were nationalized and became part of the so-called state entrepreneurial sector. That is, they became a source of state reproduction, generating funds and opening new opportunities for the exercise of state clientelism and state populism. Second, the nationalizations were defended by both federations of labor and up until recently by the Socialist Party, which was for several years the governing party. Third, given the new international conditions of capital accumulation, the monopoly sector to be reconstructed should integrate new groups, with forward-looking, nonrevanchistic attitudes and better links with transnational capital. Fourth, the privatization of the nationalized sector, when brought about, should bring some relief to the state treasury. Since 1986, when the centrist party formed a government, privatization became one of the main goals of the government program. After complex negotiations with the Socialist Party the constitutional obstacles to full denationalization were removed in 1989. The process of privatization is now in full swing and is very similar to the one adopted by Thatcher in England.

The consolidation of a new industrial and financial monopoly sector could be seen as a corelike strategy, that is, a strategy to promote a modern sector of intensive accumulation interested in upgrading the national pattern of productive specialization and international integration, a sector that would see the wage relation as a factor of realization of capital (mass consumption) rather than as a factor of valorization of capital (a cost of production)—in sum, a sector that would promote a greater coherence between the real wage relation and the fordist regulation formally in force. After all, throughout this period the nationalized sector had been the one in which greater coherence was achieved, since, for obvious reasons, the state-

as-public-administrator denied the state-as-an-entrepreneur the illegal fa-
cilities that it had granted private capital.

But though in this sector some pockets of fordist regulation are developing, the corelike pattern of accumulation and regulation has been by far
outrun by old and new periphery-like patterns of accumulation and regulation. The coexistence of contradictory patterns, supported by old and new
structural factors, has made the Portuguese economic structure highly heterogeneous and discontinuous in terms of logics and organizations of production, in terms of wage relations and labor markets, and in terms of exchange
relations. I would argue that this is the nuclear characteristic of the Portuguese economy and that the major function of the state has been to keep the
heterogeneities and discontinuities within boundaries.

After 1978, the year of the first stabilization program under the IMF,
the economic policy abandoned all structural objectives and concentrated
on the conjuncture. From then on the state policies concentrated on the
control of the external and public deficit, the control of inflation, and the
promotion of exports. Throughout the period exports grew at average rate
higher than the annual growth rate of the GDP and much higher than the
average growth rate of imports. Because of the emphasis on low labor costs,
the export sector that most benefited from these policies was the traditional, labor-intensive sector of textile and garment and shoemaking. It
grew faster than any other, and given its low technological base and its
devaluation in international terms it led to the degradation of the international value of the national production. In the 1973–80 period this value
decreased 3.4 percent. In Spain it increased 2.3 percent and, as a measure
of comparison, in South Korea, 10 percent (Reis 1989, 241).

In terms of the wage relations, this sector and civil construction are at
the base of the pyramid. They account for the majority of the employment
and are dominated by the poorest forms of wage relation: low wages, highest rates of fixed-term contracts, underground work, semiproletariat with
close ties to small-holding agriculture and rural life, high rates of young
and female labor usually worse paid than adult and male labor, low professional training, and restrictive career access.

In a detailed analysis of the labor markets, Maria Rodrigues has identified eleven subsystems of employment and has classified them according
to the relative quality of the wage relation (1988, 248). The top of the hierarchy is occupied by the production of intermediate and equipment products
and is dominated by the public enterprises (those that are now being priva-
tized). The bottom of the hierarchy is occupied by the above-mentioned
sector of export and mass-consumption products. Within each category there
is wide differentiation that occurs not only intersectorially but also

intrasectorially. For this reason the labor market is not just segmented but rather discontinuous (Rodrigues 1988, 259). The discontinuities have been reproduced in recent years under several forms and by different means.

First, clandestine work has been growing steadily, involving various forms, some more obviously illegal than others, and its role in the consolidation of a new mode of social regulation is a subject of debate. Though it is very difficult to estimate its weight in the employment system, it has been possible, for instance, to calculate the rate of unregistered workers in different sectors: 51 percent in civil construction; 20 percent in garment; 59 percent in fisheries.

Second, the growth of subcontracting is also a general trend, and for comparative purposes it is very important to distinguish among the different forms of subcontracting. Maria Marques has analyzed in great detail the patterns of national and international subcontracting and has compared them with those of other European countries. Portuguese patterns have a hybrid nature but with the distinctive predominance of peripheral traits (Marques 1989, 361).

Third, there is the growth of the feminization of the labor force. In this respect the changes of the last two decades have been tremendous. In 1960 men were 81 percent of the labor force and, in 1981, 65 percent. Between 1970 and 1981 the statistical category of domestic housewife decreased from 74.4 percent to 41.3 percent. This development has been concomitant with others equally dramatic: the rapid decline of the fertility rate—the fastest demographic transition in European history—and the fastest growth rate of domestic equipment. However, women have been the major victims of the heterogenization of the labor markets, as they tend to work in the sectors with most degraded wage relations.

Fourth, there are an increasing number of agencies that provide a range of workers for clients on a temporary basis. Though illegal until recently, these contracts are an emerging form of evading the rigidity of the fordist laws and institutions.

Finally, there is the growth of autonomous work. Portugal has the lowest proletarianization rate of Europe. In 1984, this rate was 82 percent for the EEC and 67.1 percent for Portugal. This is due to two convergent phenomena. One is the strong presence of small-holding agriculture and the other is the growth of autonomous work. In the period 1974–81 it grew 36 percent while the wage labor grew only 12 percent. So-called autonomous work is almost always not truly autonomous work, but is so defined in legal terms to avoid the labor laws and, above all, social security payments.

All these trends point to the fact that the regime of accumulation that has been emerging in the last fifteen years has favored the quantity of work in detriment of the quality of work (Portugal has the lowest unemployment rate in Europe: 4.7 percent). The dialectic of integration/exclusion has thereby in general terms favored the side of exclusion. In terms of their contribution to the national product important pockets of fordist integration have remained, mostly in the public enterprises. But the productive specialization of the economy has been lowered. As a result, the fordist laws and institutions have only been effective in highly selective terms and for that reason they have coexisted with a predominantly competitive, neoliberal regulation of the wage relation. The dramatic progress in the regulation of the wage relation obtained in the revolutionary period and in the two years thereafter have been followed by equally dramatic regressions in the real social value of labor.

The regulation theory has claimed that the changes in mode of regulation may start in any of its constitutive elements. It has also been claimed that the regulation of the wage relation is relatively autonomous in bringing about changes in the regime of accumulation. The Portuguese case indicates that the autonomy of the wage relation may, at times, be very relative indeed. Given the weight of the political factors in the configuration of the wage relation, the general conditions of its autonomy may also become the general conditions of its dependence. Indeed, in the Portuguese case, the state has produced the autonomy of the wage relation in a given moment and, in the following, its dependence. It did that through the parallel state and the heterogeneous state. The heterogeneous state, in contrast with the parallel state, does not rely on law or on its violation and is more positive than negative—it acts through administrative decisions, economic guidelines, monetary and financial mechanisms, fiscal incentives, exchange rates, subsidies, vocational training, public threats against more aggressive social actors, management of strikes in the public sector, mythmaking in the media, etc. Through all these means the state has assumed a very central role in social regulation, even if apparently it lacks an economic policy or is rather inefficient in its deployment. In my view the fragmentation and apparent incoherence of economic measures have been crucial to regulate the heterogeneity and discontinuities of the wage relations and of the accumulation process itself. Though transitional periods call in theory for the predominance of structural policies over conjunctural policies, the fact remains that the structural intervention of the state may take place, in some circumstances, through conjunctural intervention. The combination of apparently contradictory and highly fragmented and discontinuous conjunctural interventions end up producing a new structure. This process is far from being completed in the Portuguese case, but the trends cannot but be seen.

Centrality in social regulation can be therefore combined with inefficiency, which may occur by sheer inefficiency, but also by design. One of the most striking features of the official discourse of the Portuguese state is its antistatism. Throughout this period state agents have been claiming that the state is a poor administrator and an even poorer producer, this being the main reason to strengthen civil society and private enterprise. This masochistic discourse is, however, not self-indicting because the concrete state, in so discoursing, distances itself from the abstract state, the real (and thus, unreal) bête noire. Because the state has also to intervene in order not to intervene, the antistatist discourse is self-defeating. The centrality of the state reproduces itself through the discourse of the marginality of the state.

The social regulation of heterogeneity and discontinuity does not by itself make the state a heterogeneous state. The heterogeneous character of the Portuguese state lies in the fact that the heterogeneity and discontinuity in the social structure have reproduced themselves in the political and administrative matrix of the state through the range of modes of social regulation that have been attempted and the speed with which they have been replacing one another in the last fifteen years. In such a short period, the Portuguese state has evolved from state corporatism to transition to socialism, to fordist regulation and welfare state, to neoliberal regulation. Since each mode of regulation has translated itself in laws and institutions, in administrative services and ideologies, and given the inertia of these phenomena, the structure of the state at a given moment has a number of different layers, differently sedimented, some old, some new, each one with its own logic and implicit strategical orientation. Here lies the heterogeneous state.

The heterogeneous state does not limit itself to the regulation of exchange relations and wage relations. It extends to the broad field of social welfare, which I will analyze below. Before doing so, however, it is imperative to mention other dimensions of the social heterogeneity of the Portuguese society, which are crucially important to understand the field of social welfare.

The Discrepancy Between Capitalist Production and Social Reproduction: The Role of the Small-Holding Agriculture

The picture of the Portuguese society I have given so far focuses mainly on wage and exchange relations and their regulation by the state. It is a partial picture and as such it fails to capture other aspects equally relevant to understanding the society. However heterogeneous in terms of accumulation and wage relations, Portuguese society appears as a very cohesive society. For instance, it has the lowest crime rate in Europe. Though periphery-like as regards the main trends of recent economic development, Portuguese society presents many other features in which the center-orientation predominates, as in cultural life, in family conceptions, and above all in consumption patterns. Though still distant in quantitative terms, the norms of consumption are, in qualitative terms, closer and closer to European norms. The two structuring commodities of working-class mass consumption in the fordist mode of regulation—the automobile and the house—have become increasingly central in the expense planning of the working-class families. The consumption of domestic equipment has also increased dramatically, as I mentioned earlier.

These features illustrate the intriguing fact that in Portugal the social crisis has always been less serious than the economic crisis. Leaving aside other aspects of this phenomenon, I will concentrate on the question of consumption. My main argument is that there is a discrepancy or dissociation between capitalist production and social reproduction, or between the dominant norm of production and the norm of consumption. The discrepancy or dissociation lies in the fact that the norm of capitalist production is less developed than the norm of consumption and, accordingly, the latter is closer to the center than the former. This is due to a peculiar wage-income relation in which nonwage income plays an important role in the total income pull of working-class families, a phenomenon that directly or indirectly is related to the strong presence of small-holding agriculture. This characteristic seems to be common to semiperipheral countries in the European region, but it presents itself in Portugal in a particularly striking manner (Reis 1989; Hespanha 1990).

If we compare Portugal and the former FRG in terms of product and in terms of consumption in parities of purchasing power, the figures are striking: the difference in terms of product is between 2,480 (Portugal) and 13,240 (FRG), but in terms of private consumption it is between 2,846 (Portugal) and 6,175 (FRG). In other words, the GDP per capita underestimates by 2.4 times the average standard of living (Mateus 1987, 57). In order to explain this distortion it is necessary to analyze the household income and its composition. Between 1973 and 1983 the sum of wage income and income from property and entrepreneurship (including corporate profits)—that is, the two main sources of income in a capitalist society—suffered a decrease of 20.1 percent (from 85.1 percent to 65 percent). But income from savings accounts increased from 3.1 percent to 19.4 percent, which means that rentism is an important dimension of the reproduction of Portuguese families. Social-security payments and current transfers increased from 4.1 percent to 12.1 percent. External private transfers, which are basically the remittances of migrant workers, maintained throughout the period, with some oscillations, the same rate: 11 percent. If we exclude corporate profits from autonomous income (property and entrepreneurship), autonomous income is basically constituted of income derived from small-holding agriculture. Throughout the period its national average weight is around 25 percent of the household income. The regional differences are quite striking, but even more striking is the fact that the region with the highest industrial growth in the last decade is close to the national average. This shows the weight of noncapitalist incomes in the social reproduction of Portuguese workers and the peculiar complementarity between agriculture and industry. Agriculture accounts for 19 percent of the employment but more than one-third of the Portuguese families have an agricultural linkage, which shows the incidence of double class and contradictory class locations. Interestingly enough, this linkage ranges from 18 percent to 69 percent in the regions with most dynamic industrial growth.[6]

Small-holding agriculture is a structuring component of the industrialization process and, as one might expect, a rather ambiguous one in social terms. On the one hand, it has functioned as an important compensatory mechanism in periods of crisis; on the other hand, it has alleviated the pressure on wages, thereby contributing to the degradation of the industrial specialization. But the strong presence of small-holding agriculture extends beyond productive activities and influences and into such different areas as symbolic universes, electoral patterns, labor-union activism, and forms of sociability.

The dissociation between norm of production and norm of consumption means, therefore, that the heterogeneity of Portuguese society is not confined to discontinuities of the labor markets. It derives also from the coexistence and articulation of different modes of production: private capitalist production, state-enterprises production, cooperative production, production for self-consumption, and simple mercantile production. The heterogeneous state extends also to these other forms of heterogeneity.

As I mentioned earlier, the complex mixture of social heterogeneity and social cohesion in Portuguese society is also important for understanding the patterns of social welfare and, for that matter, the role of the quasi- or lumpen-welfare state. To this I turn now.

A Weak Welfare State and a Strong Welfare Society

I will argue in the following that the Portuguese state is not a welfare state in the technical sense, though in some respects it approximates this political form. I will also argue that the deficits in state welfare are partially compensated for by the social welfare that can be produced in a society which is relatively rich in relations of community, interknowledge, and mutual help. This latter phenomenon I will designate as *welfare society*.

The welfare state is the dominant political form of the state in the central countries in the phase of "organized capitalism," and, as such is part of the fordist mode of regulation. It is based on four structural elements. First, there is a social pact between capital and labor under the aegis of the state, a pact whose ultimate goal is to make capitalism and democracy compatible; second, there is a sustained, even if tense, relation between accumulation and legitimation; third, a high level of expenses in social consumption (welfare services); fourth, an administrative structure that has internalized the social rights as rights (not as state benevolence).

Judged in light of these attributes the Portuguese state falls short of the welfare state: it is a *quasi-* or *lumpen-welfare state*. For the reasons already presented, no social pact has been established and the hypertrophy of state normalization is as visible in the field of social policies as in the field of the wage relations. During the revolutionary crisis and in the two following years, there was an attempt to build an advanced welfare state, not only in terms of the extension of the risks covered and the quality of the services, but also in terms of the democratic participation of citizens' groups in the organization of those services. In that period, the social expenses increased dramatically. For instance, in the field of health, they grew from 1.9 percent of the GDP in the period of 1971–73, to 2.9 percent in the period of 1974–76. As we already know, this period was characterized by an excess of the tasks of legitimation over those of accumulation and was followed by another with inverted priorities. Accordingly, in the following years social expenses grew at a much slower rate; in some cases they even stagnated, and today they are still far behind the European average values.

As one might expect of an intermediate society, the Portuguese state approximates the welfare state of European countries in some aspects more than in others. The European welfare states are internally very diversified and it is common to distinguish between the Continental model and the Anglo-Saxon/Scandinavian model (Alber 1988, 452). The Portuguese state seems to come closer to the latter. In general terms it approximates it more in what concerns range of services and the type of instruments to provide them and the financing mechanisms, and less in what concerns scope and quality—the two features that, together with range, directly determine the quality of welfare consumption.

However, what most unequivocally distinguishes the Portuguese state from the welfare state is the fact that the public-welfare administration has not yet fully internalized the conception of public welfare as a matter of right, and in some respects goes on conceiving it as a matter of state benevolence, as was the case during the fascist regime. Indeed, the revolution of 25 April left the administration relatively untouched; even if there were changes, they took place at the level of personnel, not at the level of structures. Under these conditions the authoritarian ideology of the Estado Novo administration infiltrated the administration of the new democratic state. In the field of social services such authoritarianism translates itself in a discretionary, privatistic behavior. People are serviced differently according to the informal connections they manage to mobilize in their favor. In a sense, they are doubly clients of the state, of the state that produces the services and of the state bureaucrats that deliver them.

The degradation of the state welfare in the last ten years parallels the degradation of the wage relation analyzed above. In the field of welfare, the measures adopted to lower the welfare content of the state have been very similar to the ones that have been adopted in central countries in the aftermath of the crisis of the welfare state. It is as if Portugal is undergoing a crisis of the welfare state without ever having had a welfare state. The research I have conducted on the health services enables us to see the full range of such measures which indeed have also been adopted in other social fields (Santos 1990, 193). The National Health Service promulgated in the late seventies was based on an advanced concept of health—health as community health—and followed the British model closely. A potentially universal service, it gave full priority to public medicine and health care and that is why it was fiercely opposed by the national medical association. Partly because of this opposition and also due to the changes in government in the early eighties, the National Health Service was never fully implemented, and whatever parts of it had been implemented were soon subjected to severe criticism. The restrictive measures gained a new strength and coherence in the last four years under the centrist party rule.

These measures have included budget cuts that have led to the degradation of the services so that the better-off turn to the private sector and absorb the costs of health care in the family budget; new administrative guidelines that restrict access, thereby increasing the selectivity of a formally universal service; and several measures of cost-sharing, thereby transferring to the families part of the costs. But they have, above all, included a sliding process of privatization of the National Health Service whereby the state gradually ceases to be a producer of welfare and becomes a financing agency for welfare produced privately in the market or in the nonprofit charitable sector (Campos et al., 1986; Carapinheiro and Pinto 1987). In 1975 the private sector accounted for only 2.8 percent of the total health investment, while in 1980 it accounted for 17.2 percent and this percentage has been growing in the last ten years. The production of health care has in part been transferred from the state to the private sector. Today, more than 30 percent of public health expenses are payments to the private sector. This transfer has been following a distinctive pattern: to the private sector are transferred the profitable services, capital intensive services with high technological content and low hospitalization time, such as high-tech diagnosis, dialysis, and elective surgery. The state keeps for itself the less productive, more labor intensive services with high hospitalization content. This pattern has led to the emergence of what I call, borrowing from O' Connor, the social-industrial complex (O' Connor 1973).

The transfer of public services to the private sector has, however, taken another form. In the last decade the state has been supporting, financing, promoting, and even creating nonprofit private institutions that by means of contracts with the state provide social services that were formally provided by the state, particularly in the field of welfare for the elderly and handicapped. There is a great tradition of charitable institutions in Portugal, and these provide services under the supervision of the state and indeed are supposed to operate as quasi-public institutions. They are civil society institutions, but the presence of the state in their operation is so pervasive both in regulatory and financial terms that I designate them as *secondary civil society,* in order to stress the fact that through them the state reproduces itself in nonstate institutions. This process bears some similarities with the role of the state in the promotion of social actors in the field of wage relations, although, in the case of the secondary civil society, the institutions depend much more on the state and are supposed to operate as quasi-state institutions.

By downgrading quality and upgrading selectivity the state has limited the range of public welfare. Through cost-sharing it has partially recommodified welfare services. Through privatization it has created new areas for capital accumulation: captive or protected markets in which the state is sometimes the only consumer. In all these forms has the Portuguese national health service been under attack, though, as in England, it has so far resisted full dismantling. As with nationalizations in the field of accumulation, so the dismantling of public welfare institutions has been the ground of heated social and political struggles. Because the beneficiaries of public welfare are a broad sector of the population and are socially identifiable, it is predictable that the supporters of public welfare will have more chances of succeeding than the supporters of the nationalizations.

The degradation of the quality of public welfare has taken forms that parallel those in welfare states of Europe during the last decade. But their

social and political meaning should be different, because the threshold or
base from which the process of degradation started was, and still is, lower
in Portugal than in developed Europe. However, in Portugal the deficit of
public welfare does not manifest itself in forms as socially and politically
disruptive as we might expect in light of its extent. It is my contention that
this is due to the fact that part of the deficit of state welfare is covered by
socially produced welfare. In other words, in Portugal a weak welfare state
coexists with a strong welfare society.

By welfare society I mean the networks of relationships of interknowledge, mutual recognition, and mutual help based on kinship and community ties, through which small social groups exchange goods and services
on a nonmarket basis and with a logic of reciprocity that approximates that
of the gift relationship as analyzed by Marcel Mauss (1950). Such networks vary widely in terms of formalization, range and scope, duration,
and stability. In Portugal, due to the strength of the small-holding agriculture
and the prevalence of rural or small-town working families in residence,
the forms of the welfare society are dominated by patterns of sociability,
by class habitus, by cognitive maps, and by the symbolic universe that are
usually attributes of rural life. However, contrary to what is often believed,
such networks are not exclusively found in rural areas; they exist also in
urban areas. Moreover, they often comprise complex linkages between rural
families and communities, on one side, and urban families and communities, on the other side.

The welfare society is a form of social capital in Bourdieu's terms. Its
social valorization and realization is of more strategic importance in those
social groups and families whose life trajectories are most affected by the
deficit of public welfare. In 1981, 71 percent of the unemployed said that
their main source of income and life support was the family. The deficit of
unemployment benefits is thereby made evident.

The welfare society covers a wide range of activities that are not always easy to identify. Here are two examples from my research on the
Portuguese health services.

Over a typical weekend more than ten thousand people visit their friends
and relatives in the two central hospitals of Lisbon, and the figures are not
much lower in the central hospitals of other big cities. Furthermore, during
the week the figures, though lower, are still significant and unheard of elsewhere in Europe. The social isolation of hospital patients is a major problem in welfare states and elsewhere in Europe, the role of professional
social work in the hospitals is today a controversial issue. In Portugal, the
welfare society provides hospitals with free, informal social work that is, I
dare to say, of a much better quality.

Another example is provided by the popular or folk medicine that is available in the welfare society. It includes a wide range of goods and services: traditional self-therapy; nonmonetary exchanges of both natural and supranatural goods and services such as accompanying the sick in their homes; providing medicinal herbs and preparing tisanes; lending pharmaceutical products; pledged pilgrimages to Fátima and other sanctuaries in return for cures believed to be miraculous; monetary exchanges outside the market, like herbs and ointments; services rendered at a fee by a midwife, a folk-medicine person, a medium, a witch. Some of the goods and services are provided by specialists, be they the saints or the midwives, while others are provided by neighbors and kin.

Folk or popular medicine holds a conception of bodily and mental health that is quite different from that of allopathic medicine (M. J. F. Hespanha 1987). It therefore provides different products and services through different social relations. As a matter of fact, folk medicine involves a specific mode of production of health. I would argue that, in Portugal, health care is the result of an articulation of three different modes of production of medical services and health care: public medicine, private capitalist medicine, and popular medicine. The relations between the welfare state and the welfare society are interwoven in the dynamics of this articulation. The heterogeneity that derives from the joint operation of different and sometimes contradictory welfare logics is regulated by the state. In the social field, the heterogeneous state presents itself as a lumpen-welfare state that counts on the welfare society to compensate for its own shortcomings, thus reducing the crisis of legitimation that could derive therefrom.

Curiously enough, some social scientists in central countries of Western Europe have also recently proposed the concept of welfare society to discuss the crisis of the welfare state and its possible solutions. Thus Rosanvallon speaks of the need for a "more decentralized and more diversified form of welfare provision in many respects akin to the flexibility that the family used to provide" and calls for a re-expansion of social policy based on "publicly motivated but privately organized groups (such as charitable institutions) and the traditional family itself" (1988, 539). In the same vein, Lipietz develops the idea of the third sector, a social-utility sector, beyond the state and the capitalist private sector (1989, 108).

This discussion has brought a new interest in the research on the Portuguese welfare society. The research so far has tended to conceive of the welfare society as a premodern survival or residue. However, in the light of the discussion on new mixes between welfare state and welfare society, what was previously conceived of as a premodern residue is gradually recoded as a postmodern feature. There are, of course, differences between the Portuguese welfare society and the welfare society that is now being proposed in central countries, but there are also some striking similarities. Above all, the Portuguese case illustrates some of the positive potentialities and some of the limitations of a new combination of welfare society and welfare state. It has been argued that the welfare state put too much emphasis on equality in detriment of security; that as it developed citizenship, it also bureaucratized it; that it turned citizens into clients, thereby increasing dependency and social control; and that it eliminated commodity fetishism in the field of social welfare, only to replace it by state fetishism.

The research on Portuguese welfare society yields a few comments on this. First, it should be borne in mind that the services provided by the welfare society are never the same as those provided by the state. This is clearly illustrated by the social work involved in the visits to hospitals or by the conception of the body and of health in folk medicine. Second, the welfare society is hostile to equality or, at least, it does not distinguish as clearly as the welfare state between legitimate and illegitimate inequalities. Third, welfare society is hostile to citizenship and to legal entitlements, since welfare relations are concrete, multiplex, and based on the concrete, long-term reciprocity of sequences of unilateral benevolent actions. Fourth, welfare society also creates dependency and forms of social control, which may be more flexible and more negotiable but are also more visible. Fifth, welfare society tends to create spatial rigidity. Last but not least, most of the burden of the welfare provided by the welfare society will inevitably fall on women if dominant family practices are not changed. These comments are intended to expand the scope of the discussion on the welfare state/welfare society mix. In analytical and political terms it is crucial to distinguish between progressive mixes and regressive mixes. In my view, the discussion so far, though well intended, has fallen short of a clear distinction.

The analysis of the Portuguese welfare society as a strong welfare society coexisting with and complementing a weak welfare state and the expansion of the analysis in light of the new alternatives that have been proposed for the crisis of the welfare state illustrate the dialectic of territorialization and deterritorialization in the world system. In concrete terms, at stake are the challenges confronting national experiences increasingly interpenetrated by transnational experiences.

I have been suggesting that the Portuguese society is a very complex social formation whose social cohesion and dynamic development is premised upon the reproduction of unstable equilibria between highly heterogeneous and dissociated social, economic, political, and cultural processes, many of them inscribed in the history of the country. It is legitimate to ask what impact the integration into the Common Market will have on these equilibria, bearing in mind that, according to officially stated goals, integration does mean economic, political, and social integration. To this I turn now.

The State-as-Imagination-of-the-Center and the Integration into the European Economic Community

Portugal has been a full member of the EEC since 1986. Together with Spain, Greece, and Ireland it has benefited from a transitional period of structural adjustments aimed at increasing the homogeneity of the EEC as a whole. In its most important aspects this period ended in 1993.

One of the most remarkable features of the Portuguese process of integration in the EEC is the priority given to political considerations. When the Socialist Party in the late seventies adopted for the first time the slogan "Europe with us," the objective was that, by joining the EEC, Portugal would be able to build and consolidate a stable democratic society, a European Western society. The "excesses" of the revolutionary crisis were still present and the Leninist posture of the Communist Party was still considered potentially dangerous. The integration in the EEC would decisively contribute to eliminate these nondemocratic elements and to consolidate the young democracy.

The priority of the political (which, as I emphasized, was a general feature of the period) combined with the corporatist deficit reinforced the centrality and the autonomy of the state in the negotiations leading to the integration into the EEC. The negotiation was a complex process and the social impact of many of the agreed-upon measures is still to be felt. The state conducted the negotiations with virtually no consultation with the social-interests organizations. Repeated surveys, not only among the population in general but also among the employers, have revealed an almost total ignorance about the economic, political, and social consequences of the integration into the EEC.

The autonomy of the state has a political, an economic, and a symbolic dimension. As regards the political dimension, the autonomy of the state has been justified in terms of the national interest that is up to the state to defend. Contradictorily enough, the autonomy of the state to defend national interests is threatened by a process that considerably reduces the autonomous capacity of the state to control the mechanisms of national development. Another political dimension of state autonomy lies in the legal and institutional harmonization called for by the integration. In recent years the legal and institutional productivity of the state has been geared to the goal of harmonization, and this goal has also served as a justification to undo some of the legal and institutional innovations of the period between 1974 and 1977 or to delegitimate the social and political demands that are supposedly in contradiction with the harmonization goal. The underside of the political autonomy of the state is the distance that it has created between national social actors and the challenges of the integration into the EEC.

The economic dimension of the autonomy of the state has lain mainly in the management of the sizable structural funds that the EEC has injected into the Portuguese economy as part of the transitional program of structural adjustment and homogenization. The state has assumed total control of the distribution of the structural funds and has done it in a highly particularistic way, divorced from any strategic conception of economic development and at the mercy of the pressure of organized interests and political clienteles. This has given rise to a form of state populism that, contrary to the forms of populism in, for instance, Latin America, does not involve common people but rather enterprises and economic groups, and the relation they entertain with state power does not use the intermediation of political leaders; rather, it reaches the state bureaucracy directly.

During the transitional period, Portugal has been a net beneficiary of the integration. The structural funds, when not misused through corruption, have contributed to the general conditions of accumulation, for instance, through the construction of infrastructures and vocational training, and have also created employment in many sectors. For these reasons the economic impact of the integration has so far been positive and, consequently, the state has been able to convert autonomy into legitimation. Whether this virtuous cycle can go on after 1993 is an open question.

The political and economic dimensions of the autonomy of the state in the context of the integration into the EEC have fed on its symbolic dimension. The latter is a very complex dimension because through it the state regulates, mainly by discourse and symbolic actions, the dialectic of distance and proximity, of difference and identity, between Portugal and Europe. The regulation consists in creating an imaginary universe in which Portugal becomes an European country like any other, its lower level of development a mere transitional feature whose management is entrusted to the state as the guardian of the national interest. This symbolic construction is a strategic resource in the credible deployment of the other dimensions of the state autonomy, so much so that in my view it determines the dominant political form of the state in the context of the integration into the EEC, a political form that I will call *the state-as-imagination-of-the-center*.

The state-as-imagination-of-the-center is a political form with multiple productivity. First, it produces intelligible and credible signs of a future better life, thereby making current hardship and scarcity transitional and thus acceptable if not legitimate. Second, it enables the state to cash in on all the current benefits from the integration, relegating to a vague future any possible costs. Third, it delegitimates any specificities of national development that are not amenable to current state objectives (e.g., the state entrepreneurial sector) under the guise that they contradict European patterns of development and therefore cannot be politically sustained. Fourth, it depoliticizes the internal political process by invoking the technical inevitability of some measures in light of European constraints.

In spite of its multiple productivity, the state-as-imagination-of-the-center has a specific material base, namely, the political and economic relations that Portugal has been developing with its former African colonies. In the light of these relations, Portugal appears as a central country, a member of the EEC, and indeed in competition with other EEC countries such as France, Spain, and Italy. At the symbolic level these relations dramatize the fact that Portugal belongs to the center and indeed condition the political and the economic nature of the exchanges. However, at a deeper level, one might also see here the reconstruction, in new terms, of the colonial, intermediary, transmission-belt role: Portugal acting as an intermediary between the core and the periphery.

In my view, this reconstruction unites the colonial to the postcolonial period and it is an important ingredient of the autonomy of the state in the context of the integration into the EEC. I would argue that the autonomy of the state, which in the fascist period was based on the colonies, is now based on the integration into the EEC, of which the relations with the Portuguese-speaking African countries will be an increasingly important element. Like all the other political forms of the Portuguese state, the state-as-imagination-of-the-center is a transitional entity. According to the nature of future European development either the "imagination" or the "center" will disappear from this political form. What are then the prospects?

The future of the EEC is today, as much as ever, an open question, more open in terms of its political and social dimension than in terms of its economic dimension. The last few years have witnessed a decisive revitalization of the European Community. The treaty of Rome has been reformulated by the Single European Act, the 1992 strategy, the market without frontiers, and the Social Charter. These measures taken together point to an integrated, harmonic development of the European Community in all its dimensions—economic, political, and social. In real terms, however, the policies and the instruments that have been concretely applied reveal the clear priority of the economic dimension, the construction of the internal market. Moreover, though the political discourse stresses the goal of economic and social cohesion and, therefore, of the increasing homogenization of the European space, the economic policies being implemented have a strong neoliberal tone and are insensitive, if not altogether hostile, to the goal of social cohesion and social homogenization.

This can be illustrated by the long discussions and successive stalemates on the question of a European social policy (Streeck 1989; Teague 1989). Beyond the statutes on equal opportunity not much has been accomplished. The Val Duchesse talks on social dialogue have failed. According to the Single European Act, while all issues relating to the internal market can be decided by a majority vote, the issues relating to social policy will require a unanimous vote, with the exception of the provisions on health and safety of workers.

The Commission has been pushing for a more dirigiste social policy but without much success. The Belgian initiative on the so-called plinth-of-social-rights to be granted in all member states may have some chance of being accepted but it will not be, as some would like, a kind of European Social Constitution with binding norms directly applicable in all countries. Probably it will constitute a "social regime" in which terms the norms will be more than mere guidelines but less than legally binding obligations. If so, the goal of social homogenization will remain a remote one.

Besides, the history of the EEC makes us feel pessimistic about the feasibility of such goal. If we analyze the evolution of the real income (GDP per capita in parity of purchasing power) between 1960 and 1987 of the twelve countries that form today the EEC, three conclusions are in order (Mateus 1989, 179): first, the majority of the central countries cluster around the community average with some oscillations, upward in the case of FRG, and downward, in the case of England and Holland; second, Portugal, Greece, Ireland and Spain form a distinct group with a level of real income between 26 percent and 46 percent below the community average; third, in the subperiod of economic expansion (1970–75) these disparities decreased while in the period of economic crisis and restructuring (1975–87) they increased again. More revealing, however, is the fact that the integration only shows a potential for social homogenization in the first period of the community, the period between 1958 and 1973 when the EEC included only six countries. The subsequent enlargements of the community don't show any dynamics toward homogenization. If we analyze the evolution of the dispersion between the maximum and minimum national-income levels between 1960 and 1987, the following results are elucidating: the EEC-6 shows a dispersion of 1.32 in 1960 and a dispersion of 1.15 in

1987; the EEC-9 shows a dispersion of 1.89 in 1973 and 1.84 in 1987; the EEC-10 shows a dispersion of 1.97 in 1981 and 2.15 in 1987; and finally the EEC-12 shows a dispersion of 2.21 in 1985 and 2.15 in 1987. Except for the last value, which is probably related to the transfers of structural funds, no dynamics of homogenization is detectable in the last decade. The same results would be obtained if we compared regions instead of countries.

In light of this, the homogenization, even if only partial, is a very difficult goal and can be obtained only through courageous structural policies both at the community level and at national level, involving not only the construction of the internal market but also the building up of social cohesion and the construction of a new European state. For the time being, nothing of this sort is in sight. On one side, there are visible discrepancies between national and European structural policies and the degree of discrepancy manifests itself through nationalist regression (e.g., the cases of Great Britain and Portugal). On the other side, the less-developed countries, those that most need broad structural policies, are those that, in the context of the community, have less capacity to develop and implement them. In this respect, the danger may lie in the European attempt to gain international competitiveness at the cost of its periphery.

Europe is the motherland of social protection, as Aglietta says; it presents the remarkable social experience of a mixed economy wisely combining state intervention and broad social concertation. This is a commendable pedigree, but the disturbing coincidence—which is not really a coincidence at all—is that the discourse of social cohesion at the European level is coexisting with the dismantling of the welfare states and the increase of social inequality at the national level in all EEC countries.

Conclusion

The integration into the EEC has gradually become the single most important factor structuring the period of transition that Portuguese society has been undergoing since 1974, or better, since 1969. This transition has been a double one, taking place both at the national and at the European level, with increasing interpenetration between the two levels. Portuguese society is a highly heterogeneous society, not only in economic and social terms but also in political and cultural terms. The complex weaving and cross-neutralization of those multiple heterogeneities in Portugal—one of the oldest nation-states of Europe (at least in having had the same borders for longest time) and one of the most homogeneous in ethnic terms—has made it possible so far to combine high heterogeneity and diversity with high social cohesion. This complex process has been regulated by the state, which has inscribed in its institutional matrix the very transition and social heterogeneity that are the object of its regulation. In different spheres of social life the state has assumed different partial political forms: in the sphere of exchange relations and wage relations, the form of the parallel state followed by the form of the heterogeneous state; in the sphere of social welfare, the form of the quasi- or lumpen-welfare state; in the sphere of European integration and the values attached to it, the form of the state-as-imagination-of-the-center. All these forms are transitional and bear witness to the tensions between core orientation and periphery orientation, between international promotion and international demotion, between social integration and social exclusion. They represent the Portuguese way of living through the dynamic transformations of the world system in the last fifteen years.

This transition is far from reaching its conclusion. However, the different partial political forms of the state and their evolution seem to point to a new semiperipheral mode of social regulations.

Notes

1. Dudley Seers (1977) and Albert Hirschman (1983) were probably the first to argue that development economics and the sociology of development were only sustainable scientific disciplines if they were applied to developed countries as well as to less-developed ones. See Mateus 1987, 45.

2. This conception is also being defended in the cultural field. Most recently, Arjun Appadurai has argued that "the new global cultural economy has to be seen as a complex, overlapping, disjunctive order which cannot any longer be understood in terms of existing center-periphery models" (1990, 6).

3. This reterritorialization occurs usually at an infrastate level but can also occur at a suprastate level. A good example of the latter is the European Economic Community, which is in the process of deterritorializing social relations at the state level only to reterritorialize them at a suprastate level.

4. Moreover, the figures show the longevity of that condition in countries like Portugal, Spain, and Ireland. Thus values obtained in 1983 in recently industrialized countries such as Brazil (38) and South Korea (40) correspond, *grosso modo,* to the values of 1960 for the European countries: Ireland (28); Portugal (38); Spain (42) (Mateus 1987, 54).

5. Even more outrageous has been the practice of not delivering to the trade unions the union fees paid by unionized workers and also deducted from the wages.

6. It is then clear that the Portuguese model of agriculture is quite different from the European model after the war. As Reis has shown, the latter is characterized by a rapid and permanent rural exodus to industrial branches offering high salaries and the consequent decrease of the active rural population and of the number of farms, an increase in the average area of farms, mechanization of household agriculture through credit, and the intensifi-

cation of production and trade. On the contrary, the Portuguese model of agriculture is associated with a less massive exodus from agriculture and, in any case, without rural exodus, pendular migrations, semiproletarianization, ruralization of industry, prevalence of self-consumption or simple mercantile production, a steady high number of farms with small average areas throughout the last thirty years, and low industrial wages (Reis 1985). See also P. Hespanha (1990).

References

Aglietta, Michel. 1976. *Regulation et Crises du Capitalisme.* Paris: Calmann-Levy.

Aglietta, Michel, and Anton Brender. 1984 *Les Métamorphoses de la Société Salariale.* Paris: Calmann-Levy.

Alber, Jens. 1988. "Continuities and Changes in the Idea of the Welfare State." *Politics and Society* 16, no. 4:451.

Appadurai, Arjun. 1990. "Disjuncture and Difference in the Global Cultural Economy." *Public Culture* 2, no. 2:1.

Arrighi, G., and J. Drangel. 1986. "The Stratification of the World-Economy. An Exploration of the Semiperipheral Zone." *Review* 10, no. 1:9.

Boyer, Robert. 1986. *La Théorie de la Regulation. Une Analyse Critique.* Paris: La Sécouverte.

Broué, Pierre. 1971. *Révolution en Allemagne, 1917–1923.* Paris: Minuit.

Campos, Correia, L. Patrão, and R. Carvalho. 1986. "A privatização de um sistema público: o caso das tecnologias de diagnóstico e terapêutica em Portugal." Valência: VI Jornadas de Economía de la Salud.

Carapinheiro, Graça, and M. Pinto. 1987. "Políticas de saúde num país em mudança: Portugal nos anos 70 e 80." *Sociologia, Problemas e Práticas* 3.

Fortuna, Carlos. 1987. "Desenvolvimento e Sociologia histórica: acerca da teoria do sistema mundial capitalista e da semiperiferia." *Sociologia, Problemas e Práticas* 3:163.

Hespanha, M. J. Ferros. 1987. "O corpo, a doença e o médico. Representação e práticas sociais numa aldeia." *Revista Crítica de Ciências Sociais* 23:195.

Hespanha, Pedro. 1990. *A propriedade multiforme, um estudo sociológico sobre a evolução recente dos sistemas fundiários em Portugal.* Coimbra: Faculdade de Economia.

Hirschman, Albert. 1983. "Confissões de um dissidente; a estratégia de desenvolvimento reconsiderada." *Pesquisa e Planejamento Económico* 13:1.

Jessop, Bob. 1990. "Regulation theories in retrospect and prospect." *Economy and Society* 19:153.

Lenin, V. I. 1960. *Selected Works in Three Volumes.* Moscow: Progress Publishers.

Lipietz, Alain. 1989. *Choisir L'Audace. Une Alternative pour le XXIe siècle.* Paris: La Découverte.

Marques, Maria Manuel. 1989. *Subcontratação e Autonomia Empresarial: O caso português.* Coimbra: Faculdade de Economia.

Martin, William. 1990. "Introduction: The Challenge of the Semiperiphery." In *Semiperipheral States in the World Economy,* edited by William Martin. New York: Greenwood Press.

Mateus, Augusto. 1983. "Internacionalização, crise e recessão (a especificidade portuguesa)." *Pensamiento Iberoamericano* 3.

———. 1987. "Economias Semiperiféricas e desenvolvimento desigual na Europa (reflexões a partir do caso português)." *Economia e Socialismo* 72–73:41.

———. 1989. "'1992': A Realização do Mercado Interno e os Desafios da Construção de um Espaço Social Europeu." *Pensamiento Iberoamericano* 15:167.

Mauss, Marcel. 1950. *Essai sur le don.* Paris: Puf.

O'Connor, James. 1973. *The Fiscal Crisis of the State.* New York: St. Martin's Press.

Reis, José. 1985. "Modos de industrialização, força de trabalho e pequena agricultura: para uma análise da articulação entre a acumulação e a reprodução." *Revista Crítica de Ciências Sociais* 15/16/17:225.

———. 1989. *Os Espaços da Indústria: A regulação económica e a mediação local numa sociedade semiperiférica.* Coimbra: Faculdade de Economia.

Rodrigues, Maria João. 1988. *O Sistema de Emprego em Portugal: Crise e Mutações.* Lisboa: Dom Quixote.

Rosanavallon, Pierre. 1981. *La Crise de l'État-Providence.* Paris: Seuil.

———. 1988. "Beyond the Welfare State." *Politics and Society* 16, no. 4:533.

Santos, Boaventura de Sousa. 1979. "Popular Justice, Dual Power and Socialist Strategy." In *Capitalism and the Rule of Law,* edited by Bob Fine. London: Hutchinson.

———. 1990. *O Estado e a Sociedade em Portugal, 1974–1988.* Porto: Afrontamento.

Seers, Dudley. 1978. "Pour une nouvelle orientation des recherches sur le développement." *Economie et Humanisme* 242:42–54.

Streeck, Wolfgang. 1989. "The Social Dimension of the European Economy." Paper delivered at Meeting of the Andrew Shonfield Association, Florence, Italy.

Teague, Paul. 1989. "Constitution or Regime? The Social Dimension to the 1992 Project." *British Journal of Industrial Relations* 27:310.

Trotsky, Leon. 1963. *The Basic Writings of Trotsky.* New York: Vintage Books.

Wallerstein, Immanuel. 1974. *The Modern World-System.* New York: Academic Press.

———. 1984. *The Politics of the World-Economy.* Cambridge: Cambridge University Press.

2
Overviews

From Revolution to Apocalypse: Two Decades of Portuguese Poetry

FERNANDO J. B. MARTINHO
Translated by Anna Klobucka

The decade of the seventies clearly stands out as a period of great changes in Portuguese political and cultural life. First and foremost, in April 1974 the country experienced the fall of the authoritarian regime, and profound changes led to the establishment of democracy and the decolonization of former Portuguese possessions in Africa. The abolition of censorship and the disappearance of repressive mechanisms of the New State freed up literary discourse, poetry, and other literary genres, and led to publication of things that had previously constituted either a linguistic or ideological taboo: eroticism, scatology, or, more broadly, anything bearing the mark of *marginality*. In a review article written on the tenth anniversary of 25 April, I summed up the changes that took place in Portuguese poetry in the wake of the revolution:

> April 25 [. . .] immediately put an end to all limitations with regard to topics or ways of developing them. Poets, although less harassed than writers of fiction or essayists, had also been victimized by the repressive apparatus of the old regime, as proven by the eloquent example of the ludicrous court suit provoked [in the sixties] by the publication of an *Anthology of Erotic and Satiric Poetry in Portugal.* Certain allusive and metaphoric precautions (for instance in the treatment of such a red-hot topic as the colonial war during the final stages of the regime) have become unnecessary. (1984, 19–20)

Portuguese poets were also among the first to greet in verse the liberating *madrugada* of the revolution, as, for instance, in Sophia de Mello Breyner Andresen's poem, "25 de Abril":

Esta é a madrugada que eu esperava
o dia inicial inteiro e limpo
Onde emergimos da noite e do silêncio
E livres habitamos a substância do tempo

[This is the dawn I was waiting for
The first day whole and pure
When we emerged from night and silence
Alive into the substance of time][1]

(Breyner 1988, 56)

The vicissitudes of the revolutionary process during the period immediately following 25 April likewise found alert and committed witnesses among
poets who expressed their respective political and ideological perceptions.
Following are two brief, if conveniently polarized, examples. First, Miguel
Torga's anguish, in the 1975 poem "Lament," about the dangers threatening his "fatherland" and the "madness" of revolutionary radicalization:

Pátria sem rumo, minha voz parada
Diante do futuro!
Em que rosa dos ventos há um caminho

. . . .

De inédita aventura,
Que o poeta, adivinho,
Veja com nitidez
Da gávea da loucura?

[Fatherland adrift, my voice has stopped
Before the future!
What mariner's compass shows the way
Of uncharted adventure,

. . . .

That the poet, the seer,
Might see clearly
From the crow's nest of madness?]

(1977, 136)

Second, José Gomes Ferreira's obstinate defense of the revolutionary
utopia's "unreal purity" in the face of the apparently irreversible "agony of
the Revolution":

aqui vou a teu lado
eu, o poeta operário de palavras

— as palavras 'sonho', 'bandeira', esperança', 'liberdade' —
ferramentas de pureza irreal
que tornam a Realidade
ainda mais real
e transformam os bairros de lata
em futuras cidades de cristal

[here I come by your side
I, the poet, worker of words
—the words "dream," "flag," "hope," "freedom"—
tools of unreal purity
that make Reality
more real still
and transform shantytowns
into future cities of glass]

(1978, 316)

Aside from reflecting the radical transformation of social and political reality in the wake of 25 April, Portuguese poetry of the seventies also reflected a shift of aesthetic expectations. These expectations guided the work of later writers who had a certain new awareness, which some critics would identify later as postmodern. This aesthetic transformation followed many decades of formal and conceptual stability characteristic of most twentieth-century Portuguese lyric discourse. In 1952, in the journal *Brotéria,* Manuel Antunes had published an article entitled "The Persistence of Modernism," in which, referring to a recent publication of several literary reviews predominantly devoted to poetry, the author called attention to a "fact" that he viewed as evident: "the constancy of modernism" (Antunes 1987, 181). Antunes argued that Portuguese modernism, already substantially aged since its beginnings in the second decade of the century, had started to undergo a process of stabilization. He described the "new" poets associated with the reviews discussed in the article as interested in "continuation" rather than "disruption," and appearing to be moved by a "desire to expand and purify" modernism, renewing it "from the inside" (182). Nevertheless, in the conclusion of his article, Antunes did not fail to predict the inevitable passage, the death of that modernism to which the emerging fifties generation appeared to hold on: "As all the other schools, so the modernism shall pass" (183). Antunes's prediction took a while to come true: the modernist paradigm was to last at least two more decades before showing signs of exhaustion. During the fifties, most poets adhered to this paradigm through *continuation* rather than through the way of avant-garde *disruption;* in fact, only surrealism, which arrived in Portugal quite belatedly, showed the influence of the avant-garde, harking back to the national models provided by the more decidedly nonconformist figures of the first modernism. In the sixties, with the emergence of such groups as Poesia 61 and Poesia Experimental, the modernist paradigm in its most radical guise found a new vitality, paralleling the neo-avant-garde trends operating then on the international scene.

The first signs of the "new awareness" mentioned above were carried by the book debuts of João Miguel Fernandes Jorge[2] and Nuno Júdice[3] in *Sob sobre voz* (Under over voice, 1971) and *A noção de poema* (The notion of poem, 1972) respectively. The groups Poesia 61 and Poesia Experimental were concerned with material aspects of language, emphasized on the understanding of the poem as a *verbal reality,* and the poetics of expressive concentration. They ceded priority to a freer, more detached attitude toward language, while still holding on to "discursive tradition" (Cruz 1973, 164). They also displayed an interest in everything that might, to quote Nuno Júdice, "develop [the poem] beyond itself." The discursive orientation of Fernandes Jorge and Júdice stood in clear contrast to the antidiscursive poetic practice dominant in the sixties. Herberto Helder and Ruy Belo also wrote against the grain of the decade's prevailing trends, largely continuing the "discursive tradition" and revitalizing it in a spectacular way. Indeed, it was not by chance that Belo would sign the introductory note to Fernandes Jorge's volume of poems.

In one of the most significant passages of that introduction, Belo justified his support of the then-young poet "due to his following in the steps of the best poets of *Poesia 61,* a publication which, aside from its intrinsic merit, had the virtue of preventing the appearance of concrete poetry in our midst" (Belo 1984, 253). There are two immediately relevant points to be discerned in Belo's words: first, that he saw Fernandes Jorge as a follower of *Poesia 61* (which would further on make him say that the young poet's work inscribed itself "not in the sphere of the signified but in that of the signifier" [253]); second, that *Poesia 61* was supposed to prevent concrete poetry from emerging in Portugal. The second point makes it obvious that Belo's preferences, with regard to the two avant-garde directions present in the sixties, were for *Poesia 61*'s authors. On the other hand, it is implicit in his words that the "virtue" of *Poesia 61* lay in not having gone as far as Poesia Experimental in avoiding, thanks to a "homeopathic" (so to speak) use of its defamiliarizing devices, the utmost fragmentation of discourse to which the "experimentalists" were led by their avant-garde radicalism. With regard to the two ways of embracing *the new* that emerged on the Portuguese poetic scene in the sixties, *Poesia 61* did not, in fact, prevent concrete or experimental poetry from exercising its influence on such poets as Herberto Helder or António Ramos Rosa. Still, it is not difficult to comprehend the reservations felt toward concrete poetry's avant-garde extremism by a poet whom Eduardo Lourenço described as a voice "less flamboyant and more classically dialectical" at a time when that modernity was parting ways "with itself" (Lourenço 1987, 199). Ruy Belo erred, however, in placing Fernandes Jorge in the wake of *Poesia 61,* precisely because the author of *Sob sobre voz,* instead of absolutely privileging the "signifier," preferred to place it in a balanced harmony with the "signified." Witness the following sonnet from his first collection, in which the novelty does not derive from syntactic contortions or discursive discontinuities, but rather from the discreetly allusive straightforwardness employed in describing the painter Amadeu de Sousa Cardoso:

Quero falar de Amadeu,
talvez nascido a 11 ou 12
de novembro. Era 1919 e
tinha já então muito de

velho. As mulheres gostaram
dele (seduzindo-o na sua
própria vida de cigano) e
do outro lado da montanha

percebiam como sabia de
crisântemos, azuis (do
mesmo azul das dunas).

Ainda o visitam, mas o
tempo de Amadeu é agora
uma ilha perdida de Böcklin.

[I want to speak of Amadeu,
born perhaps on the eleventh or twelfth
of November. It was 1919 and
he already was a lot

like an old man. Women were fond
of him (seducing him in his
own gypsy life) and
from the other side of the mountain

they perceived how he knew of
chrysanthemums, the blue ones (of
the same blue of the dunes).

They still visit him, but the
time of Amadeu is now
a lost island by Böcklin.]

(Jorge 1982, 18)

Belo's assessment of the continuity existing between Fernandes Jorge and the "best poets of *Poesia 61*" would, more than a decade and a half later, serve to support Luís Miguel Nava's claim, in the conclusion of an article on the poetry of the sixties in Portugal, that "there is no break whatsoever between the poetry born in the sixties and that which was to appear in the seventies" (Nava 1988, 157). In his view, poets such as Gastão Cruz, Luiza Neto Jorge, or Fiama Hasse Pais Brandão, all of them contributors to *Poesia 61,* could be credited with "blazing the trails" to be followed later by poets who began to write in the seventies. Some who rooted their poetry under Ruy Belo's influence, "in a return to the real and to the heart," were supposed to receive from their predecessors a legacy of a language "pure and capable of supporting sentimental and commonplace discourse" (157). Nava's thesis is not without foundation, insofar as there is no such thing in literature as an absolute break with the past and since the linguistic experimentation carried on by the *Poesia 61* poets was obviously not to be ignored by their immediate successors. We should also take into account the evolution manifest in highly individualized poetic courses to be taken by the authors of those five slim brochures, published in 1961 in Faro, that constituted *Poesia 61*. The difference that the inaugural volumes of João Miguel Fernandes Jorge and Nuno Júdice represent can be perceived especially with regard to the most *programmatic* aspects of *Poesia 61*'s phase of collective affirmation. According to Gastão Cruz, the *Poesia 61* poets and those akin to them, such as Armando Silva Carvalho, rearticulate "the issue of poetic realism and, essentially, the issue of the relationship between realism and the avant-garde" (Cruz 1973, 188). If so, then Júdice's poems in *A noção de poema,* in which the subject makes no effort to disguise its fictional status, have nothing to do, in their staged reveries and extraordinary narratives, with the realist tradition. Witness the following fragments of the poem "Exílio" (Exile):

As planícies áridas de uma inspiração antiga deram-me a conhecer
o seguinte — que eu era um poeta único, o Anunciado, o Iluminador
das tardes

violetas do Bósforo e Antineia . . . e que ninguém, durante os anos
criadores de uma imaginação múltipla, regressaria às fórmulas
arcaicas/que os medíocres ousaram — furiosos de Resto . . .

. . . .

Cheguei a um continente erótico. Os ventres
bojudos das árvores atraem os animais. Ouço os gritos
de uma terra por habitar. O céu é uma superfície vegetal
que dá música e choro. Na sombra, os insectos congeminam grandes
    devastações no interior solar das figueiras descarnadas.

[The arid plains of an ancient inspiration let me know
what follows—that I was the only poet, the Foretold, the Illuminator
    of violet
evenings of Bosphorus and Antinoë . . . and that no one, during the
    creative
years of multiple imagination, would return to the archaic formulae
dared by the mediocre — furious Besides . . .

. . . .

I have arrived at an erotic continent. The rounded
bellies of trees attract animals. I hear screams
of an unsettled land. The sky is a vegetative surface
which pours music and lament. In the shade, insects ponder great
    devastations in the solar insides of lean fig trees.]

(1991, 16–17)

Likewise, Fernandes Jorge, although to some extent assimilable to poetic realism, does not appear particularly interested in reconciling it with the avant-garde, at least not with the kind Gastão Cruz associates with "new linguistic experiences"; in his writings, Jorge comes closer to the "common language" than to that "deviation" from it which is supposed to constitute "the language of poetry" (Cruz 1973, 80).

In an essay included in his *O processo poético* (The poetic process), "Remembrance of Discourses Past: Recent Directions in Poetic Language," Nuno Júdice calls attention to what he considers to be a "limitation" of *Poesia 61,* resulting "from a supposedly antirhetorical prejudice hindering complete development of the poem." As he adds immediately afterwards, it befell to the poets of the seventies "to restore, in clear opposition to that prejudice, proper dignity to rhetoric and discourse" (1992, 154). In Júdice's particular case, the rehabilitation of the discourse entailed also the use of inordinately long verse, emphasizing lack of distinction between poetry and prose (when it is not prose pure and simple that clearly prevails). In any case, Júdice's work falls within one of the dominant tendencies in the postsixties Portuguese poetry and succumbs to the fascination of narrative discourse, whose free flow was largely obstructed by the scrupulous control of "all discursive elements" (Cruz 1973, 185) aimed at by the poets of Poesia 61. Witness the initial sentences of his "Segundo poema sobre a morte" (Second poem about death) in *A noção de poema:*

> Procurando a paz no coração, Maria Pleyel veio a refugiar-se no castelo, nas montanhas, um século antes de eu o ter visitado. Nenhuma solicitação exterior a atraiu, durante os últimos anos da sua vida; nenhum apelo do transitório e do material; nenhuma superstição a afastou. Nas noites em que o vento e a chuva assolavam a montanha costumava ela sentar-se ao piano, na sala enorme que a lareira apenas iluminava, e compor as sinfonias desconcertantes que alguém, nos anos desencantados, procurou depois reproduzir.

> [Seeking peace of heart, Maria Pleyel took refuge in the mountain castle, a century before my visit there. No outside force tempted her in the last years of her life; no appeal of the transitory and the material; no superstition diverted her. In the nights when wind and rain ravaged the mountains, she used to sit at the piano, in the enormous room barely illuminated by the fireplace, and compose perplexing symphonies that later, in disenchanted years, someone attempted to reproduce.]

> (1991, 23–24)

Another feature of the seventies poetry is an inclination toward intertextual dialogue with varying degrees of ironic detachment that relies on either accurately cited or invented quotations (Magalhães 1981, 263). This discourse is not limited to the world of literature, but branches out instead into the most diverse cultural areas, often irrespective of hierarchies traditionally separating "high" and "low" culture. Thus, in a poem by Fernandes Jorge in *Turvos dizeres* (Troubled sayings, 1973), after an epigraph from Bach's *Passio secundum Mathaeum,* we find references to Klee, Janis Joplin, Hölderlin, and Jim Morrison. Another poet, António Franco Alexandre,[4] one of the most important voices of the decade, goes as far as to indicate, in his *Sem palavras nem coisas* (Without words or things, 1974), under the guise of bibliographic references, which texts were employed in writing his own (they also appear quoted in their original languages within the poems themselves).[5] In "Arqueologia história possível" (Archaeology possible history), the author embarks upon a dialogue with history, represented by three documents—two "reports" and one "speech" in Spanish. These are submitted to the devices of an *ars combinatoria* in order to carry out (with "possible" veracity) an "archaeology" of a historical phenomenon, namely, that of slavery in the last quarter of the eighteenth century and the first years of the nineteenth century; and also to highlight the inevitable distance separating a modern viewpoint from the ideology dominant in the period from which, in the poem, "history" is made. One of the poets manifesting the most appreciable predilection for intertextuality is doubtlessly Vasco Graça Moura.[6] Having started to write in the sixties, he did not develop a truly authentic voice of his own until the following decade. In *Instrumentos para a melancolia* (Instruments for melancholy, 1980), a volume assembling "series" of poems written and published in the late seventies, Moura included a brief introductory note in which he spoke "of himself in the third person." With that lack of inhibition which has become characteristic of the Portuguese poets' insistence on the intellectual nature of their work, he says that he "seeks to absorb into his writing a lot of interrelated stuff" and "that he understands creation as an assembly of cultural emersions to which he relates through an existential solidarity." The volume concludes with a section of endnotes destined to clarify some of the allusions found in the poems, a device also used by Moura in *A variação dos semestres deste ano; 365 versos seguidos de A escola de Frankfurt* (A variation of this year's semesters; 356 verses followed by The Frankfurt School), published the following year. As Óscar Lopes rightly observed, in Moura's and other poets' intertextual practice there is obviously a great deal of "playful exercise," as well as a great deal of disillusioned irony, as documented by a poem from Moura's latest volume (with its title borrowed from Montale), *A furiosa paixão pelo tangível* (The furious passion for the tangible):

> Quando marina tsvetaeva escreveu a
> rainer maria rilke, ele tinha morrido
> havia poucos dias. tornara-se
> o poeta emigrado lá no reino
>
> onde a leitura é um puro contacto da alma
> e nenhuma mulher o sustentava.
> imagina-se a carta: podia ser em cirílico,
> terminando, como essenine, num patético
>
> do svidania, drug moi, do svidania.
> imagina-se rilke, rindo silenciosamente sob
> a terra, e a pensar: estas gajas. imagina-se
> a resposta que ele teria dado.
>
> tratando-a por madame (fürstin seria um exagero) e
> falando obliquamente de rosas e anjos, volúpias de

outono, falta de dinheiro, e de gaspara stampa,
com muito tacto e delicadeza. o entusiasmo, o falhanço,

viriam depois, . . .

[When Marina Tsvetaeva wrote to
Rainer Maria Rilke, he had died
a few days before. he'd become
a poet exiled to that kingdom

where reading is a pure contact of souls
and no woman supported him.
One imagines the letter: it could be in Cyrillic,
ending, like esenin, in a pathetic

do svidania, drug moi, do svidania.
One imagines Rilke, laughing silently under
the ground, and thinking: those broads. One imagines
the reply he would have given.

Addressing her as madame (fürstin would have been
    too much) and
talking obliquely of roses and angels, voluptuous
autumns, lack of money, and of gaspara stampa,
with much tact and sensitivity. The enthusiasm, the failure

would come later . . .]

(1987, 12–13)

Irony dominates also Manuel António Pina's[7] intertextual "exercise" in his first book of poems, whose unusually long title betrays already the ironic agenda pursued throughout the volume: *Ainda não é o fim nem o princípio calma é apenas um pouco tarde* (It's not over yet nor is it beginning take it easy it's just a little late, 1974). In "As pessoas" (Persons), one of the best-known poems in the collection (attributed, very much in keeping with Fernando Pessoa's legacy, to a sort of heteronymous author), the indebtedness to other poets is announced right in the epigraph:

> Fernando pessoa
> uma vez, Fernando Lemos
> uma vez, Mário Cesariny
> duas ou três

[Fernando Pessoa
once, Fernando Lemos
once, Mário Cesariny
twice or thrice]

(1974, 45)

The total effect of the parodic collage composed from fragments of their poems is to emulate the mode of laid-back mockery preferred by that one among the poets with whom Pina identifies the most: the surrealist Cesariny. An ostentatiously parodic effect is also what Nuno Júdice aims at in his *Rimbaud inverso* (Rimbaud inverted), written in 1985 and published for the first time six years later, in a volume of collected poems *(Obra poética, 1972–1985)*. *Rimbaud*'s epigraph leaves no doubt as to its parodic intent: "The pastiche is a *pastis*." The parodic desecration of one of the most revered modern texts, *Une saison en enfer*, is carried out essentially by means of inversion (a device already indicated in the title), whose most evident signs can be found in the titles of poems: "Um inferno na estação" (A hell of a season), "Inferno da noite" (Hell of night), "A virgem infernal e o esposo doido" (The infernal virgin and the mad husband), "Delírios do verbo — alquimia" (Delirium of the word—alchemy), "Possível" (The possible), "Adeus, relâmpago matinal!" (Farewell, morning lightning!). A particular form of intertextuality is practiced by Joaquim Manuel Magalhães[8] (who debuted in 1974, with *Poemas* [Poems] and *Consequências do lugar* [Consequences of the place]) in his texts from the volume *Uma exposição* (An exhibition, 1980). Although they refer to paintings by Edward Hopper, Magalhães's poems only ostensibly belong to the tradition of *Bildgedicht*— describing a work of art. In spite of their essentially descriptive, even hyperrealist mode (paralleling, in fact, Hopper's own visual technique), the viewpoint throughout the text seems to forgo the mediation provided by the paintings, in order to create images of "desolate" cities or suburbs that belong much more to our time of urban disaster than to Hopper's own, despite the undeniable premonitory power of his works. The poet may say, in one of the texts from the volume, "o eu dos pronomes pessoais não sou eu" (the I of personal pronouns am not I); but he is unable to disguise the violent indignation with which his adopted "viewpoint" reacts to the disfiguration of physical space brought about by the mass society, as in the poem "Rooms by the sea," which clearly refers to post-25 April Portuguese reality:

Foi então que a democracia começou
a trazê-los aos punhados para as praias.

Amarrotados nas furgonetas ou calcados
em matrículas emigrantes e essas tintas
de casas que não serviam lugar nenhum.
Trouxe-os a democracia, o fascismo
tinha-os feito assim. Deram-lhes
a liberdade para isso, estragar o mar.

[It was then that the democracy started
to bring them by handfuls to the beaches.
Crumpled in minivans or pressed
into emigrant license plates and those colors
of house paints that served no place.
Democracy brought them, fascism
had made them like that. They were given
freedom for this, to ruin the sea.][9]

(1987, 213)

The aesthetic renovation that started to gain ground in Portuguese poetry in the early seventies was later on to be interpreted by some as "postmodern." One of the first critics to give it such a label was Eduardo Prado
Coelho, during a conference organized in the mid eighties by the Gulbenkian
Foundation's Cultural Center in Paris.[10] Meanwhile, the terms and concepts of "postmodernity" and "postmodernism" had already been shaping
up in Portuguese critical discourse, as proven by a number of books published in recent years: Fernando Guimarães's *A poesia contemporânea
portuguesa e o fim da modernidade* (Contemporary Portuguese poetry and
the end of modernity, 1989), Fernando Pinto do Amaral's *O mosaico fluido—
modernidade e pós-modernidade na poesia portuguesa mais recente* (The
fluid mosaic: Modernity and postmodernity in recent Portuguese poetry,
1991), and Américo António Lindeza Diogo's *Modernismos, pós-modern-
ismos, anacronismos—para uma história da poesia portuguesa recente*
(Modernisms, postmodernisms, anachronisms: Toward a history of recent
Portuguese poetry, 1993). Prior to Prado Coelho's use of the word, the
adjective "postmodern" may be found, for instance, in Joaquim Manuel
Magalhães's discussion of Poesia Experimental, although with a meaning
quite different from the one currently attributed to the term: "The
postmodernist cultism [of the group] became stagnated in unoriginal attempts to transplant linguistic inventions being developed, in the wake of
the early twentieth-century vanguard movements, in more fertile cultural
environments and by better minds" (1981, 259).
When Magalhães, whose critical writings made him into something of

a spokesman for the new generation of poets emerging in the seventies, wants to stress the difference separating them from the dominant orientations of the preceding decade, he speaks of "surpassing," of "discursive change," "transformation of the [poetic] process," and of "qualitative turnabout." He does not, however, refer to the exhaustion of the modernist paradigm. Neither does he fail to point out the "conceptual and thematic rarefaction" brought about by the "supposedly anti-discursive rhetoric" of Poesia 61, and the stagnation suffered by the experimentalists in their "inevitable posteriority" (Santos 1987, 87) with regard to the "early twentieth-century vanguard movements" (Magalhães 1981, 259). While emphasizing the "changes" effected by the generation of the seventies and the "novelty" it represents (259), he also follows an undeniably modernist logic (Frow 1991, 132). In addition, his poetic contribution, together with that of António Franco Alexandre, Helder Moura Pereira, and João Miguel Fernandes Jorge, to the provocative publication *Cartucho* (Paper bag, 1976), in which the poems were printed on loose sheets and stuffed inside a paper bag, shows that the example of the vanguards is not all that distant. Eduardo Lourenço (1987, 199) was one of the first critics to perceive the onset of a "crucial moment in which Modernity" was to part ways "with itself." Curiously, Diogo Pires Aurélio, whose first book of poems, *A herança de Hölderlin* (Hölderlin's legacy, 1978), was closely attuned to the new poetic sensibility prevailing in the seventies, in spite of his ironic remarks (in an essay published that same year) about the lack of synchrony existing between an "avant-garde" project put forward at that time by a literary review and the contemporary Portuguese reality, never associates the poets of his generation (Magalhães, Fernandes Jorge, Júdice, António Franco Alexandre, and Rui Diniz, whom he discusses in his book *O próprio dizer* [1984]) with postmodernism (Aurélio 1984, 13).

Whether or not the term "postmodernism" is evoked in discussing this group of poets, all critics agree on their difference from the previous generation. For Aurélio, the "break with earlier poetry consists [. . .] in a return to a certain kind of discursivity" (1984, 67). For Júdice, what differentiates the poets of the seventies from those of the sixties is, aside from intensified practice of intertextuality, the restoration of "dignity to discourse and rhetoric," on the one hand, and "the return of a certain narrativity," on the other (1992, 154–55). We owe the most complete characterization of the general features of the "new generation" to Joaquim Manuel Magalhães, despite the overtly polemical quality of some of his remarks, which is understandable in view of his placing himself in opposition to what he saw as the poetic establishment of the time:

The poetry published during the following decade [the seventies] owes its particular inflection, corresponding to an effective emergence of a new generation, to the fact that its authors left behind the syntactic fear of discourse, the lyric fear of the confessional mode, and the abject restriction placed, in the name of trivial melodiousness or paltry experimentalism, on declarative eruptions. Against the then necessary rarefication of feeling, imagination and articulation, the most recent poetry displays a renewed desire to tell, to adopt, directly or under disguise, a discourse whose tensions are less verbal than explicitly emotional. This brings forth candid openness about the body, affirmation of desires and intentions, stories of confrontations with the established order, all couched in a discourse more interested in declaring than in synthesizing or visualizing. (1981, 258)

Finally, Eduardo Prado Coelho says the seventies were characterized "by a great diversity of styles and tendencies and by a marked absence of a generational spirit" (1988, 128). The author of *A noite do mundo* also calls attention to an aspect repeatedly mentioned in recent literary criticism in Portugal: the difficulty, or even impossibility, of writing a history of Portuguese poetry in the last decades in terms of groups, movements, and reviews presenting their aesthetic and literary programs. Instead, the tendency manifest on our literary scene for the past few years has been toward the affirmation of radical uniqueness of individual *writings,* in the sense that Meschonnic gives to the writing of a "solitary," "subjective historical adventure" (Meschonnic 1985, 68–69).

More or less at the same time when this new poetic orientation was gaining ground in Portugal, Octavio Paz wrote the following words:

The poets of the modern age searched for the principle of change; we, poets of the age which is beginning now, search for this invariable principle which is the foundation of all change[. . . .] The aesthetic of change stressed the historical nature of the poem; we ask ourselves now: might there exist a point where the principle of change becomes confounded with the principle of permanence? . . . The poetry beginning in this end of a century does not really begin, and neither does it return to the point of departure: it is a process of constant renewal and incessant return. The poetry beginning now, without really beginning, seeks an intersection of times, a point of convergence. (1990, 53–54)

It would be difficult to find words to describe poetic developments of the seventies in Portugal more adequately. This description also applies to the eighties since, as Nuno Júdice observed, the symbolic line separating the seventies and the eighties is less sharply defined than the divide between the sixties and the seventies (1990, 155). The direction that the most prominent poets of that period followed was indeed that of an "art of convergence," a "poetry of reconciliation," and an "imagination incarnated in a timeless now" (Paz 1990, 54). Paz prefers to speak of the poetry of "intersection" and "reconciliation" in terms of an "art of convergence" (51–53), shunning labels such as "postmodern era" and "postmodernism" that have been commonly used to describe our times and current artistic production. His definition does not greatly differ, however, from the interpretations some authors have given of postmodernism as a period based in a "different temporality: not novation but stasis" (Frow 1991, 132), and a period that "with the end of the 'new'" would privilege "perpetual recycling of quotations, styles, and fashions," resulting in "an uninterrupted montage of the 'now'" (Chambers 1986, 137). What seems particularly important to stress here is that "the new" is no longer regarded in absolute terms, even as the logic of "radical innovation" underlying the modernist paradigm is replaced by the logic of "renovation" (Calinescu 1987, 276). The postmodern is thus founded "on an aesthetic of repetition rather than an aesthetic of originality" (Frow 1991, 140). The point is not, however, to see in iteration "the basis of all textuality," since any intertextual system is inevitably constituted by a "complex mix of repetition and deviation" (141), but rather to consider "repetition" and "citation" as being "integral to all forms of writing," or, in other words, to recognize that "reproduction" and "quotation," far from representing "forms of textual parasitism," are in fact something "constitutive of textuality" (Wollen 1986, 141–42).

The first signs of a crisis of modernity in contemporary Portuguese poetry, which could be observed in the early seventies, consisted essentially in that "decline of the aesthetic of change" described by Octavio Paz (1990, 51). The modernist aesthetic, based "on the cult of change and disruption," had little appeal left for some of the authors then making their debut in Portugal. This is demonstrated by Diogo Pires Aurélio's already cited 1978 text: the author, referring to a project put forth by a literary review and presented as "the first coherent attempt [in] the second half of the seventies to propose an avant-garde," calmly assumes an "anti-vanguard" stance not only because he does not consider the review's contributors to be truly innovative but also because he denies the publication "any possible meaning within the [. . .] social and cultural state of affairs in Portugal" at that time. The avant-garde concerns of the review's editors were no longer in tune with the contemporary "social and cultural state of affairs" and therefore betrayed the unmistakable taste of reheated leftovers (Aurélio 1978, 79).

The "contemporary social and cultural state of affairs," referred to by Aurélio, has not fallen outside the thematic concerns of the new poetic generation. Having emerged during the decade that witnessed the establishment of democracy, the new poets took it upon themselves to voice vehement criticism of the new status quo and to react to the betrayal of hopes awakened by the revolution, to the persistence of "sameness" underneath the rhetoric of "change," and to the lack of concern for the quality of everyday life, by presenting themselves as a "dissatisfied generation." "A Dissatisfied Generation" was, in fact, the title of a text by Joaquim Manuel Magalhães (included in *Os dois crepúsculos*), which served as something of a manifesto of that generation, at the time when the already distant "euphoria" of the days following 25 April was replaced by a disenchanted realization that "culturally, neither side makes sense, nor has made new sense" and that "politically, nothing was invested in any kind of cultural creativity" (1981, 368). The text forms a kind of statement of belief in the "poets' word": "The poets' word needs to inhabit again the meaning of things that are becoming lost and of those which are slow in coming" and is an appeal to poets, asking them not to withdraw into silence, to affirm "clearly" their rebellion, their dissatisfaction, and to denounce the "emptiness" of the present moment (367–69).

While the poets emerging during the seventies did not fail to "denounce the present," they expressed their discontent quite differently from those who adhered to the example of social and political commitment set by the neorealists. The word that best captures their attitude, and that also conforms to their professed individualism, might be "rebellion," which not by accident appears in Magalhães's manifesto (366–67). The poet who most vocally expounded their privately rebellious attitude was Al Berto, with his 1977 poetic debut.[11] His poems were at first written in prose or allowed the expansive flow of a biblical verse, and only later submitted to strophic discipline. They express, among the unrestrained proliferation of metaphors, the turmoil of life, the "hallucination" of liminal experiences set in a "nauseating," "catastrophic," and, at the same time, "fascinating" scenery of "night cities." A more withdrawn, intimate scenery, registering the daily life with its "routine," its "little joys" and simple gestures, is found in the poems of Helder Moura Pereira,[12] whose first individual volume, *Entre o deserto e a vertigem* (Between the desert and the vertigo) was published in 1979, following his 1976 contribution to *Cartucho*. The poems' simplicity makes no less pungent their visions of memory-laden spaces being destroyed by urban growth, or their rendering of the wordless pain of "abandonment":

Escrevias pela noite fora. Olhava-te, olhava
o que ia ficando nas pausas entre cada
sorriso. Por ti mudei a razão das coisas
faz de conta que não sei as coisas que não queres
que saiba, acabei por te pensar com crianças
à volta. Agora há prédios onde havia
laranjeiras e romãs no chão e as palavras
nem o sabem dizer, apenas apontam a rua
que foi comum, o quarto estreito . . .

. . . .
·. . . Este abandono
custa. Porque estou contigo e me deixas
a tua imagem passa pelas noites sem sono,
está aqui a cadeira em que te sentaste
a escrever lendo. Pudesse eu propor-te
vida menos igual, outras iguais obrigações.
Havias de rir, sair à rua, comprar o jornal.

[You used to write all night. I would watch you, I watched
what remained in the pauses between each
smile. For you I changed the reason of things,
pretended not to know things you don't want
me to know, ended up thinking of you with children
all around you. There are buildings now where there used to be
orange trees and pomegranates on the ground and the words
are silent, they just point to the street
that was common, the narrow room. . . .

. . . .
. . . This abandonment
hurts. Because I'm with you and you leave me
your image passes through sleepless nights,
this is the chair in which you sat
reading and writing. If only I could offer you
a less equal life, other equal duties.
You would laugh, go out to the street, buy the paper.]

(1990, 17)

Another author, Rui Diniz,[13] brings to this assembly of poetic voices belonging to "a generation doomed to dream of unfulfillment" (in the words of his friend, Nuno Júdice [1977, 8]), the (Pessoan) "disquiet" of a self multiplying its masks and personae throughout a boundless migration of times and spaces. He evokes a self torn between an attitude of ironic detachment and an empathic desire to follow, despite everything, into the steps of the "writers of unhappiness," and to continue the desperate adventure of a modernity injured by "solitude" and "exile," and abandoned to a "never-ending melancholy." Among the figures summoned from the modernist repository there are, for example (in the poem "Morbus sacer"), the dadaists, the first ones to discover the radical uselessness of art, "the tireless desolation of every word" (1977, 56–57).

Yet another poet, José Agostinho Batista,[14] a self-declared heir to romanticism (the title of one of his most important volumes is precisely *O último romântico* [The last romantic]) and indelibly marked by a nostalgic longing for the lost "island," seeks the impossible solace for his Sehnsucht in imaginary voyages to times and spaces surrounded by a mythic aura (Mexico, ancient Egypt, the American West), recounting them in poems of lofty diction, always mindful of the sacred and ritual origins of poetry. In his latest book, *Paixão e cinzas* (Passion and ashes, 1992), the romantic pathos reaches its highest point, even as it becomes affected by a pessimism very much attuned to our fin de siècle, expressing a belief in the "absolute certainty of disasters." Another beneficiary of the romantic legacy is Diogo Pires Aurélio, whose single book of poems (*A herança de Hölderlin,* 1978) bears an epigraph from Pessoa's heteronymous creation Álvaro de Campos

> Produtos românticos, nós todos . . .
> E se não fôssemos produtos românticos, se calhar não seriamos nada
>
> Romantic products, all of us . . .
> And if we weren't romantic products, we might just be nothing
> (Aurélio 1978, n.p.)

in a pointed reminder of a long-accepted view that finds in romanticism the origins of poetic modernity as well as postmodernity. Aurélio's poems, however, rely far more heavily on the memory of literary systems, playing the intertextual game with visible delight. Another of the volume's epigraphs is from Barthes: "[T]he intertext is not necessarily a field of influences; it is rather a music of tropes, metaphors, of words-thoughts; it is where the signifier plays the role of a *siren*." We find among them rereadings (as in the poem entitled "Rereading Durrell"), misreadings (for example, the title "Nem toda a noite a noite" is a deliberate distortion of Vitorino Nemésio's title *Nem toda a noite a vida*), and, finally, glosses: in what is perhaps the most important text of the volume, "Pranto para Sá de Miranda" (A lament for Sá de Miranda), Aurélio abandons himself to the irresistible

melody of the often paraphrased sonnet "O sol é grande, caem co'a calma
as aves" by the sixteenth-century poet:

> Caem co'a calma as aves e as coisas morrem. Um manto hierático, solene
> e sem avesso vai cobrindo lentamente as cores, a vida. O tempo veio e
> apagou os vestígios da deusa, esqueceu nas praias o extremo das águas e
> na floresta o recorte das folhas. Veio, veio vindo nas veias dos homens e
> misturou-lhe a loucura nas searas, pôs-se aquém e além das palavras,
> deixou nas aves a calma. . . .

> [The birds fall in calm air and things die. A hieratic mantle, solemn and
> with no seamy side, is slowly covering colors, the life. Time came and
> wiped out traces of the goddess, on the beaches forgot the extremity of
> waters and in the forest the outline of leaves. It came flowing in men's
> veins and blended madness into the harvest, lay on this and that side of
> words, left calmness in the birds. . . .]

(1978, 45–46)

Two poets whose texts had appeared in literary reviews of the fifties,
António Osório[15] and José Bento,[16] did not publish their respective first
volumes of poetry until the seventies, when the conditions for a full acceptance of their poetic projects became more propitious. Osório's affinity
with the spirit of the decade expresses itself most of all in the spare, unadorned nature of his poetry, devoid of formal complications and always
closely attuned to life's beat and to the multiple signs flashed by the outside world, into which his poems seem to throw themselves in a kind of
fragile and helpless contingency. For him, we might say, the "duty" of the
poet—always close to others, always mindful of "suffering," theirs as well
as his own—consists in welcoming and giving shelter to that suffering, and
in "distributing it later / limpidly" in a language that is accessible and
ready to be shared. This is what happens in Osório's magnificent mono-
dramatic poem, "Parking Lot Attendant Speaking," where the voice of the
lyric subject is ceded to one of those who do not have a voice of their own:

> Assustado com a miséria e estes anos,
> pouco espero de Deus e dos homens.
> Não mendigo, olho de soslaio, adivinho,
> sem gratidão guardo no bolso os óbolos.
> E fui pescador, depois faroleiro: longe
> deitava a alma, relâmpago
> sobre falésias, em estrelas tocava,

a sirene era meu grito de amor.
Transluzente e distante e bom
como clarões de um farol nunca foi fácil:
algo se afundava debaixo de mim,
desconhecida culpa. Odeio, sim, odeio
este parque onde chuva e sol impõem as mãos
e na pele penetram sem bálsamo.
Primeiro a luxúria, depois vinho,
escuridão. No fundo de um poço
cujas paredes ressumam lágrimas e avencas.
Custa ganhar a vida e perdê-la.
Tudo foi defraudado, sou eu
— eu ou alguém por mim — quem aperta
desde a infância o nó que me estrangula.

[Frightened by poverty and these years,
I expect little from God or men.
I don't go begging, I watch from the corner of
        the eye, I make guesses,
accepting without gratitude the obols in my pocket.
I used to be a fisherman, a lighthouse keeper next:
        far away
went my soul, a lightning
over the cliffs, it touched the stars,
the siren was my love cry.
Translucent and distant and good
like beacons of a lighthouse, my soul was never
        at ease:
something was sinking underneath
unfamiliar guilt. I hate, yes I hate
this lot where rain and sun subject the hands
and harshly penetrate the skin.
First lust, then wine,
and darkness. At the bottom of a well
whose walls ooze tears and maidenhair.
It's hard to earn one's living and lose it.
Everything was swindled, it is me
—or someone for me—who has tightened,
since childhood, the knot that strangles my neck.]

                                    (1978, 86)

As for José Bento, his encounter with the poets of the seventies is made
possible due particularly to the discursive orientation that characterizes his
texts. They are entirely unconcerned with restraining the power of impres-

sions and feelings experienced by a self who never faces reality with indifference. Witness the following poem, preceded by epigraphs from two great poets of the city, Álvaro de Campos and his master, Cesário Verde:

Onde a cidade aos borbotões perde o seu nome
e o crepúsculo recupera a amplitude das suas pulsações
—entre tímidos arbustos, cômoros de sucata,
pátios onde crianças armam álacres campos de batalha—,
foi abatida uma casa:
abriu-se uma ferida
que ninguém sabe quanto irá doer
ao avaro coleccionador de imagens memoradas
que em afanosas buscas defende o seu frágil património.

[Where the city gushingly loses its name
and the twilight regains the amplitude of its beat
—amidst timid shrubbery, mounds of junk,
courtyards where children set up eager battlefields—,
a house was torn down:
a wound has opened
and no one knows how much it will hurt
the thrifty collector of remembered images
who in toilsome searches defends his fragile patrimony.]

(1992, 62–64)

In a way Nuno Guimarães (1942–73) managed to effect a transition between the sixties and the seventies with the two books he published in the early seventies, *O corpo agrário* (The agrarian body, 1970) and *Os campos visuais* (The visual fields, 1973). While the former was still strongly influenced by the formalism of the Poesia 61 poets (particularly by Gastão Cruz), the meticulous structure of the poems from the latter volume barely manages to contain the yearning—thematized there as "imprecision," "insecurity," and "instability"—for a less rigid prosody, such as the kind adopted at that time by Fernandes Jorge and Júdice. The year 1970 also saw the publication of the first book of poems by Alberto Pimenta,[17] whose poetic course would continue to follow the experimental goals of the sixties, tempering them with a playful attitude and a provocative sense of humor, traits destined to find resonance in some of the new poets in the eighties (for example, Adília Lopes).

As I have stressed before, the transition between the seventies and the eighties in Portuguese poetry was much less evident than had been the one effected a decade earlier. The same could be said with regard to the nineties. In fact, in neither case are there any true signs of change. What can be distinguished is a tendency toward pluralism, considered proper of the postmodern era and consisting in a stylistic scattering and a "proliferation of styles and private languages" (Jameson 1975/76, 208). Having diverse traditions at their disposal, the poets seize upon whatever they see as useful and appropriate in view of their particular objectives.

Amidst the extreme "heterogeneity" of individual voices that characterize the most recent Portuguese poetry (Nava 1991, 22), a few may be recognized with some assurance. In speaking of the poets who made their debut in the eighties, the name to be mentioned first must be Luís Miguel Nava,[18] editor of an anthology that systematically presents the last thirty years of Portuguese poetry (*Antologia de poesia portuguesa, 1960–1990*, 1991). At a time when the social and personal mores, as well as the languages used to describe them, were undergoing profound changes in Portugal, Nava's own poetry (since his first volume, *Películas* [Films, 1979]) distinguished itself due to the importance it attributed to the thematics of the body. In it, the "ars poetica" becomes, without euphemisms, an "ars erotica" ("Eu amo assim: com as mãos, os intestinos. Onde ver deita folhas" [I love like this: with hands, intestines. Where seeing sheds leaves]), and, in an inversion of Roland Barthes's famous phrase ("Le langage est une peau"), skin itself is made into a language. Another poet, Fátima Maldonado,[19] gives a central place in her poetry to the city; in travels through urban scenery, her poetic viewpoint, moved both by memory and by transfiguring imagination, divides itself between unsparing, at times even cynical, perceptiveness, and a tenderness that, in the end, it finds impossible to disguise. The following is a fragment of her poem "Elvas/79."

> Na cidade deixada a descoberto
> as pedras que pisamos são vitrais.
> Os roxos, os vermelhos são perfis
> de uma velha aliança:
> Belial que rege os borregos metálicos,
> os férreos touros
> de bocas guarnecidas por mica incombustível.
> A cor da rocha deixada pela maré
> espalha-se no chão da cidade deserta
> por festas de família, presépios, consoadas,
> mesas que as mães não deixam retirar,
> guardando-as intactas para que cada morto
> tire o seu sonho escorrido da calda,
> fatia de peru, o naco de perdiz, o prato de arroz doce
>
> . . . .

Passeando na cidade
repara-se na sua fortaleza,
frágil mecanismo potente de minúcia.
Em cada torreão há uma fechadura,
a cidade é uma chave inglesa ornamentada,
funcional, organizada na sua virulenta precisão.

[In the city left uncovered
the stones we tread are stained-glass windows.
The purples, the reds are profiles
of an old alliance:
Belial who governs metallic lambs,
ferruginous bulls
of mouths garnished with fire-proof mica.
The color of a rock abandoned by the tide
spreads on the floor of the city deserted
by family celebrations, Nativities, Christmas Eves
tables which mothers don't let us clean
keeping them intact so each one of the dead
may get his sweetmeat dripping with syrup,
some turkey, a piece of partridge, a dish of rice pudding
. . . .
Walking through the city
one notices the fortress,
fragile and potent mechanism of minuteness.
In every turret you'll find a lock,
the city is an ornamented wrench,
functional, organized in its virulent precision.]

(1980, 45–46)

In many of Gil Carvalho's[20] texts, his "private" language becomes virtually a secret code: their interpretation is made particularly difficult by multiple allusions crossing the tight textual space, which is often punctured by ellipses. His poems seem thus determined to emphasize that which, in all poetry, falls within the sphere of undecipherable mystery. Nevertheless, Carvalho's poetry also manages to recapture occasionally such traditional themes as the pleasures of the open air, the experience of being within the natural environment, among its plant and animal inhabitants. This is a trait which differentiates it clearly from most of the eminently urban Portuguese poetry of the last decades. A more explicit ecological concern may be found in Jorge de Sousa Braga's[21] volume *Os pés luminosos* (Luminous feet, 1987), whose author, like Carvalho, has also produced a number of variations on Oriental poetry.[22] Adília Lopes's[23] brief narrative poems may be said to follow a direction similar to Sousa Braga's early ironic mini-parables: her poetry embarks upon a fanciful and perversely innocent parodic dialogue with the literary canon, be it represented by the *Letters of a Portuguese Nun* or by Diderot's *Jacques le fataliste*. Her volume *O poeta de Pondichéry* (The poet from Pondichéry) revolves around the young poet who is mentioned in Diderot's book and advised to leave for Pondichéry; the following is a fragment of one of the poems in which the young poet himself speaks (note that the intertextual dialogue reaches out to other texts as well, namely to Álvaro de Campos's famous poem "Todas as cartas de amor são ridículas" subjected here to a parodic inversion):

> Tenho as gavetas cheias de papéis escritos
> poemas e cartas que não cheguei a mandar a Diderot
>
> . . . .
>
> as cartas estão fechadas e têm selo
> escrevi-as num papel nem muito caro nem muito barato
> para não constranger Diderot
> nunca escrevi cartas de amor
> mas costumo pensar que escrevi cartas ridículas
> e por ter a mania de pôr o carro à frente dos bois
> acho que todas as cartas ridículas são cartas de amor
>
> [My drawers are full of papers covered with writing
> poems and letters unmailed to Diderot
>
> . . . .
>
> sealed and stamped
> written on a paper neither too expensive nor too cheap
> so they wouldn't embarrass Diderot
> I never wrote love letters
> but I guess I have written ridiculous letters
> and since I have this obsession of putting the cart before
>   the oxen
> I think that all ridiculous letters are love letters]

(1986, n.p.)

Among Fernando Pessoa's heteronyms, it is Alberto Caeiro whose example appears to attract João Camilo,[24] given the unadorned language and free rhythm that he prefers in his poems:

> O espírito, tranquilo,
> diz-me: descansa, olha; Alberto Caeiro
> não te ensinou a olhar as montanhas e os rios?
>
> . . . .

No comboio, a olhar para as paisagens,
recupero o olhar dele como se lhe tivesse emprestado
a minha alma . . .

. . . . . .

A minha vida não sei para onde vai.
Mas o comboio há-de chegar
a uma estação. E eu hei-de descer.
Querer saber mais do que isso parece-me fútil.

[The spirit, tranquil,
tells me: calm down, look; didn't Alberto Caeiro
teach you to look at mountains and rivers?

. . . .

On the train, looking at the landscapes,
I regain his gaze as if I had lent him
my soul . . .

. . . . .

I don't know where my life is going.
But the train will arrive
at a station. And I will get off.
Wanting to know more than that seems to me useless.]

(1989, 18)

Gil de Carvalho, João de Sousa Braga, and Adília Lopes are all fea-
tured in *Sião* (Siam, 1987), an anthology edited by Al Berto, Paulo da Costa
Domingos, and Rui Baião, and published by Frenesi, an enterprise situated
on the margins of the publishing system. Since the early eighties, Frenesi
has distinguished itself by bringing out volumes of poetry from the new
generations of authors, particularly favoring works that, through challenging the political, social, or cultural establishment, most overtly identify
themselves with countercultural currents. The anthology, including poets
born between 1942 and 1960 and as "extremely partial" as the one edited
two years earlier by Herberto Helder *(Edoi lelia doura—antologia das vozes
comunicantes da poesia moderna portuguesa),* does not, however, share
its predecessor's undeniable coherence, obviously lacking any criterion for
some of its exclusions and inclusions. In spite of its flaws and imbalances,
Sião may be useful in identifying some of the traits that define the artistic
sensibility gaining ground in Portugal in the seventies and early eighties. I
have described elsewhere the skepticism, disillusion, individualism, narcissism, and urgency to live one's own life that arose in the wake of the crisis
of modernity and the beginning of an era dominated by uncertainty (Martinho
1990, 27). Among the younger authors included in the anthology, two

women poets may be mentioned in particular: Isabel de Sá[25] and R. Lino,[26] both with volumes published by Frenesi. Above all else, Sá sees in her writing a closure against the "flowing of senses" and a means to "obscure the words": "Não sou mais aquele que escreveu um verso claro, mas alguém que decidiu obscurecer as palavras, de tal modo as reduziu a nada" [I am no longer the one who wrote a clear verse, but someone who decided to obscure the words, to such an extent they were reduced to nothing] (1991, 7). As for R. Lino, her transfiguring inquiry of other times and spaces plunges her into an "always recurring 'work of memory'" (Amaral 1991, 178); the following is a fragment of a poem from her book *Daquira,* in which the "other time" explored is that of the Arab-Andalusian civilization:

> Raça misturada de deuses
> na rasura do seu chão,
> esta terra é para nós
> parte mais longe e mais verde,
> magníficas as figueiras,
> o atlântico do seu mar
> e as alfarrobeiras.
>
> [Race blended with gods
> on the flatness of its ground,
> this land is for us
> a part greener and further away,
> magnificent are the fig trees,
> the Atlantic of its sea,
> and its carob evergreens.]

(1988, n.p.)

As we approach the end of the century and the end of the millennium, these poets acquire an increasingly keen awareness of the end of all times: the Apocalypse. The apocalyptic consciousness is particularly manifest in the poems of Paulo Teixeira,[27] one of the most powerful revelations in the last ten years of Portuguese poetry. His texts, often dramatic monologues, employ a lofty poetic diction, which goes entirely against the grain of the artistic rehabilitation of everyday banality, so common in the latest Portuguese lyric. They rely on a confluence of the most diverse veins of literary tradition, as well as of traditions belonging to other arts. Teixeira is the author of a volume entitled *Conhecimento do Apocalipse* (Knowledge of the Apocalypse, 1988), which emphasizes a "feeling of twilight" and a "certainty" of "the end." The speaker in the poem wears one of the oldest masks of a poet, that of a prophet announcing the imminent "overturning" of all there is, in a more explicit allusion to St. John's Apocalypse. The cover of his other book, *Inventário e despedida* (Inventory and farewell, 1991), bears a reproduction of Dürer's famous *Visions of the Apocalypse*, while an epigraph from Eustache Deschamps suggests a reading of our time as a "time of tribulation." The poems gathered there present it as a poet's chore to make an inventory" of the "old world" before it disappears. One of the most expressive texts in the volume is the eloquently titled "Obituário" (Obituary):

> O coração imóvel, a língua tua infecunda,
> reverencia a deduzida luz do mundo,
> as prodigiosas mandíbulas do crepúsculo.

> Congrega duas mãos cheias de pó no vento
> e lança-as sobre o teu nome como as palavras
> de um obituário, como as cinzas que se perdem
> de volta à nudez agradecida do espaço exterior.

> [With heart unmoving, and your tongue barren,
> venerate the diminished light of the world,
> the prodigious jaws of twilight.

> Assemble in the wind two handfuls of dust
> and throw them over your name, like the words
> of an obituary, like ashes disappearing
> as they return to the grateful nudity of the world outside.]

>   (1991, 105)

The elegiac awareness of "the end of times," "the end of the world," "the night" of "the world," and damnation "without forgiveness" weighing heavily upon our cities informs also many of the poems by Luís Filipe Castro Mendes[28] (with their epigraphs borrowed from Borges, Rimbaud, and Rilke), particularly those in his latest book, *Viagem de Inverno* (Winter journey). The volume's significant closure is a *finda* in the form of a triptych of poems, all of them sonnets attesting to a renewed attractiveness of classic molds and confirming the increasing remoteness of formal effronteries of the avant-garde ("Fim do dia" [The day's end], "Finisterra," and "Fin de siècle [epílogo]"). The third title makes manifest the poet's insistence that the connection between the end of the century and the "epilogue" of all time not be forgotten:

O século que finda já nos deu,
para além das palavras mais vazias,
a estrela d'alva aonde morre o céu
em vãs constelações por demais frias.

Manhã se diz a treva iluminada
que ri no limiar do pensamento,
como se à terra nua e devastada
coubesse o culminar do firmamento.

Como um deus que se esconde na folhagem,
o vão poeta nasce desta imagem.

[The closing century already gave us,
beyond the hollowest of words,
the morning star where the sky is dying
in vain, excessively cold constellations.

As morning poses the lighted dusk
laughing on the edge of thought,
as if the earth, desolate and naked,
were to be the climax of the firmament.

Like a god hiding among the leaves
the vain poet is born from this image.]

                                                                    (1993, 95)

Even more closely bound to fears and anxieties of the "time of tribulation," time shadowed by ravages of AIDS and by urban violence and destruction, is the awareness of the approaching end in Joaquim Manuel
Magalhães' latest volume, *A poeira levada pelo vento* (Dust gone in the
wind, 1993), full of apocalypses befalling human beings in scenarios of
generalized catastrophe. The following is a fragment of a poem entitled
"Terra trabalhada pelo sal" (Earth wrought by salt):

A vida usual tem um cheiro suicida.
Falharam tudo. Vou morrer sem o que procuro.
Deixo a poesia dizer? Ela que não é para mim?

Levanto-me cada vez mais cedo.
Em redor da cidade um trânsito estacado.
Horas que me não pertencem a ninguém me trazem.
Estou fechado nesta armadilha que sou eu
se não encontrar a detonação.

[Regular life smells of suicide.
They failed in everything. I'll die without finding
    what I'm looking for.
Should I let poetry say it? She who is not for me?

I get up earlier day by day.
All around the city the traffic is jammed.
Hours that are not mine bring me to no one.
I'm locked in this trap that is myself
if I don't find a detonator.]

(1993, 58)

"Among the ruins" of a world that "ended" (Pitta 1991, 41),[29] or among the "ruins of the soul" (Amaral 1990, 82),[30] the vision of poets of our time thus wanders and "wavers," "shortly before / the end of the century" (Gonçalves 1991, n.p.),[31] only on rare occasions allowing a hope for "new skies" to overcome the "anxiety / and despair of final destruction" that no words are capable of "show[ing] and embody[ing]" (Belchior 1985, 87).

I have attempted to sketch a necessarily incomplete picture of the "new" Portuguese poetry being written since the early seventies; it should be obvious, however, that poets belonging to earlier generations have also been active during this time.[32] Many of them, ranging from those closely involved in a directly confrontational dialogue with the new voices to those who remain entirely removed from disputes arising on the literary scene, have even published some of their most important volumes during the last two decades. By creating their own traditions, however, the new poets have significantly altered the literary landscape, establishing other models and other masters, and, as often happens in such cases, reclaiming past figures either forgotten or, according to them, insufficiently appreciated. They have embarked upon a process of interaction with contemporary poetry, meaning not only that they have absorbed an influence of their chosen precursors but also that their example inspired in turn some of the older poets to alter their own course. Like all poetic generations, they have argued with their ghosts and have experienced that unease which Harold Bloom had famously called the "anxiety of influence."

As we have seen, the generation of the seventies, conforming to the model that, since romanticism, has shaped literary evolution, defined itself to a great extent through an opposition to the preceding generation. The same cannot be said with regard to the generation of the eighties, however. This is a significant fact in its own right in view of what has been said earlier about the crisis of modernity and postmodernism. Portuguese poetry of the eighties and nineties could be thus defined in terms of what

Ortega y Gasset called, in contrast to "eliminatory and polemical epochs", a "cumulative epoch," that is, a time when the new generations' experience a "substantial homogeneity between what they have received and what is unique to them" (1981, 80–81).

Notes

1. [Unless otherwise noted, all translations included in the text are my own. *Trans.*]
2. Born in 1943. Poetry: *Obra poética - 1* and *Obra poética - 2*, 1987; *Obra poética - 3*, 1988; *Crónica*, 1977; *Actus tragicus*, 1979; *O roubador de água*, 1981; *O regresso dos remadores*, 1982; *À beira do mar de Junho*, 1982; *Poemas escolhidos*, 1982; *Um nome distante*, 1984; *Tronos e dominações*, 1985; *A Jornada de Cristóvão de Távora primeira parte*, 1986; *A Jornada de Cristóvão de Távora segunda parte*, 1988; *Pelo fim da tarde*, 1989; *A Jornada de Cristóvão de Távora terceira e última parte*, 1990.
3. Born in 1949. Poetry: *Obra poética, 1972–1985*, 1991; *A condescendência do ser*, 1988; *Enumeração de sombras*, 1989; *As regras da perspectiva*, 1990; *Um canto na espessura do tempo*, 1992.
4. Born in 1944. Poetry: *A distância*, 1969; *Sem palavras nem coisas*, 1974; *Os objectos principais*, 1979; *Visitação*, 1983; *A pequena face*, 1983; *As moradas 1 & 2*, 1987; *Oásis*, 1992.
5. See, for example, the poems "Universo animal," "L'oubli" (whose main references are the texts of William Carlos Williams, Charles Olson, Newton, Guillevic, and Gide), "Arqueologia história possível," and "Lançando papagaios junto ao rio," in Alexandre 1974.
6. Born in 1942. Poetry: *Modo mudando*, 1963; *Semana inglesa*, 1965; *Quatro sextinas*, 1973; *O mês de Dezembro e outros poemas*, 1976; *Recitativos*, 1977; *Sequências regulares*, 1978; *Instrumentos para a melancolia*, 1980; *A variação dos semestres deste ano: 365 versos seguido de A escola de Frankfurt*, 1981; *Nó cego, o regresso*, 1982; *Os rostos comunicantes*, 1984; *A sombra das figuras*, 1985; *A furiosa paixão pelo tangível*, 1987.
7. Born in 1943. Poetry: *Algo parecido com isto, da mesma substância - Poesia reunida, 1974–1992*, 1992.
8. Born in 1945. Poetry: *Os dias pequenos charcos*, 1981; *Segredos, sebes, aluviões*, 1985; *Alguns livros reunidos*, 1987; *Uma luz com um toldo vermelho*, 1990; *A poeira levada pelo vento*, 1993.
9. It is important to note here that the interest in intertextuality, which Portuguese poets have displayed during the last decades, was no doubt greatly influenced by the example of Jorge de Sena who, at least since the publication of *Metamorfoses* in 1963, had engaged his poetry in a stimulating dialogue with the world of culture at large.
10. The text of Prado Coelho's presentation, entitled "Poesia portuguesa contemporânea," has been included in the essays in Coelho 1988.
11. Born in 1948. Poetry: *O medo [poesia reunida, 1974–1991]*, 1991.
12. Born in 1949. Poetry: *De novo as sombras e as calmas — Poesia, 1976–1990*, 1990.
13. Born in 1949. Poetry: *Ossuário (ou: a vida de James Whistler)*, 1977.
14. Born in 1948. Poetry: *Deste lado onde*, 1976; *Jeremias o louco*, 1979; *O último*

romântico, 1981; *Morrer no Sul*, 1983; *Autoretrato*, 1986; *O centro do universo*, 1989; *Paixão e cinzas*, 1992.

15. Born in 1933. Poetry: *A raiz afectuosa*, 1972; *A ignorância da morte*, 1978; *O lugar do amor*, 1981; *Décima aurora*, 1982; *Adão, Eva e o mais*, 1983; *Aforismos mágicos*, 1985; *Planetário e Zoo dos homens*, 1990.

16. Born in 1932. Poetry: *Silabário [poesia reunida]*, 1992.

17. Born in 1937. Poetry: *Obra quase incompleta*, 1990.

18. Born in 1957. Poetry: *Poemas [poesia reunida]*, 1987; *O céu sob as entranhas*, 1989.

19. Born in 1941. Poetry: *Cidades indefesas*, 1980; *Os presságios*, 1983; *Selo selvagem*, 1985; *A urna no deserto*, 1989.

20. Born in 1954. Poetry: *Alba*, 1983; *Aboiz*, 1985; *De Fevereiro a Fevereiro*, 1987.

21. Born in 1957. Poetry: *O poeta nu [poesia reunida]*, 1991.

22. Gil de Carvalho: *Uma antologia de poesia chinesa* (1989). Jorge de Sousa Brage: *Matsuo Bashô: O gosto solitário do orvalho* (1985); idem, *Li Po e outros poetas chineses*; idem, *Sono de Primavera* (1987); idem, *Matsuo Bashô: O caminho estreito para o longínquo norte* (1987).

23. Born in 1960. Poetry: *Um jogo bastante perigoso*, 1985; *O poeta de Pondichéry*, 1986; *O Marquês de Chamilly (Kabale und Liebe)*, 1987; *A pão e água de colónia*, 1987; *O decote de dama de espadas (romances)*, 1988; *Os 5 livros de versos salvaram o tio*, 1991; *Maria Cristina Martins*, 1992.

24. Born in 1943. Poetry: *Os filmes coloridos*, 1978; *O T de Tu*, 1981; *Na pista, entre as linhas*, 1983; *Para a desconhecida*, 1983; *A mala dos Marx Brothers*, 1989; *A mais nobre das artes*, 1991.

25. Born in 1951. Poetry: *Esquizofrenia*, 1979; *O festim das serpentes novas*, 1982; *Desejo ou asa leve*, 1982; *Bonecas trapos suspensos*, 1983; *Restos de infantas*, 1984; *Autismo*, 1984; *Nervura*, 1984; *Em nome do corpo*, 1986; *Escrevo para desistir*, 1988; *O avesso do rosto*, 1991.

26. Born in 1952. Poetry: *Palvras do Imperador Hadriano*, 1984; *Atlas paralelo*, 1984; *Paisagens de além Tejo*, 1986; *Daquira*, 1988.

27. Born in 1962. Poetry: *As imaginações da verdade*, 1985; *Epos*, 1987; *Conhecimento do Apocalipse*, 1988; *A região brilhante*, 1988; *Inventário e despedida*, 1991; *Arte da memória*, 1992.

28. Born in 1950. Poetry: *Recados*, 1983; *Seis elegias e outros poemas*, 1985; *A Ilha dos Mortos*, 1991; *Viagem de Inverno*, 1993.

29. Born in 1949.

30. Born in 1960. Poetry: *Acédia*, 1990.

31. Born in 1951.

32. The following names particularly deserve to be mentioned, regardless of their distance from, or closeness to, the poets who, in the last decades, joined them in continuing the rich tradition of Portuguese poetry: José Gomes Ferreira (d. 1985), Vitorino Nemésio (d. 1978), Miguel Torga, Ruy Cinatti (d. 1986), Jorge de Sena (d. 1978), Sophia de Mello Breyner Andresen, Carlos de Oliveira (d. 1981), Eugénio de Andrade, Mário Cesariny, Alexandre O'Neill (d. 1986), Natália Correia (d. 1993), António Ramos Rosa, David Mourão-Ferreira, Alberto de Lacerda, Fernando Guimarães, Fernando Echevarria, Ana Hatherly, Pedro Tamen, Herberto Helder, E. M. de Melo e Castro, Ruy Belo (d. 1978), M. S. Lourenço, Rui Knopfli, Fiama Hasse Pais Brandão, Gastão Cruz, Luíza Neto Jorge (d. 1989), Casimiro de Brito, Maria Teresa Horta, Fernando Assis Pacheco, Armondo Silva Carvalho, and Manuel Alegre.

References

Alexandre, António Franco. 1974. *Sem palavras nem coisas*. Lisboa: Iniciativas Editoriais.

Amaral, Fernando Pinto do. 1990. *Acédia*. Lisboa: Assírio & Alvim.

————. 1991. *O mosaico fluido — Modernidade e pós-modernidade na poesia portuguesa mais recente*. Lisboa: Assírio e Alvim.

Antunes, Miguel. 1987. "Persistência do modernismo". In *Legómena*, 179–83. Lisboa: Imprensa Nacional-Casa da Moeda.

Aurélio, Diogo Pires. 1978. *A herança de Hölderlin*. Lisboa: Assírio & Alvim.

————. 1984. *O próprio dizer*. Lisboa: Imprensa Nacional-Casa da Moeda.

Belchior, Maria de Lourdes. 1985. *Gramática do Mundo*. Lisboa: Imprensa Nacional-Casa da Moeda.

Belo, Ruy. 1984. *Obra poética*. Vol. 3. Lisboa: Presença.

Bento, José. 1992. *Silabário*. Lisboa: Relógio d'Água.

Breyner, Sophia de Mello. 1988. "25th April 1974." In *Marine Rose: Selected Poems*, translated by Ruth Fainlight. Redding Ridge, Conn.: Black Swan Books.

Calinescu, Matei. 1987. *Five Faces of Modernity*. Durham, N.C.: Duke University Press.

Camilo, João. 1989. *A mala dos Marx Brothers*. Lisboa: Caminho.

Chambers, Iain. 1986. *Popular Culture: The Metropolitan Experience*. London: Methuen.

Coelho, Eduardo Prado. 1988. *A noite do mundo*. Lisboa: Imprensa Nacional-Casa da Moeda.

Cruz, Gastão. 1973. *A poesia portuguesa hoje*. Lisboa: Plátano.

Diniz, Rui, ed. 1977. *Ossuário (ou a vida de James Whistler)*. Lisboa: & etc.

Ferreira, José Gomes. 1978. *Poeta Militante, 3° volume*. Lisboa: Moraes.

Frow, John. 1991. "Postmodernism and Literary History." In *Theoretical Issues in Literary History*, edited by David Perkins, 131–42. Cambridge: Harvard University Press.

Gonçalves, Manuel Fernando. 1991. *As horas certas é que me enervam*. Lisboa: Frenesi.

Jameson, Fredric. 1975/76. "The Ideology of the Text." *Salmagundi* 31/32 (fall/winter): 208. Quoted in Astradur Eysteinsson, *The Concept of Modernism* (Ithaca: Cornell University Press, 1992), 137.

Jorge, João Miguel Fernandes. 1982. *Poemas escolhidos*. Lisboa: Assírio & Alvim.

Júdice, Nuno. 1977. "Apresentação do texto." In *Ossuário (ou a vida de James Whistler)*, edited by Rui Diniz (Lisboa: & etc.).

————. 1991. *A noção de poema*. Lisboa: Publicações Dom Quixote.

————. 1992. *O processo poético*. Lisboa: Imprensa Nacional-Casa da Moeda.

Lino, R. 1988. *Daquira*. Lisboa: Frenesi.

Lopes, Adília. 1986. *O poeta de Pondichéry*. Lisboa: & etc.

Lourenço, Eduardo. 1987. *Tempo e poesia*. Lisboa: Relógio d'Água.

Magalhães, Joaquim Miguel. *Os dois crepúsculos*. 1981. Lisboa: A Regra do Jogo.

————. 1987. *Alguns livros reunidos*. Lisboa: Contexto.

————. 1993. *A poeira levada pelo vento*. Lisboa: Presença.

Maldonado, Fátima. 1980. *Cidades indefesas*. Coimbra: Centelha.

Martinho, Fernando J. B. 1984. "Dez anos de literatura portuguesa (1974–1984) — Poesia." *Colóquio/Letras* 78 (Março): 19–20.

———. 1990. "Poesia portuguesa a partir dels anys 60." *Daina* (València) 7.

Mendes, Luís Filipe Castro. 1993. *Viagem de Inverno*. Lisboa: Quetzal.

Meschonnic, Henn. 1985. *Les états de la politique*. Paris: PUF.

Moura, Vasco Graça. 1987. *A furiosa paixão pelo tangível*. Lisboa: Quetzal.

Nava, Luís Miguel. 1988. "Os anos 60 — realismo e vanguarda". In *A phala. Edição especial — Um século de poesia (1888-1988)*, edited by Fernando Pinto do Amaral, José Bento, Gil de Carvalho, and Manuel Hermínio Monteiro, 150–57. Lisboa: Assírio & Alvim.

———, ed. 1991. *Antologia de poesia portuguesa — 1960–1990*. Lisboa and Leuven: Caminho & Leuvense Schrijversaktie.

Ortega y Gasset, José. 1981. *El tiema de nuestro tiempo*. Madrid: Revista de Occidente en Alianza Editorial.

Osório, António. 1978. *A ignorância da morte*. Lisboa: Edição do Autor.

Paz, Octavio. 1990. *La otra voz — poesía y fin de siglo*. Barcelona: Seix Barral.

Pereira, Helder Moura. 1990. *De novo as sombras e as calmas—Poesia, 1976–1990*. Lisboa: Contexto.

Pitta, Eduardo. 1991. *Arbítrio*. Lisboa: & etc.

Sá, Isabel de. 1991. *O avesso do rosto*. Lisboa: Caminho.

Santos, Maria Irene Ramalho de Sousa. 1987. "Da crítica à ficção: Harold Bloom no centro e na margem." In *Ficção narrativa—Discurso crítico e discurso literário*. Actas do III Encontro da Associação Portuguesa de Estudos Anglo-Americanos. Porto: Associação Portuguesa de Estudos Anglo-Americanos.

Teixeira, Paulo. 1991. *Inventário e despedida*. Lisboa: Caminho.

Torga Miguel. 1977. "Lament." 136 in *Diário XII*. Coimbra.

Wollen, Peter. 1986. "Ways of Thinking About Music Video (and Postmodernism)." *Critical Quarterly* 28, nos. 1/2 (spring/summer).

The Historical Parable in Contemporary Portuguese Drama

JOSÉ OLIVIERA BARATA
Translated by Helena Kaufman and Anna Klobucka

Pertinence of a Theme: History and Literature

As literary criticism has begun to move beyond the inconsequential excesses of textual analysis, an increased appreciation of the historical context has become apparent, independently of its actual material realization in the work of art. Such development would seem inevitable, in fact, regardless of fashion or of specific operational models. After all, literary convergence of reality and fiction is always produced within a historical framework manifested in characters. Through them, the ingredients of history are rearranged, their arrangement predicated not on any particular historical truth, but rather on specific practices of narrative representation, characteristic of different genres, and yet never distanced from the crucial problematics of representation of reality through a fictional universe.

This "chronotopic" quality of literature—as defined by Bakhtin essentially with regard to the novel—may be ascribed to other genres as well, particularly to drama.[1] In drama, a protagonist is construed as a function of action rather than narration—action that, since Aristotle, has been conceived as the *interpreter* (in the precise sense of "translator") of emotions and situations solely possible to contextualize in a present that is unique and fleeting, but also historical in its uniqueness: the present of representation.

The phenomenon of ongoing contamination between history and literature is neither new nor even traceable specifically to romanticism, with its renewed valuing of the "different" national histories. It may be instead considered as a constant feature of various literatures, a reflex of the literary creation's function as a carrier of values and emotions, thus reaffirming the Bakhtinian notion of the chronotope as the critical instrument that determines the artistic unity of the literary work.

Leaving aside the discussion of the rise of history in Portuguese drama, it is important to note that historical themes have maintained a strikingly vigorous presence in Portuguese literature, demonstrating how literary creation has accompanied and shared in recurrent crises of national identity, crises so common in Portugal's peripheral culture.

The manner in which Portuguese literature represents Portugal, and in which Portuguese history *allows itself* to be represented by literature, becomes manifest in what António Quadros calls "the conflicted way of our being with ourselves" (1989, 21). Symptomatically, it was at times of crisis—as during Spain's occupation of Portugal from 1580 to 1640—that epic poems such as Rodrigues Lobo's *O Condestabre de Portugal* sought to retrieve the historical and mythical past of the nation, embodied in its most representative heroes. While a particularly rich, direct, and critical confrontation with national history took place during Portuguese romanticism, later generations never shrank from that challenge either, beginning with the Geração de 70 and continuing with the twentieth-century movements of Renascença Portuguesa or Presença, not to mention individual works, such as Guerra Junqueiro's *Finis Patriae* or Fernando Pessoa's *Mensagem*, to give but a few examples.

The political and institutional rupture of 25 April has brought a number of new perspectives: on the one hand, an examination of the most recent history has become possible; on the other, many writers have engaged in a critically divided retrieval of past events and characters through the prism of present ideologies.

Portuguese drama has always shared in these complicated exchanges between literature and history. On these latest, postrevolutionary historical crossroads it has once again become necessary to "rethink Portugal," and a number of recent Portuguese plays confirm the words of the great playwright Georg Büchner, written with regard to his *Death of Danton*, a critical rereading of the events of the French Revolution:

> The dramatic poet is, in my eyes, nothing but a writer of history, except that he stands above the latter in that he creates history for the second time; he transplants us directly into the life of another time, instead of giving us a dry account of it; instead of characteristics, he gives us characters; instead of descriptions, he gives us living figures. (1963, xviii)

Staging History

The parallel roads traveled by history and literature from antiquity until the eighteenth century—the time when new concepts of history emerged, together with new ways of viewing the "contamination" of literature by historical concerns—bore questions that, having risen to a new prominence in the last half century, led to the study of interpenetration between narrative and history, going as far as to include direct affirmations of a purely narrative character of historical "facts." It is particularly in some recent research on the historical novel that one finds direct echoes of these ideas, resulting in analyses of how the notions of narrativity and historicity become articulated within a literary design informed by concrete ideological and aesthetic assumptions.

As Heiner Müller puts it with regard to the interference of history in the theater, "History can only be represented as a coexistence in time of the past, present and future, and this is how it becomes intelligible." The noted German playwright thus expresses that the contemporary experience of the long tradition of historical theater, from Aeschylus to Brecht (and passing through the virtually endless list of the likes of Shakespeare, Racine, Büchner, Schiller, Goethe, Kleist, or Sartre), has attempted ever new mythical rereadings of national or universal history. Similarly, as demonstrated by a number of Portuguese plays from romanticism to the present, the recuperation of national history for the benefit of dramatic literature has generally centered around weighty mythical nuclei.

But even when the dramatic transposition of events coincides with the viewer's ignorance of the facts, thus obstructing the apprehension of the meaning (or meanings), the essence of history emerging in drama always aims at "the continuity between past and present" as "a central assertion in history plays of all times and styles" (Lindenberger 1975, 6). This continuity is not, however, dictated by chance or by mere opportunistic perception: the retrieval of history into drama almost always corresponds to moments of intense national consciousness and to the extent and significance of its crisis.[2]

The fundamental procedures the playwright follows in bringing history to the stage can be designated as *transforming* and *transcoding*. Operating on the level of the story, transformation leads to the construction of a dramatic *parable*, in which the actual historical names are abandoned so as to focus more intensely on the function of the historical moment itself. As for transcodification, its parallel action brings about changes in the order of genre, including all the questions of time and space that such a procedure implies: for instance, the need to move from a one-dimensional narrative space into the multidimensional space of dramatic representation.

It is important to note, however, that any discussion of historical drama, whose objectives are as much ethical and ideological as aesthetic, needs to pursue a double thread of analysis: on the one hand, the study of its formal, literary features; on the other hand, an investigation of the *poetic transmutation* that the historical events undergo as they are presented to a contemporary audience. To delve into the rich evidence of this process found in Portuguese literature contributes toward a collective self-knowledge or, in other words, toward the formulation of an *imagology*, defined by Eduardo Lourenço as a "critical discourse about the images that we have wrought for ourselves" and particularly about "the multiple perspectives, countless portraits that have been consciously or unconsciously created and imprinted upon the common consciousness by those who are by nature predisposed toward collective self-knowledge (artists, historians, novelists, poets)" (1978, 14).

This kind of analysis, complemented by a *mythocritique* (as described in Durand 1979), requires naturally a constant awareness of the historical context, since history is par excellence the site where a narrative becomes concrete (Ablamowicz 1984). Even more evident is the need to take into account the performative aspect of drama and the context of social communication in which the theatrical spectacle functions.

The Portuguese Theater: Decline and Resistance

I am Portuguese, a writer, and I am forty-five years old. I have lived this way. This way we have lived in Portugal. I am forty-five years old and . . . I am fed up, tired, I do not believe in anything anymore. This will be my last play. This performance is—I would like it to be—a good-bye. A loveless good-bye. I lost everything. I am not interested anymore in what can happen to you, the spectators, even the youngest ones. Hope, progress, struggle, future, beauty, camaraderie, people, youth, for me represent roles long gone. They took everything from me. I cannot continue anymore. This will be, I repeat, my last play. An autobiographic play. I wrote it in prison. (Santareno 1974, 42)

These words by Bernardo Santareno, written in a play that was completed in March 1974, are singularly expressive. His outburst of personal desperation simultaneously conveys the mute protest of many people of the theater (writers, producers, actors) who witnessed progressive stifling of the liberties that made a politically interventionist creativity possible. Performed in July 1974—shortly after the events of 25 April—this work, written by one of Portugal's most representative playwrights, was not appreciated exclusively for its dramatic merits, but was immediately transformed into an unavoidable homage to the Portuguese theater, which had suffered censorship.[3] The atmosphere of short but intense euphoria that usually follows moments of political and institutional rupture explained why, soon after 25 April, everything that had been prohibited until then underwent a process of revision and restaging. This explanation applies also to the Brechtian boom, with its multiple performances of plays that could not be staged previously and its endless discussions about the relationship between the theater and power. Many of those plays were original texts that had suffered double censorship (one of text and the other one of performance). Portuguese drama, on the other hand, continued to follow a historical and pedagogic line established to evade the mechanisms of censorship and in a time of freedom continued to revisit and reread history.

An initial and necessary observation about theater censorship reveals that its principal perpetrators understood perfectly the power of social intervention contained in the performance itself. As early as 1926, soon after the military coup of 28 May, there was an attempt to reestablish and broaden the scope of censorship. It reached beyond specific occurrences in cultural life to include the totality of civic manifestations that could challenge the principles of the newly established Estado Novo. However, the decisive moment came with the 1933 constitution. Coupled with a ban on unions and political parties, the Secretariat of National Propaganda under the authority of António Ferro (a major representative of the Portuguese intelligentsia in the Salazar era), in close collaboration with other repressive institutions, set in motion mechanisms deemed necessary to avoid "a very real threat of infection of the country's organic tissue that could lead to disease and even death," as affirms António Quadros (1989, 83).

In general, the years 1933 and 1934 showed a decline of the national theater. As a result of that decline, new European movements and aesthetic trends that had been influential in Portuguese dramatic writing and performance until then became more distant. The triumph of the "light genres" (from *revista* to operetta and including the ambiguity of comedy) demonstrates the support bestowed on a certain type of theater based on a comic typology of customs and situations.

Progressively, the anemic state of the national repertoire became more accentuated and did not register any new developments. Even such major artistic events as the movements of Orfeu, Presença or neorealism had almost no effect on dramatic production.[4] A major exception has to be made, however, for the cultivated vitality of Luís Sttau Monteiro's play *Felizmente Há Luar!* (Fortunately there is moonlight!): first published in 1961 and reprinted constantly, it has achieved a paradigmatic status within contemporary Portuguese drama. Today, well over thirty years since the play's publication, it is clear that the favorable critical judgment it received at the time was not dictated just by the contemporary political circumstances.[5]

Nevertheless, it was not until much later, well after 25 April, that *Felizmente Há Luar!* was staged in the Teatro Nacional D. Maria. Regardless of the continuing validity of arguments that make the play, with its new and innovative techniques put to use in the treatment of an episode of Portuguese history, a successful example of historical drama, it is easy to perceive why Sttau Monteiro's aiming at a situated objective may deprive his play of some of its efficacy today. In other words, *Felizmente Há Luar!*, written and designed to be effective in a specific historical context, can no longer boast didactic effectiveness, once its points of reference have changed. This problem, obviously, is not unique to *Felizmente Há Luar!*. It is shared by many other plays whose political purpose determined the dramatic strategies privileged by the playwrights. In view of the profound changes undergone by Portuguese society after 25 April, works such as those of Sttau Monteiro (apart from *Felizmente Há Luar!* itself) appear to us as irreparably dated. In some cases, they present the audience with the burden of excessively difficult (or ambiguous) interpretation. The spectators, ignorant of points of reference that are essential to decode the entire subtext (hidden in multiple veiled allusions) can hardly be expected to see the plays' deliberate parallels for what they were intended to be: "contemporary" metaphors referring to daily reality.

Felizmente Há Luar! was subtitled a "tragic apotheosis," in contrast to "grotesque apotheosis," a designation chosen by José Cardoso Pires for his first play *O Render dos Heróis* (The surrender of the heroes). In comparison with *O Render dos Heróis*, Sttau Monteiro's play represents a notable qualitative leap that can be demonstrated by a close reading of the text, with particular attention devoted to bringing forth the social and historical referents that sustain it. In fact, and contrary to Cardoso Pires's epic experiment, the entire structure of *Felizmente Há Luar!*, written in the year when the first outbursts of violence foreshadowed the colonial war, was designed to correlate with very concrete references within Portuguese society. However, besides and in spite of its deliberate complicity with the present moment, its deeply committed (but never demagogic) *clin d'oeil* directed toward the Portuguese audience of the sixties, *Felizmente Há Luar!* is also, formally, an adaptation of a historical-narrative structure to the language of drama.

The great homogeneity of the play expresses itself essentially through the perfect harmony achieved between form and content. It is not by accident that its stage directions appear as detailed indications of how a line should be said, a gesture made, and an impression conveyed. One might say that Sttau Monteiro's directions are no longer limited to the traditional function of a secondary text, but rather assume the role of a musical score designed to direct, according to Brechtian notions of alienation and *Gestus*, the potential interpreters of *Felizmente Há Luar!*[6] Long before the achievement of Santareno with *O Judeu* (The Jew, 1966), *Felizmente Há Luar!* may be considered a magnificent example of a reconciliation between the nationalistic didactic goals of a text and the techniques drawn from French and English translations of Brecht's writings on theater. In fact, the easiest way to prove the unique value of *Felizmente Há Luar!* is to look at Sttau Monteiro's other dramatic works. The desire for political relevance and the contact with such models as the "documentary theater" of Peter Weiss or Erwin Piscator shaped the unsuccessful (because lampoonish) examples of *Guerra Santa* and *Estátua*, clearly influenced by Weiss's *Song of the Lusitanian Bogey*, staged all over Europe but unpublished in Portugal until after 25 April.

The "historical parable" of *Felizmente Há Luar!* was not meant, however, to merely evoke or bear witness to a moral truth or a sociological experience. It aimed, instead, at helping the audience gain insight into their own world so that they might be empowered to transform it. While history supplied the meanings, it also greatly surpassed, in the words of Sttau Monteiro himself, its more traditional function of a "perspective for the future": "History is more than just a perspective: it is the present moment itself seen through the prism of its constituent elements" (1969, 179).

While the appearance of *Felizmente Há Luar* marked a unique moment in contemporary Portuguese drama, it should be stressed that it shared its thematic allegiance to national history with many other works, beginning with Cardoso Pires's *O Render dos Heróis* and culminating in Santareno's *O Judeu,* a symbolically charged landmark in the history of Portuguese theater.

Before and After 25 April

Although Portuguese drama has clearly evolved in new directions and discovered new forms of expression since the Revolution of Carnations, its continuing vitality owes a great deal to its past record of resistance. It has its roots in independent and student theater, amateur theatrical productions (with noteworthy examples of communities choosing drama as a privileged form of cultural militancy), and, finally, short-lived professional companies often operating almost clandestinely.

In spite of the unfortunate scarcity of documentary records with regard to the most recent history of Portuguese theater, it is possible to name the principal protagonists of this lived experience of resistance: companies such as Comuna, Grupo 4, Cornucópia, TEUC (Teatro dos Estudantes da Universidade de Coimbra), CITAC (Centro de Iniciação Teatral da Academia de Coimbra), and TUP (Teatro Universitário do Porto), as well as Cénico da Faculdade de Direito, TEC (Teatro Experimental de Cascais), and Lisbon's Teatro Estúdio, among many others. All were born and shaped their activity in clear opposition to the dictatorial regime and to the stifling rules of conduct it imposed, even as it disguised the dictatorship occasionally with a pretense of partial political thaw, as in the case of the so-called *primavera marcelista* ("Marcelo's [Caetano] spring").[7]

Persecution directed against certain Portuguese playwrights, who were imprisoned, put on trial, and forbidden to practice their profession, was a matter of common knowledge. But the regime went further: the written work was also subject to oppression as its publication was prohibited or, once published, ordered to be withdrawn from the market. And if someone challenged the country's rulers by courageously staging the text in question, difficulties immediately piled up.

During the most oppressive years of the fascist regime, a play was subjected to various readings before its staging could be authorized. The commission in charge of censoring dramatic texts was at liberty to cut out sections of dialogue and entire scenes, or, indeed, to suppress the play itself. The ostensibly more liberal and flexible Caetano regime realized that the old mechanisms of censorship, in spite of their apparent stringency, did not allow for sufficient control over the content of the performance. Thus, while the reading stage of the censorship process was somewhat liberalized (the readers were now members of the theatrical community), a second step was added, requiring an examination of the staged performance. Many plays were never performed in front of an audience, in spite of having been staged with substantial monetary and creative expense, due solely to the censor's negative verdict, which could not be appealed. Needless to say, the Portuguese theater was thus being slowly asphyxiated, not only because original Portuguese productions became fewer and fewer but also due to the absence of external stimulation, which can, in turn, be attributed to the scarcity of performances of plays by the foreign authors who were at the time exercising decisive influence in European theater.

The following brief statistical overview, aside from documenting the reasons for the stagnation of Portuguese theater, will also point to such crucial aspects of its situation as the difficulties in establishing a distinct repertory or the cautious approach to starting a new production that theatrical companies have tended to adopt.

Some Statistics

To begin with, let us scrutinize the list of authors and plays completely forbidden during the tenure of the Censorship Commission. It is important to emphasize that these were works suppressed in their entirety: countless others suffered partial mutilation that, in most cases, distorted their essential significance. Among foreign dramatic authors who were censored in Portugal, three names stand out: Bertolt Brecht, Jean-Paul Sartre, and Peter Weiss. A substantial portion of Jean Anouilh's work was also prohibited. The list of forbidden authors included names such as Arrabal, Dürrenmatt, Max Frisch, Ionesco, Alfred Jarry, Pablo Neruda, Sean O'Casey, Piscator, Sastre, and Boris Vian, among many others (works by the likes of Ernst Toller, Armand Gatti, John Arden, Hochhut, or Kipphart never even made it to the censors' desks, since in their case the verdict was fully predictable). The Portuguese censorship also classified as "dangerous" the plays of Machiavelli, Shakespeare, Sophocles, and Gil Vicente, along with works by such French *boulevard* playwrights as Sauvajon or Salacrou.

The data available for the last five years of the Caetano regime eloquently and unequivocally contradict its vaunted claim of "liberalization" that some were at the time inclined to believe. In 1969, ten original Portuguese dramas were staged (including five published more than five years before); in 1970, there were five such productions; in 1971 four (three of which were published more than ten years before); and in 1972 only one original Portuguese play was brought to the stage. In general, the number of performances given by the seventeen theatrical companies existing at the time (and destined, in principle, to serve eight million potential spectators) was extraordinarily scarce. The year of 1970 saw, in all, sixty-six theater performances (a number including both valuable productions and commercial subproducts); in 1971 there were only forty-eight and in the following year forty-six.

While a thorough analysis of this situation has yet to be made,[8] a few additional observations may be advanced to help explain the lamentable state of Portuguese theater on the eve of 25 April. A crucial factor was the macrocephalic distortion of the country's cultural map. While census data showed the existence of about 320 halls where theatrical performances could be staged, in fact only one-third fulfilled this function, the majority opting for the far more lucrative employment as movie theaters. A mere sixteen performance halls functioned exclusively as theaters: of those, thirteen were located in Lisbon, two in Porto, and one in Cascais, on the outskirts of Lisbon. Thus, until 1974, there was one theatrical performance per each 143,000 inhabitants of Lisbon, and one per 5,385,000 inhabitants of the rest of the country. Not until after 25 April did this state of affairs begin to change, owing to a decentralizing project carried out by theater activists marked by a French experience during their years of exile. The role of independent theater companies prior to 1974 needs to be stressed as a first agent of change toward the creation of new performance venues, renovation of the repertory, and, finally, a greater permeability to artistic precepts developed and perfected by the European theater of the fifties.

Completing this sad picture were such factors as lack of, or uneven distribution of, institutional support and material incentive, persecution directed against world-famous figures of international theater attempting to work in Portugal (Ricardo Salvat, Victor García, Luís de Lima, and Adolfo Gutkin, among others), progressive degradation and insufficient recognition accorded to the National Conservatory, state protectionism reserved for the weakest sectors of professional theater, and constant marginalization of independent, student, and amateur companies. No wonder therefore that in Santareno's penultimate play, *Português, Escritor, quarenta e cinco anos de idade* (1973–74), guarded as a tempting but forbidden fruit, the author's despair should be so overwhelming when faced with the dismal scenario of contemporary Portuguese culture.

In Search of an Answer: The Historical Parable

Confronted with severe restrictions placed on their freedom of artistic expression, Portuguese playwrights attempted diverse solutions. Not few among them experienced the painful reality of self-censorship; others took refuge in allusion and innuendo, which nearly always resulted in compromising the efficacy of their message. Many wrote in hopes that their text, once staged and thus given additional emphasis by the immediate impact of the performance, would serve as a *pre-text* for conveying meanings that could not be expressed in words. Others yet, influenced perhaps by a greater familiarity with aesthetic lessons absorbed during exile in France, Sweden, Holland, Germany, or Italy, found precisely in the *historical parable* a formula for the recuperation of the popular roots of rebellion and a rethinking of national history.

The Brechtian Boom

The onset of predilection for historical themes coincided with the clandestine entry of Brecht's writings into Portugal, an event that can be approximately traced back to 1960. As defined by Brecht in his "Short Organum for the Theater," the formula of historical parable does not oblige the writer to factually follow the events gathered in history; on the contrary, the play's effectiveness resides instead in a certain discontinuity it cultivates with regard to historical record, thus producing disruptions that allow the author to introduce, in proper form and at the right moment, the process of distancing (Brecht 1964).[9]

As many Portuguese playwrights have since learned, the validity of Brecht's project is far from unquestionable. At the time, however, they were caught by surprise by the Brechtian revelation, which appeared to provide a powerful working tool, simultaneously entertaining and pedagogically effective. Brecht's long-lasting preeminence in Portuguese theater was not always based on a thorough understanding of his writings: at times, a superficial reading of Brechtian doctrine would result in unbearably didactic performances. Another important limitation of the Portuguese reception of Brecht may be linked to the fact that the German author's theory was always meant to be tested in the theatrical praxis, which Brecht himself subjected to a gradual, thorough process of revision. While Portuguese playwrights and directors were generally familiar with Brechtian *theory*, only a small minority had a comparable knowledge of his *praxis*. Nevertheless, Brecht was accorded fully, if tardily, the status of a paradigmatic mentor of Portuguese theater, whose influence would later be complemented and reinforced by the impact of figures such as Piscator, Peter Weiss, or Gatti.

Central Historical Themes

An important point to be made while outlining the "before and after" situation of Portuguese theater with regard to 25 April is that the spirit of opposition animating its protagonists during the years of dictatorship has continued beyond the watershed date of 1974. The attitudes assumed are obviously no longer those of resistance fighters facing the enemy from behind a barricade. The theatrical praxis is now placed in the service of revising imaginary constructs that shaped the understanding of Portuguese history within the framework of collective national consciousness conditioned by the forty-eight years of Salazarist propaganda. What follows therefore is a necessarily concise inventory of chief thematic nuclei that have stimulated artistic reflection—and the varying meanings of political intervention—since 1960.

Sebastianism

The subject of Sebastianism has long been a central theme in Portuguese culture—and in Portuguese theater. Earlier examples include Almeida Garrett's play *Frei Luís de Sousa* (according to the interpretation proposed by Luciana Stegagno Picchio in her *História do Teatro Português*), Fernando Pessoa's dramatic sketch *O Encoberto*, and José Régio's *El-Rei D. Sebastião*. The myth of the young king defeated in the 1578 battle at Alcácer-Quibir, who is to return one foggy morning as the country's savior, has been repeatedly appropriated by authors in search of a certain concept of nationalism. Generally associated with the myth of the Fifth Empire, D. Sebastião's figure thus becomes the protagonist of a new national restoration.

Not surprisingly, the theme of Sebastianism tends to return to the stage at times of national crisis. The fatalistic import of this messianic myth, with its defining belief in providential historical figures, becomes linked either to a nostalgic longing *(saudade)* for the dead or dying past, or, conversely, to a despairing recognition of that very past's undying persistence in the nation's present.

To give but one example, Natália Correia's political and artistic agenda in writing her *O Encoberto* (published in 1969) is quite clear: to unmask, once and for all, the belief in historical ghosts that are brought back to life at the precise moments when their intervention is judged to be an effective tool toward erasing public awareness of concrete social reality. Correia's play, based on the formula of theater within the theater, deliberately sought to address the ideological project of the many contemporary defenders of Portuguese colonial expansion. These colonialists staunchly stood by the idea of the empire and the providential figure of a soldier who is strong and revered even in his defeat. While *O Encoberto*, which was not brought to stage until after 25 April, stands out as the most successful among contemporary dramatic rewritings of the Sebastianist theme, other plays also deserving a mention are Jorge de Sena's *O Indesejado* (1951) and *Encantado do Nevoeiro* (1980), a didactic play with magical elements written for children's theater.

Independence and National Crises

The Sebastianic myth, in addition to providing a platform from which to address questions of Portuguese historical destiny and present-day reality, points also in the direction of another weighty theme that appears to hold particular interest for Portuguese playwrights: the subject of national independence. The question of the country's independent existence commonly finds its attendant motif in the issue of Portuguese national identity. As if heeding the call of a character in Sttau Monteiro's *Felizmente Há Luar!*, who reacts to Freire de Andrade's sacrifice by exclaiming that some men are destined to compel others to see themselves in a new light, numerous playwrights have sought material for reflection in national historical events such as the nineteenth-century civil wars or popular revolts.

Plays of particular importance in the general context of Portuguese theater are Sttau Monteiro's *Felizmente Há Luar!* and Cardoso Pires's *O Render dos Heróis*. Both works examine the dynamics of popular rebellions, seeking to comprehend the mechanisms that unleashed them, as well as to point out, from a historical distance, the mistakes and uncertainties that contributed to their failure. It is easy to understand the reasons of the playwrights' predilection for the early nineteenth-century Liberal upheavals (such as the 1817 revolution in *Felizmente Há Luar!*), or for the later uprising of *Maria da Fonte* (in *O Render dos Heróis*). Portuguese playwrights confront the commonly voiced conviction that no revolutions ever took place in Portugal and that, on the contrary, national insurrections were from the beginning doomed to failure and ultimately co-opted by the agents of regeneration. Therefore they also focus their critical spotlight on the question of the (im)possibility of revolutions. What follows is a partial enumeration of the most insistently dramatized aspect of revolutions, present already in *Felizmente Há Luar!* and *O Render dos Heróis* and later instrumental in plays such as Miguel Franco's *Motim* (1965) or *A Legenda do Cidadão Miguel Lino* (1970), as well as, to some degree, in Virgílio Martinho's *Filopópulos*, with its clear allegoric references to *primavera marcelista*:

1. Representation of "the people" as a class of analphabets, largely devoid of political consciousness, pure in their beliefs and intentions, but incapable of becoming organized.

2. Constant tension between the enthusiastic spontaneity of popular movements and their inability to organize themselves, resulting in a clash of unequal forces in a confrontation with the established regime.

3. The role of the state, the church, and various repressive mechanisms (a constant theme, with an immediate resonance for Portuguese audiences from the forties to the seventies).

4. The confrontation, in the area of religious interpretation, between traditional Roman Catholic views and progressive tendencies influenced by the teachings of Pope John XXIII and by the reformist documents approved during the second Vatican Council.

5. The sordid reality of informers selling their services to the regime, the Inquisition, or the foreign occupant, in a clear allusion to contemporary practices of the Portuguese political police.

6. The emotional charge associated with the issue of national independence, almost instinctively—and sometimes suicidally—leading the population to resist the foreign occupant (as during the Napoleonic invasions).

7. The exaltation of forgotten martyrs who fell in an unequal struggle and need to be rehabilitated as an example for the present time.

8. The co-optation of revolutionary movements, at a later stage, by social groups that, not having participated in them from the beginning, come to take advantage of their outcomes, bypassing risks and reaping dividends.

Soon after the 25 April revolution, a phenomenon that is both curious and symptomatic took place: Portuguese playwrights returned to the theme of great national crises, but in a manner that was no longer veiled and allusive. On the contrary, political references and aims of works such as Jaime Gralheiro's *Arraia-Miúda* (1977) or Virgílio Martinho's *1383* (1977) became increasingly well-defined; in the case of some plays, it seems possible to carry out a full process of identification, matching each figure with its double on the contemporary Portuguese political scene. A subtler, but nevertheless noticeable trend manifests itself in the treatment of a more universal problem of the relations between the individual and the state. Examples include historical protagonists such as Leonor Teles, a queen but also a woman; Inês de Castro, "revisited" from a psychoanalytic angle by Luso Soares in *A Outra Morte de Inês* (1968); Bocage, seen not only as a man and a poet but also as a citizen of a country attempting to leave behind its obscurantist past and embrace Reason. A central theme here is the nonconformist stance adopted by free, creative individuals in opposition to the closed-mindedness characterizing retrograde representatives of the political power, as happens in the 1974 play *Bocage* by Sinde Filipe, in Romeu Correia's *O Andarilho das Sete Partidas* (1983), and in Luzia Maria Martins's earlier play *Bocage Alma Sem Mundo* (1967). In an important production of Hélder Costa's play *D. João VI* (1979), it is the Portuguese king himself who becomes the symbol of power that is, in effect, powerless: the court fool reigning over a country straight out of an operetta.

The Marginalized

A no less fertile source of inspiration for Portuguese playwrights has been the search for anonymous, marginalized agents of history, whose names have not been preserved and who represent the other side of the coin of official culture. Such is the case of the protagonist in Hélder Costa's *Zé do Telhado* (1978): a highwayman and a criminal banned from society, who must nevertheless be understood in light of the social determinants that conspired to make him an outcast. Another example of this dramatic exploration of society's margins is provided by the 1982 Barraca production of *Fernão, Mentes*: the play reappropriates an authentic historical figure, that of the *pícaro* Fernão Mendes Pinto, the sixteenth-century traveler and author of *Peregrinação*, and exposes the manifold contradictions in the politics of colonial expansion. The play does not renounce the importance of Portuguese cultural and historical achievements in the golden age of the Renaissance, but offers a questioning of such major aspects of the national past and present as the problem of emigration; the imperial and postimperial transformations of Portuguese identity; and, finally, religious obscurantism and inquisitorial terror.

The somber shadow of the Inquisition has become another thematic constant in contemporary Portuguese theater. Playwrights thoroughly reexamine and dissect its significance, in some cases choosing to emphasize one of its martyrs. The audience is thus invited to recollect the past in order to be able to confront the present from a critical and militant standpoint. An important work in this vein and, simultaneously, an event that signaled the decisive arrival in Portugal of Brechtian epic theater was *O Judeu* by Bernardo Santareno (1966), greeted at the time of its publication as a truly revolutionary mark in the development of contemporary Portuguese drama. The play dramatizes the infamous inquisitorial trial of the eighteenth-century playwright António José da Silva. It both exposes the brutality of the repressive apparatus and foregrounds "illuminated" attitude, exemplified by the figure of Cavaleiro de Oliveira, whose intervention made it possible to reestablish, in a dialectical fashion, the historical truth on its way into the future.

Mythical Revisions

The urgently felt need to "reread" Portuguese history has resulted, particularly since 25 April, in a process of systematic rethinking of cultural significance carried by such mythically charged historical figures as Camões, D. João II, or Damião de Góis. Among the plays written to commemorate the fourth centenary of the great poet's death, José Saramago's play *Que farei com este livro?* (1980) needs to be mentioned, along with Natália Correia's *Erros Meus, Má Fortuna, Amor Ardente* (1980), Luzia Maria

Martins's *O Homem que se julgava Camões* (1980), Hélder Costa's *A Viagem* (1980), and Jaime Gralheiro's . . . *Onde vaz, Luiz?* (1981). The "Perfect Prince," D. João II, becomes the focus of the historian Borges Coelho's incursion into drama (*Príncipe Perfeito* [1988]), while the Renaissance diplomat and scholar Damião de Góis is remembered in the Barraca production of Hélder Costa's play *Um Homem é um Homem*.

The appropriation of mythical figures and narratives includes dramatic nationalist rereadings of universal Western myths (as in Augusto Abelaira's *Anfitrião, Outra Vez. Telecomédia* [1980] or in Norberto Ávila's *A Paixão segundo João Mateus* [1983] and *Dom João no Jardim das Delícias* [1987]), as well as new interpretations of Portugal's own cultural icons (for example, Agustina Bessa Luís's *A Bela Portuguesa* [1986]) and regional mythologies (Jaime Gralheiro's *A Longa Marcha para o Esquecimento*). Jaime Gralheiro contributed also toward a didactic mythification of the history of anti-Salazar resistance in his *O Homem da Bicicleta* (1982) or *Vieram para Morrer* (1980), a play dealing with life in the Tarrafal prison camp in Cape Verde. The same direction was taken by José Cardoso Pires in his return to theatrical writing with *Corpo-Delito na Sala de Espelhos* (1980), which revolves within the sinister world of Salazar's secret police. In addition, José Saramago in *A Noite* (1979) brings to stage the 25 April revolution itself as it unfolds in the editorial offices of a Portuguese newspaper. Another author writing in the similar vein is Abel Neves, with his *Amadis* (1987) and an exploration of the bullfighting lore in *Touro* (1986).

Finally, a playwright deserving special mention at the close of this list, which is by no means exhaustive, is Joaquim Pacheco Neves, whose still insufficiently appreciated theatrical works (*Lenda da Berengária* [1980], *Bobby Sands* [1981], *O Conde-Duque de Olivares* [1981], and *Fanny* [1987]) find inspiration in a vast treasury of historical and contemporary, Portuguese and European, and cultural and literary references.

Although historical themes and the formula of the historical parable have, over the years, lost some of their political and artistic effectiveness, the need to evoke crucial moments in national history is still a defining constant of the collective imagination that Portuguese playwrights share. Such is the key to interpreting the work of Miguel Rovisco, a young author whose premature death cut short a promising career. His plays demonstrate how historical plots are no longer targeted at political intervention but are a free adaptation that privileges the psychological molding of characters (*O Arco de Sant'Ana* [1986], *O Homem Dentro do Armário* [1986], *Uma Comédia de Quinhentos* [1986], *Trilogia Portuguesa* [1987] and *Retrato de uma Família Portuguesa* [1989]).

Some Conclusions

1. The discovery and exploration of historical themes as a source of inspiration for a considerable portion of Portuguese theatrical literature has accompanied, in a synchronic fashion, chief political and cultural developments that have taken place in contemporary Portugal. However, Portuguese playwrights, recognizing their civic responsibility as representatives of the country's intelligentsia, have not always been able to surmount the obstacles they have faced both in writing and in theatrical praxis, obstacles due primarily to lack of information and contact with European culture, the country's traditional source of cultural imports.

2. The attractiveness of the formula of "historical parable" may be demonstrated with all of its advantages and shortcomings. Given the polysemic potential inherent in the interpretation of historical events, evocations of various episodes of Portuguese history could help in the fight against the dictatorship, or in the days immediately following 25 April, or even today.

3. In terms of public appeal and marketability, the consequences of the exploration of historical themes have been in general positive for Portuguese theater, resulting in some of the most successful and best-received productions in the last decades. In some cases, however, due to the authors' lack of distinction between the essential and the accidental, coupled with an inability to capture the internal dynamic of historical events, the outcomes have tended toward mere topical satire or caricature.

4. The study of contemporary historical theater in Portugal allows us to document the influence exercised by a highly diverse group of authors and aesthetic projects: from Anouilh, Sartre, or Ionesco to Brecht, Piscator, Peter Weiss, or Gatti.

5. Many of the historical parables written before 25 April have not retained their original effectiveness. Not surprisingly, they also may be easily misunderstood, given the radical transformation of social and political conditions that originally motivated their composition. Nonetheless, they constitute important documents toward a history of twentieth-century Portuguese culture.

To conclude: in the gentle climate of that tourist haven that is Portugal, the country's theater, once a victim of manifold difficulties and pressures, can finally show, like the barometer it has always been, that the atmosphere has become less unfavorable and that the present time is not just a devouring *kronos*, but rather a *temps vécu*, a lived, participatory time of shared political and cultural freedom.

Notes

1. Bakhtin defines the notion of chronotope as follows: "In the literary artistic chronotope, spatial and temporal indicators are fused into one carefully thought-out, concrete whole. Time, as it were, thickens, takes on flesh, becomes artistically visible; likewise, space becomes charged and responsive to the movements of time, plot, and history. This intersection of axes and fusion of indicators characterizes the artistic chronotope" (1981, 84).

2. "Indeed historians have generally attributed the 'inspiration' for these plays to moments of intense national consciousness" (Lindenberger 1975, 7).

3. A review of the play, written by Carlos Porto, pointed out weaknesses in its staging. At the same time, a certain sense of justification transpires from the criticism, complying with the historical circumstance: "It seems more important to stress the fact that *Português, escritor, 45 anos de idade* is a performance worthy of the new Portugal, which, like the play itself, comes wrapped in contradictions, weaknesses, and indecision. It is, therefore, a performance to be seen, and seen again, to be discussed, and, if one so decides, to be rejected. But it is a performance that cannot fail to attract and interest those who believe at the same time in theater and in freedom" (Porto 1974).

4. Although dramatic writing obviously did exist within those movements, it should be pointed out that it does not appear as particularly expressive when confronted with other genres chosen as means of social intervention. All the same, Alves Redol's work needs to be taken into account, as well as, more importantly, that of Romeu Correia.

5. As Mário Vilaça wrote, "Luís de Sttau Monteiro, author of two novels, published a play three months ago that I consider to be of higher note than anything produced by our playwrights in the last few years. Admirably written, intensely dramatic, structurally well wrought with Brechtian influences, *Felizmente Há Luar!* belongs to our best historical theater by its extraordinary force and contemporary appeal. It deserves to be immediately, and intelligently, brought to stage, provided the reactionary winds of censorship allow it. It is difficult to judge at such a close temporal distance, before a historical perspective can develop, but *Felizmente Há Luar!* is without any doubt a play that honors Portuguese theater and theater in general" (1967, 160).

6. See, as an example, the opening indication: "The question is accompanied by a gesture which reveals the character's helplessness in face of the problem. This gesture is openly 'represented'. The audience has to understand, from the outset, that everything that is to happen on the stage has a precise significance. And, moreover, that gestures, words and the scenery are just elements of a language to which their perceptions have to adjust" (Monteiro 1963, 13).

7. A first, well-wrought synthesis of what Portuguese theater life was like during the period of transition from censorship to freedom of expression may be found in Porto and Menezes 1985, 15–155.

8. Materials and important data toward such an analysis have already been partly published. See Rebelo 1977.

9. See the exhaustive study of Brecht's reception in Portugal in Delille 1991.

References

Ablamowicz, Aleksander. 1984. "Réalité historique, création romanesque et identité nationale: Pologne et Québec". In *Récit et histoire*, 203–13. Paris: PUF.

Bakhtin, M. M. 1981. *The Dialogic Imagination*. Edited by Michael Holquist. Translated by Caryl Emerson and Michael Holquist. Austin: University of Texas Press.

Brecht, Bertolt. 1964. *Estudos sobre Teatro. Para uma Arte Dramática Não-Aristotélica*. Lisboa: Portugália.

Büchner, Georg. 1963. *Complete Plays and Prose*. Translated by Carl Richard Mueller. New York: Hill and Wang.

Delille, Maria Manuela Gouveia. 1991. "Bertolt Brecht em Portugal antes do 25 de Abril de 1974. Um capítulo na história da resistência ao salazarismo." In *Do Pobre B.B. em Portugal. Aspectos da Recepção de Bertolt Brecht Antes do 25 de Abril de 1974*, edited by Maria Manuela Gouveia Delille. Aveiro: Estante.

Durand, Gilbert. 1979. *Figures mythiques et visages de l'oeuvre*. Paris: Berg International.

"Entrevista com Luís de Sttau Monteiro." 1961. *Seara Nova* 134:179.

Lindenberger, Herbert. 1975. *Historical Drama: The Relation of Literature and Reality*. Chicago: The University of Chicago Press.

Lourenço, Eduardo. 1978. *O Labirinto da Saudade. Psicanálise Mítica do Destino Português*. Lisboa: Dom Quixote.

Monteiro, Luís Sttau. 1963. *Felizmente Há Luar!* Lisboa: Ática.

Porto, Carlos. 1974. "Viagem ao fim do desespero." Crítica de teatro. *Diário de Lisboa*, 9 de Julho.

Porto, Carlos, and Salvato Teles de Menezes. 1985. *10 anos de tetro e cinema em Portugal, 1974–1984*. Lisboa: Caminho.

Quadros, António. 1989. *A Ideia de Portugal na Literatura Portuguesa dos Últimos 100 Anos*. Lisboa: Fundação Lusíada.

Rebelo, Luís Francisco. 1977. *Combate por um teatro de combate*. Lisboa: Seara Nova.

Santareno, Bernardo. 1974. *Português, escritor, quarenta e cinco anos de idade*. Lisboa: Ática.

Vilaça, Mário. 1967. *Teatro Contemporâneo. Problemas do Jogo e do Espírito*. Coimbra: Vértice.

On the Contemporary Portuguese Essay

ONÉSIMO T. ALMEIDA

Introduction

If we were to survey that minuscule segment of the Anglo-American readership with some knowledge of Portuguese letters, we could easily predict that, in the final analysis, poetry would rank the highest with two names: Camões and Pessoa. The second category would be the novel, with Eça de Queiroz, possibly followed by José Saramago. And that would be the end of it. Anything beyond should give rise to the suspicion that one is in front of a specialist, or at least a very special case in need of an unusual explanation. The truth of the matter, however, is that there exists a wealth of other writers and poets concentrated in the most interesting centuries in Portugal—the sixteenth, nineteenth, and twentieth. Besides, and parallel to creative works, there is a significant body of prose, usually classified under the broad heading of "essays."

In order to write about the last two decades of the Portuguese essay, it is necessary to provide a general background for the English-speaking reader, since, to my knowledge, there are no surveys or commentaries in English on the Portuguese essay. References to the essay genre in Iberian letters are usually limited to Unamuno and Ortega y Gasset, with the typical silence about their Portuguese counterparts, even when the list of essayists is long and detailed.

Although until recently Portuguese poetry has attracted more attention than any other literary genre, the number and quality of writers of prose nonfiction is nevertheless far from negligible. Indeed, the tradition is old. At the end of the Middle Ages, King Duarte wrote *Leal Conselheiro,* which, according to a much respected historian of Portuguese thought, Joaquim de Carvalho, can be classified under the essay genre, unlike other contemporary works, such as *Virtuosa Benfeitoria*, by his brother Prince Dom Pedro, whose structure and style make it fall within the traditional genre of doctrinal treatise.[1]

Given the philosophical view that meaning is use, the term "essay" is used in this article to classify a wide variety of nonfictional prose, notwithstanding Alexander Pope's *Moral Essays* in verse. In Portuguese, as in some European languages, the meaning of the term has become so extensive as to make useless any normative discussion. Not even a liberal definition such as *Britannica*'s can encompass all the works self-defined as essays: "a literary composition of moderate length, dealing in an easy, cursory way with a single subject, usually representing the writer's personal experience and outlook."[2] This definition adequately fits Montaigne's *Essais*[3] but leaves out a sizeable quantity of volumes of self-entitled essays on single subjects, not only in English but also in Portuguese, including a two-hundred-page volume on the essay (one could call it a metaessay) by the Portuguese Sílvio Lima, who sees the demarcating characteristics of Montaigne's new genre as an exercise in personal critical thinking about universal realities.[4]

Virginia Woolf puts it straightforwardly: "[T]he family [of the essay] is widely spread. . . . The form, too, admits variety. The essay can be short or long, serious or trifling, about God and Spinoza, or about turtles and Cheapside. . . . Of all forms of literature, however, the essay is the one which least calls for the use of long words. The principle which controls it is simply that it should give pleasure" (1990, 37).

Such a liberal definition notwithstanding, one cannot consider as essay writings the impressive list of works by scientific-minded authors from the sixteenth century, such as Pedro Nunes, Duarte Pacheco Pereira, and Dom João de Castro, or Garcia de Orta, among others, even though their mental attitude is definitely defiant of Scholastic and classical knowledge. These works are of a quite diverse nature, ranging from treatises and dialogues to logbooks and travel accounts. But they do comprise an impressive body of literature characterized by a rejection of the truth handed down by authority, as well as an innovative attitude toward the exploration of the new areas of knowledge made possible by the travels of the Portuguese navigators of the fifteenth and sixteenth centuries over all four corners of the globe.[5] They were also the object of a considerable number of essays at the end of the nineteenth century, during the second quarter of our own century, as well as in the last ten years.

It was up to Francisco Sanches to combine a critical attitude with a corresponding style, and thus become a precursor of Montaigne, the coiner of the term "essay" and the acknowledged father of the genre. The skepticism defended in Sanches's *Quod nihil scitur*, published in Lyon in 1581, a book known to Descartes, provoked strong reactions from seventeenth-century German theologians, who considered Sanches "the most ruinous of the Sceptics."[6]

Francis Bacon, who borrowed the classification of the new literary genre created by Montaigne but who developed a personal kind of essay writing, had, as it is well known, an enthusiastic follower in eighteenth-century Spain—Benito Feijoo, with his *Theatro Critico* and the five volumes of *Cartas Eruditas*. But he also found echo in Portugal. One of his admirers, Luís António Verney, became, in the words of the above-mentioned Sílvio Lima, "a propagandizer of the critical essayism of modernity" by virtue of his *Verdadeiro Método de Estudar* (Lima 1944, 156). The same can be said about the physician Ribeiro Sanches and his *Cartas Sobre a Educação da Mocidade*.[7]

The nineteenth century was fertile in reflections on the state of the nation vis-à-vis Central and Northern Europe. Among them, *Causas da Decadência dos Povos Peninsulares*, by the mentor of the so-called 1870 generation, Antero de Quental, stands out as one of the greatest essays written in the Iberian Peninsula.[8] Quental also wrote other remarkable pieces that can be considered within the genre, such as *Tendências Gerais da Filosofia na Segunda Metade do Século XIX* (1890).[9]

The name of António Sérgio stands out as the great cultivator of the genre in the first half of the twentieth century. The title of his eight volumes of *Ensaios* (1920) are a conscious affiliation with Montaigne and Bacon. The essay was also cultivated by members of the modernist Orpheu group, with Fernando Pessoa as its greatest representative, even though most of his writings are unfinished pieces. His *Livro do Desassossego* only appeared for the first time in 1982, almost fifty years after the author's death. Resembling Nietzsche's books, it is a collection of prose manuscripts that could very well be considered a series of condensed essays.[10]

The genre proliferated, multiplied in a rich and diversified variety of themes and styles. Almost all Portuguese major writers—novelists and poets—have written essays, mostly in the literary field. In this respect, the best tradition of the genre—for example as practiced by T. S. Eliot, Edgar Allen Poe, E. M. Forster, Aldous Huxley, Baudelaire, George Bernard Shaw, Edmund Wilson, and Paul Valéry, to name just a few—has plenty of cultivators in Portugal. Names like Vitorino Nemésio, Jorge de Sena, Vergílio Ferreira, David Mourão-Ferreira, and José Régio immediately come to mind, together with others whose work privileged the essay genre: Joaquim de Carvalho, Eduardo Lourenço, António José Saraiva, Joel Serrão, Manuel Antunes, Jacinto do Prado Coelho, and Oscar Lopes, names that would emerge on the top ten of any comprehensive survey or list. Sílvio Lima, a mandatory addition to the group, was the author of the remarkable *Ensaio sobre a Essência do Ensaio* (Essay on the essence of the essay) earlier cited, which could be included in any world anthology on the genre.[11]

In the last decade of the Salazar-Caetano dictatorship, which ended in 1974, the essay became heavily politicized. Cinema joined literature as a main topic, but both were a pretext for social and political commentary. During the years immediately following the so-called 25 April revolution, literature was somewhat abandoned and the essay became uninterestingly doctrinal, with a prose heavily stuffed with Marxist jargon. Little by little, however, the voices of the established writers reemerged. Reviewing a decade of the Portuguese essay (1974–84) for the journal *Colóquio-Letras*, Eduardo Prado Coelho recognizes that

> a narrow definition of essayism would certainly include Eduardo Lourenço—without any doubt the great essayistic presence of the post April 25th period—Vergílio Ferreira, some [Jorge de Sena], two or three books by António José Saraiva, the dispersed reflections of Father Manuel Antunes, or Nuno Teixeira Neves, a certain kind of cultural intervention of a Miguel Serras Pereira, but little else. (1984, 43)

Practically all of these authors had their reputations established before the arrival of the democratic state in 1974, hence Prado Coelho's broadening the definition of the essay to encompass all nonfictional prose. It was only in the early eighties that literature recovered its importance in Portugal and that Portuguese authors actually began to receive attention in their own country, unmatched in any previous period.

An assessment of the last decade leaves us with practically the same names at the top of the list, if we are to take the essay in the strict sense. An important shift occurred in the Portuguese literary scene, however: the academicization of the essay, which practically forsook its name for that of the English "paper." The proliferation of conferences, national as well as international, standardized Portuguese writing according to international norms of the academic paper. Only the old generation continued cultivating the old-fashioned essay. The leading essayists were thus still Eduardo Lourenço, Vergílio Ferreira, António José Saraiva, and Jorge de Sena (who died in 1978).

Two Representatives: Eduardo Lourenço and Vergílio Ferreira

Although each of the just-mentioned four essayists deserves close study, I will concentrate on those two whose essays not only fall well within the mainstream tradition of the genre but also have had the strongest impact on their generation.

Eduardo Lourenço was born in 1923. He studied philosophy in Coimbra, where he worked with Joaquim de Carvalho. While still in his twenties, he published a remarkable book of essays that would become a reference point both in his life and in the history of Portuguese intellectual life. *Heterodoxia I* (Heterodoxy, 1949), a collection of essays, reveals a heterodoxical mind caught between two main forces—Marxism and Catholicism—that pulled Portuguese intellectuals in two different directions. Lourenço carved out a personal space·in which to build a cohesive and powerful worldview. Phenomenology and existentialism would become the other two pillars of his edifice. After several years of teaching in Coimbra as an assistant professor, he started teaching abroad as a lecturer in Portuguese—first in Hamburg and Heidelberg, and later in Montpelier. He moved to Brazil to teach philosophy at the University of Bahia, but shortly thereafter he returned to Europe, where he taught Portuguese literature and culture in Grenoble and Nice, retiring in 1988. In permanent contact with Portugal's literary, intellectual, and political life, he always wrote essays that bear the mark of a universal man in touch with the philosophical themes and concerns of his times. Yet he never ceased being a passionate citizen of his native country.

Lourenço is indeed the quintessential Portuguese essayist, in the best tradition of the Iberian essay. When one reads him, Ortega y Gasset comes to mind. Lourenço's style possesses, however, a distinct and unique brilliance, whether dialoguing with the great European minds of his time or rethinking the key topics of Portuguese cultural history.[12] His essays have graced a wide variety of publications, and his books are basically collections of essays organized thematically. *Poesia e Metafísica* (1983) collects pieces on the greatest of Portuguese poets—Camões, Antero, and Pessoa. The last of these has received special attention in seminal essays, some of them now standards—*Fernando Rei da Nossa Baviera* (1986.)[13] Another collection, *Ocasionais—I* (1984), gathers earlier essays, whose unity lies not in theme but in the style and the mental attitude of their author. His subjects in this work range from Sade to Lorca and from Gilberto Freyre's luso-tropicalismo to Europe and death.

Portugal and the path of Portuguese cultural history vis-à-vis Central and Northern Europe (almost an obsession in Iberian essay writing for the last two centuries) has been a major concern of Lourenço's. His best-seller *O Labirinto da Saudade—Psicanálise Mítica do Destino Português*, first published in 1978, went through various editions throughout the eighties. The themes of that volume were dealt with from a more theoretical perspective in *Nós e a Europa ou as Duas Razões* (1988), for which Lourenço received the Charles Veillon European Essay Prize in 1988, awarded in Lausanne, Switzerland.[14]

The full collection and reprinting of Eduardo Lourenço's essays is far from complete.[15] He has appeared in all sorts of colloquia and conferences. In the volumes of proceedings his contributions are systematically characterized by an absence of footnotes or bibliography, but also by his consistently superior personal thinking, more often than not reaching brilliance.

In the interview that opens a special issue of the journal *Prelo* dedicated to the study of his work, Lourenço explains the formative boundaries of his thought in Portugal of the forties:

> Of no little importance was the fact that I lived in a country and in a cultural atmosphere in which vital attitudes and spiritual or ideological choices were conditioned by the hegemonic presence of Catholicism, creed, ideology and almost state religion and, even more important, the ancestral practice of the Nation. Out of that background, and as a kind of anti-church, emerged what one could grossly call Marxism, less important as a political reality than as a sign of opposition to, and rejection of the official cultural discourse. (1984, 8)

Explaining his turn from mainstream philosophy, Lourenço says:

> [I]t is true that my resistance to the philosophical temptation to engage in an absolute discourse found a basis in what is usually referred to as "existentialism." In the last analysis, it was the figure of Philosophy itself that at a given moment appeared to me suspect. Almost at the same time, my discovery of Pessoa and Kierkegaard took me in the same direction, one exemplifying the illusion of consciousness as "consciousness of itself" existing ontologically; the other, the incommensurability of personal existence vis-à-vis any other type of existence. In either case, end of philosophy. (9)

Still in the same interview, Eduardo Lourenço explains the importance of literature in his life and to his thought:

> [M]y disillusionment with philosophy . . . does not mean that I have encountered in literature the "truth" that in philosophy was denied to me. I encountered only a reality more in agreement with the general sentiment I look for in life and in the world, something which imposes itself precisely because in it (I speak of great literature) life manifests in terms of paradoxical (poetic) splendor the nature of our relationship with reality, which is fictional. (9)

To the question of how Lourenço sees himself, since some literary critics consider him to be a metaphysician and some metaphysicians consider him to be a literary person, he replies:

> I would like to deserve the always undeserved epithet of "metaphysician" in the two senses the pseudo-Baptists attribute to it. Unfortunately, this is not the case. As a more adequate label, I accept that of "literato," if that means love or passion for the written world (imaginário). However, the absence of idolatry in regard to that same imaginário perhaps will make me unjust with myself... I never desired, nor do I desire, any kind of status. The most I could accept is, vaguely, "essayist," if one considers form, and "mystic without faith," if one considers content. (17)

Vergílio Ferreira, one of the most acclaimed Portuguese novelists of this century, is also an essayist of the first rank. Born in 1916, he studied classical philology at the University of Coimbra. He earned his living as a high school teacher in Évora and in Lisbon. Like Lourenço, he emerged very early as a great writer. First joining ranks with neorealists, who paid close attention to social themes, he soon departed from them over their closing of ranks with social realism, as well as his own discovery of existentialism. Vergílio Ferreira, under the influence of Dostoyevsky, Malraux, Sartre, and Camus, built for himself a path, combining his personal reflections upon the modern themes of the absence of meaning and value in a post-Nietzchean broken world without foundations, with a fine, yet powerful, sense of the aesthetic dimension of life. In its written form, the language he inherited from the prose of the Portuguese nineteenth-century master novelist Eça de Queiroz was a guiding inspiration for Ferreira, who envisioned the ideal writer as someone who could combine for his times in Portugal the best of Dostoyevsky, Eça de Queiroz, and Malraux.[16]

There is, indeed, a strong philosophical bent in the writings of this compulsive author, who has maintained a steady flow of volumes (forty so far) of fiction, essays, and, since 1980, a journal, *Conta-Corrente* , which is filled with entries easily classifiable as essays.[17] Although his novels can be seen as philosophical novels, full of metaphysical obsessions (and, in that sense, they are essays), there are also plenty of volumes with essays *tout court* in which Ferreira's thought is expanded in an analytical, yet quite poetic style. Of them, perhaps *Do Mundo Original* (1957) could be read as the key to understanding the mind of this thinker, "a kind of Manifesto of his essayism," as Lourenço put it, even though Vergílio Ferreira would like to add *Invocação ao Meu Corpo* (1969) as a very representative work (Lourenço 1994, 120).[18]

Eduardo Lourenço has written extensively about Vergílio Ferreira, much to the liking of the novelist, who considers Lourenço, "because of his exceptional capacities as well as solid affinity of ideas," to be his best interpreter (Ferreira 1981b, 85).[19] Lourenço, who has pointed out the reactive nature of Vergílio's essayistic discourse, written always in response to someone else's writing, asked himself about the originality of his thought, answering in the following terms:[20]

> Vergílio Ferreira's essayism does not really proceed either from inner demands that are philosophical—in the generic or the metaphysical sense—or, even less so, sociological or political. The only vital object of meditation, the one in which in questioning he questions himself, in which in inventing justifications he justifies himself, is the one of Art. It is the living experience of Art—as an incomprehensible creative impulse, an incandescence of being and not the mere result—that constitutes the matrix of all of Vergílio Ferreira's thought. (1994, 119)

A reading of any volume of his journal can be a pleasant entrance to the world of this artist and thinker, who writes fiction but who still needs to blend both in a journal. Actually, recently he decided to subdivide his journal-keeping into two genres—one intellectual, addressing ideas and philosophical themes, the other more mundane, in which he speaks of the quotidian. Of the former, *Pensar* was published in 1992. Its title and format reveal an obvious affiliation with Pascal's *Pensées*.[21] The other segment of the division has already resulted in four volumes—*Conta-Corrente, Nova Série*. But whether he writes about the ordeal of Lisbon traffic or about a TV program he happened to watch, the reader recognizes quickly that Vergílio never abandons his penchant for the reflective.[22] About the essay as a genre he wrote:

> The essay [in Portugal] basically informs; but what is important is that the essay discuss, that it problematize. . . . Infinitely more useful is the fertile error than the sterile truth. But there is an element which it is urgent to incorporate in the essay and that particularly approximates it to literary art—one that particularly makes it a candidate to succeed the novel: emotiveness. (Ferreira1981, 186)

In another interview he explained:

> For me, the novel and the essay are always parallel activities. On the one hand, I do not see the essay as a process, a means, with a merely pedagogic objective. I cultivate the essay, seeking to explicate problems trough it. I

must make clear that the problematics which preoccupies me in my essays is more or less the same as in the novels. The ideal essayistic activity is the one that extends the work of the fictionist, and not the one which is subsidiary or that happens in the intervals.

. . . I prefer the novel to the essay, because, among other reasons, the novel places me immediately in life and in myself—one exists before, and only after one speaks about what one is. (203)

Continuing to write both essays and novels, Vergílio is still obsessed with the same themes. In 1987 Vergílio published the fourth volume in his collection of essays under the general title of *Espaço do Invisível*, dealing still again with figures such as Malraux, Eça, Sartre, Kafka, and Foucault, and topics such as art, the critic, the I, death, the novel, disquietude, and the nude. Vergílio is a novelist who never ceases being a philosopher and an essayist, who never stops being a writer of narratives.

ॐ

It would be unfair to ignore many other essayists. What follows goes little beyond mentioning their names, but it can be a guiding suggestion to those who want to know more about contemporary Portuguese intellectual life.

Jorge de Sena, a superb poet of the generation of Vergílio Ferreira and Eduardo Lourenço, wrote in every genre with the desire to write about everything (close to a hundred books published despite his having died at the age of fifty-eight), including numerous essays. In spite of his death, he is alive and well in his works, which continue to be published thanks to the energy of his wife Mécia de Sena. In 1992, one more volume appeared for the first time: *Amor e Outros Verbetes*, a collection of entries written upon request for the *Britannica, Funk & Wagnalis New Encyclopedia, Great Encyclopedia of World Literature in the Twentieth Century*, and others. In the introduction, Mécia de Sena explains that the volume contains the Portuguese version of the pieces as Jorge de Sena wrote them and not the abridged and edited versions that appeared in English. Mécia refers to some incidents with the editors and throws a barb at the peculiar demands of writing English, which she calls "non-style" and Jorge de Sena had classified as "mono-style." The pieces in the volume are excellent samples of his particular style—an outpouring of facts, woven with comments, asides, derivations that sometimes take pages, but done always with a fascinating force conducting the reader through the labyrinths of a great mind.[23] The entry "Amor," for instance, is a remarkable essay in Sena's free style.[24]

Half the volume (150 pages) is taken up by fourteen entries for a Portuguese encyclopedia, all for the letter A. One imagines that had Sena not been the victim of such an untimely death, he would have written his own encyclopedia.

Among the recent volumes of Sena's posthumously published works containing pieces that are or may be called essays are *Sobre o Romance—Ingleses, Norte-Americanos e Outros* (1985), and *Maquiavel, Marx e Outros Estudos. Ensaio.*[25]

The outpouring of Sena's works continues. Another impressive collection of essays appeared in 1994. His sheer range of topics is impressive: Rimbaud, Cavafy, Antonio Machado, T. S. Eliot, Sartre, Rilke, Ungaretti, expressionism, modernism, Don Juan, Garcilaso, among others. Sena's torrential style is both refreshing and overwhelming.

Another member of this generation of essayists is the cultural and literary historian António José Saraiva, whose creative mind never let him remain within the straitjacket of professional scholarship. He wrote freely and loved toying with the ideas of great thinkers and writers. A very good example of his essay-writing was published in 1990, three years before his death. *A Tertúlia Ocidental* (1990) is a pleasant excursion into the lives and thought of renowned figures of the "1870 generation." But one cannot read Saraiva's studies, old and more recent, such as *Poesia e Drama, A Cultura em Portugal* (1982–84), *Ser ou Não ser Arte* (1993), and *Filhos de Saturno* (1980) without feeling that Saraiva was, above all, an essayist. And a very good one indeed.

An original, hard-to-classify essayist, with a paradoxically modern classical prose and a penchant for venturing into uncommon territory in Portuguese letters (e. g., virtue, tolerance, God, Latin comedy), is Agostinho da Silva. Two good collections of his writings—essays in the strictest sense—are *Dispersos* (1988) and *Considerações e Outros Textos* (1988).

Scholars have often stepped outside the boundaries of their specific fields to widen their frontiers in a personal way. This is true of Joel Serrão in history of culture, Maria de Lourdes Belchior in literary study and Manuel Antunes in history of ideas.[26]

Of the younger generation, Eduardo Prado Coelho, Arnaldo Saraiva, and José Augusto Seabra, writers as well as academics and scholars, are excellent cultivators of the genre, publishing their pieces in literary and cultural supplements of major newspapers. Prado Coelho has published a journal that is really a reader's reaction to books.[27] Saraiva is a heterodox writer who writes in a rather engaging style about national anthems, graffiti, advertisements, epigraphs, and polemics. All of these can be found in the second volume of his *Literatura Marginal/izada—Novos Ensaios* (1980), a delightful collection in the best tradition of the forefathers of the genre. Seabra's subjects are more conventional, and his style more academic, but some of his writings are definitely essays, as in the volume *Cultura e Política ou a Cidade e os Labirintos* (1986).[28]

In an introduction to the 1992 edition of *The Best American Essays*, Susan Sontag writes:

> An essay is not only an article, nor a meditation, nor a book review, nor a memoir, nor a disquisition, nor a diatribe, nor a shaggy dog story, nor a monologue, nor a travel narrative, nor a suite of aphorisms, nor an elegy, nor a piece of reportage, nor a—But can be any or several of the above. (1992, xiii)

And, after saying that "an essay could be about anything" she adds:

> While precision and clarity of argument and transparency of style are usually regarded as norms for essay writing . . . the most compelling tradition of essay writing is a form of lyrical discourse. (xvii)

Moreover, Sontag also claims, "all great essays are written in the first person," and essay writing "is one of the strong American literary forms," emerging "out of the sermon and its secular transposition, the public lecture" (xviii).

This chapter was written for Anglo-American readers. Therefore, it follows a mainstream conception of the genre and avoids the much broader use of the term, which is current in Portugal as well as in the United States. Rather than include everything published in that category, the selections follow the narrower definition used by the editors of anthologies such as Sontag's, John Gross's *The Oxford Book of Essays* (1992), Andrew McNeillie's *The Essays of Virginia Woolf* (1988), and Frank Delaney's *The Hutchinson Book of Essays* (1990).

By contemporary Portuguese literary standards, this survey is rather conservative, keeping to established figures of the older generations and short on women writers. This is due to the fact that presently, the younger generation of men and women (and there is a considerable increase in the female presence in the Portuguese literary scene after 1974) is either in the process of establishing academic careers (and thus writing scholarly papers), or writing excellent newspaper articles and *crónicas* (a favorite genre, lighter than the essay) for such dailies as *Diário de Notícias*, and *O Público*, and the weeklies *Expresso* and *Jornal de Letras*, and have not yet published books collecting their best pieces.

Notes

1. Sílvio Lima disagrees, for he conceives the essay as a product of the Renaissance, whereas King Duarte's worldview is still medieval: "free, but within orthodoxy" (Lima 1944, 134). Lima sees the personal critical attitude of the author toward any received views as the fundamental characteristic of the essay genre.

2. The entry gives as American examples of the genre Thoreau's *Walden* and Emerson's *Essays*, but adds that in the twentieth century "the essay has been reborn as a playful kind of literature, and such humorists as James Thurber and Dorothy Parker excelled in the art" (*Encyclopaedia Britannica, Micropaedia*, s.v. "Essay").

3. Even though Francis Bacon borrows the term from Montaigne, a quick glance at Bacon's *Novum Organum* and Montaigne's *Essais* is enough to reveal significant differences between the two works.

4. In Spain, where the genre has been widely cultivated, the prevailing conception seems to be along Ortega y Gasset's summation: "[T]he essay is science minus the explicit proof," or "the essay is as much or more a work of art as it is a work of thought" (cited in Aullón de Haro 1987, 109). In the prologue to an anthology of the Spanish essay in English translation, Pilar A. Sanjuan attempts a definition of the genre: "[A]n intimate and subtle literary form, it is the more personalized, half poetic, and half didactic form of expression of those Hispanic minds that are pregnant with ideas and at the same time possessed of an inspired imagination." Still according to Sanjuan, it is the "lack of limits and rules which gives the essay its particular characteristic of flexibility" for the essay is a "lyrical form"; hence the essayist is defined as "a poet who writes prose" (Sanjuan 1954, 7-9).

Some critics defend a rather narrow conception of the genre. Guillermo de Torre, for instance, considers Ortega its "true creator" in the Spanish language, dismissing Unamuno, Ganivet and Feijoo's writings as either polemical or doctrinal. (See Torre 1956, 44.) As Juan Marichal points out, however, in Spain the word *ensaio* has throughout the years acquired a *maleabilidad camaleónica* (a chameleonic flexibility) that seems to be a simple matter-of-fact recognition. (See Marichal 1984, 15.)

5. I have dealt with this particular literature in Almeida, forthcoming.

6. Richard Popkins deserves the credit for bringing Sanches's work to the attention of the English-speaking world. Having included him in his widely acclaimed *The History of Scepticism from Erasmus to Spinoza* (1979), he apparently has provoked the interest that has led to the first English translation of *Quod nihil scitur—That Nothing Is Known*. See Sanches 1988.

The works of the Conimbrincenses (of the Collegium Conimbricensis), however, which were widely used in colleges throughout Europe in the seventeenth century, should not be considered essays. In spite of some innovations, they did not venture out from the close commentary on Aristotle. (See various references in Schmitt and Skinner, 1988.)

7. The physician Jacob de Castro Sarmento, another admirer of Bacon, suggested to King John V the translation into Portuguese of *Novum Organum*.

8. On this essay, which was never translated into any language and which I have seen mentioned only once in the huge Spanish bibliography on the topic of the decline of the Iberian Peninsula, see Almeida 1989.

9. The essay is not translated into English, but it is available in French as Quental 1991.

10. There is an English translation by Alfred Mac Adam in Pessoa 1991. By the same token, the volume of essays by the painter Almada Negreiros, Pessoa's contemporary and

friend, appeared in the decade covered by this survey: Negreiros 1992. Curiously, the book has an introduction by Eduardo Lourenço, entitled "Almada, ensaísta?" (9-20).

11. A 203-page-long work can hardly be made part of an anthology, but a few pages could easily have been included in the wonderful collection in Delaney 1990.

Eduardo Nicol has also written an interesting essay on the essay. A much shorter exercise, it gives no indication as to whether its author knew Lima's book. For Nicol, the essay is "almost literature, almost philosophy" (Nicol 1961, 61).

12. Eduardo Lourenço has lived most of his life in France, even though he has published his books, until very recently, only in Portugal.

13. Lourenço's other collection of essays on Fernando Pessoa, *Pessoa Revisitado,* appeared also in a new edition (Lourenço 1980). The first edition is from 1973.

14. An essayist such as Lourenço had to have a particular interest in Montaigne. He confirmed to me that such interest started quite early, during his student years at the University of Coimbra. Incidentally, he first heard about Montaigne from Sílvio Lima, mentioned earlier in this survey. Lima's essay on the essay devotes almost half of his pages to the essay as practiced by Montaigne. Lourenço went on to write his own views on the father of the name of the genre, a particularly beautiful essay entitled "Montaigne ou la Vie Écrite," in Lourenço and Botineau 1992. The reader who knows Portuguese and is interested in knowing more about someone who has long deserved to be translated and widely read in the English-speaking world should read Lourenço's more philosophically minded essays collected under the revealing title of *Heterodoxia.* The first volume was published in 1949, and the second in 1967. Some classical reflections on the Portuguese political world of before and after the 1974 "revolution" are gathered in *O Fascismo Nunca Existiu* (1976), and *O Complexo de Marx—ou o Fim do Desafio Português* (1979).

15. Lourenço has recently published a superb collection of essays in Lourenço 1994, with his most important essays on literary theory and on Portuguese fiction. Vergílio Ferreira is the writer whose works receive most attention—fifty-two pages.

16. More than once he referred to these authors as the ones he most admired. Once he said that he had not yet read the ideal novel, which would be a synthesis of Eça, Malraux, and Hemingway. (See Ferreira 1981b, 158.)

André Malraux is one of his most admired authors, not so much as a novelist, but as an essayist. As he put it, "the Malraux of the novels aged quite a bit; the essayist I find still very stimulating, almost as stimulating as listening to Bach." (1981, 170). Ferreira is also the author of a work on André Malraux (Ferreira 1963).

17. Five volumes, averaging 450 pages, published between 1980-87. All of Vergílio Ferreira's works are published or reprinted by Livraria Bertrand, Lisbon.

18. Lourenço 1994, 120. Perhaps the epithet of manifesto could be better applied to Ferreira 1981a for its tone and brevity. In any event, it is an excellent introduction to Vergílio Ferreira's themes, as is *Um Escritor Apresenta-se* (1981b), a volume with thematically organized replies given by Ferreira in interviews.

The bibliography on Ferreira is extensive. There is a good collection of essays and reviews in Godinho 1982.

19. In another interview, when asked "What critic could better write an essay presenting your work?" Vergílio answered, "Eduardo Lourenço"(1981b, 54).

20. In Portugal an author may be known by his first name only, if it is less common than his surname. Antero (de Quental) and Eça (de Queiroz) can serve as well-known examples.

21. Vergílio explicitly mentions Pascal and his *Pensées* after he says of his volume

that "it is a sort of journal of the haphazard of thinking" (*ir pensando* in Portuguese expresses better the idea of continuity and openness). Nietzsche's opus was made of fragments, and today the fragmented nature of Pascal's work is compared favorably to the completeness Pascal intended for it.

22. For Vergílio Ferreira, the "pure" essay is creative and problematizing *(problematizante)*, as in Antero's *Tendências Gerais...* mentioned earlier. He establishes a difference between the "purely informative or analytical essay on someone else's work and the 'problematizing essay', " which should turn to itself and should itself be an aesthetic creation, i. e., something in which "ideas detain themselves and stay where the work of art dwells," and thus "the essay becomes close to the artistic work." The closer the essay is to the work of art the less questionable it becomes, "because one does not argue about emotions" (Ferreira 1993–94, 2:267).

The poet Miguel Torga has also written a much-celebrated journal, started in 1941 and running to seventeen volumes. A remarkable body of literary and political work, it does not fit however an even broad conception of the essay.

23. A good perspective on Sena's essays written by an admirable essayist is Rebelo 1993, 50–53. In English, there is a very good study on the poet's worldview in Fagundes 1988.

24. The piece is simply composed of two paragraphs, but they take 42 compact pages. I have written about Sena's essay style in Almeida 1993.

25. We could continue the list with his collection of studies and essays on Camões, Fernando Pessoa, Brazilian literature, theater, Portuguese literature and culture, England, and so on. Most of his works have been published by Edições 70, Lisbon.

26. See for instance Serrão 1989, Belchior 1980, or Antunes 1987.

27. Prado Coelho 1992. The title, *Everything I Did Not Write*, was borrowed from Wittgenstein. See also Prado Coelho 1984.

28. The list of names to be included is still long and one must be selective. Besides, the border between essay and scholarly study has become thinner and thinner. Yet, in all fairness, some names cannot be omitted, such as Óscar Lopes, Luís de Sousa Rebelo, Natália Correia, Eugénio Lisboa, David Mourão-Ferreira, Fernando Cristóvão, Helder Macedo, José Martins Garcia, Maria Alzira Seixo, Vasco Graça Moura, José-Augusto França, João Medina, Alexandre Pinheiro Torres, Fernando Guimarães, António Ramos Rosa, João Barreto, and Diogo Pires Aurélio. Selections are always hard and dangerous to make. I recognize the unfair treatment given to some of these authors. The alternative would be to write a long and fastidious list of authors and books, but it would require a volume like the one Pedro Aullón de Haro did for Spain—Aullón de Haro 1987.

Among many other deliberate omissions, I have left out names like Fernando Gil and José Enes, for their essays are predominantly philosophical papers. Likewise I have deliberately omitted historians like José Mattoso, Vitorino Magalhães Godinho, or J. S. Silva Dias. In every field of the humanities and social sciences there is a group of scholars with impressive publications, but I feel they belong to a survey of the individual disciplines.

References

Almeida, Onésimo T. 1989. "Antero de Quental and the Causes of the Decline of the Iberian Peoples: A Revisitation." In *Iberia and the Mediterranean*, edited by Benjamin F. Taggie and Richard Clement, 131–44, Warrensburg: Central Missouri State University, 1989.

————. 1993. "O ensaio teórico a la Jorge de Sena." *Colóquio-Letras*, no. 125–26:119–28.

————. Forthcoming. "Portugal and the Dawn of Modern Science." In *Portugal: The Pathfinder,* edited by George Winius. Madison, Wisc.: Hispanic Seminar in Medieval Studies.

Aullón de Haro, Pedro. 1987. *Los Géneros Ensayísticos en el Siglo XX*. Madrid: Taurus Ediciones.

Antunes, Manuel. 1987. *Legómena*. Lisboa: Imprensa Nacional - Casa da Moeda.

Belchior, Maria de Lourdes. 1980. *Os Homens e os Livros*. Lisboa: Editorial Verbo.

Delaney, Frank, ed. *The Hutchinson Book of Essays*. London: Hutchison, 1990.

Fagundes, Francisco Cota. 1988. *A Poet's Way with Music: Humanism in Jorge de Sena's Poetry*. Providence: Gávea-Brown.

Ferreira,Vergílio. 1957. *Do Mundo Original*. Lisboa: Bertrand.

————. 1963. *André Malraux—Interrogação ao Destino*. Lisboa: Editorial Presença.

————. 1969. *Invocação ao Meu Corpo*. Lisboa: Bertrand.

————. 1981a. *Carta ao Futuro*. Lisboa: Bertrand.

————. 1981b. *Um Escritor Apresenta-se*. Apresentação, Introdução e Notas de Maria da Glória Padrão. Lisboa: Imprensa Nacional - Casa da Moeda.

Godinho, Helder. 1982. *Estudos Sobre Vergílio Ferreira*. Lisboa: Imprensa Nacional - Casa da Moeda.

————. 1993–94. *Conta-Corrente. Nova Série*. Lisboa: Bertrand.

Gross, John. 1992. *The Oxford Book of Essays*. Oxford: Oxford University Press.

Lima, Sílvio. 1944. *Ensaio sobre a Essência do Ensaio*. 2d ed. Coimbra: Colecção Studium.

Lourenço, Eduardo. 1949. *Heterodoxia I*. Coimbra.

————. 1978. *O Labirinto da Saudade*. Lisboa: Edições Dom Quixote.

————. 1980. *Pessoa Revisitado*. Lisboa: Moraes Editores.

————. 1983. *Poesia e Metafísica*. Lisboa: Sá da Costa Editora.

————. 1984a. *As confissões de um místico sem fé*. Interview conducted by Diogo Pires Aurélio. *Prelo*, Special Issue, May, 9–11.

————. 1984b. *Ocasionais I*. Lisboa: A Regra do Jogo, Edições.

————. 1986. *Fernando Rei da Nossa Baviera*. Lisboa: Imprensa Nacional-Casa da Moeda.

————. 1988. *Nós e a Europa ou As Duas Razões*. Lisboa: Imprensa Nacional-Casa da Moeda.

————. 1994. *O Canto do Signo. - Existence and Literature (1957-1993)*. Lisboa: Editorial Presença.

Lourenço, Eduardo, and Pierre Botineau. 1984. *Montaigne, 1533–1592*. Photographies de Jean-Luc Chapin. Bordeaux: L'Escampette Éditions.

Marichal, Juan. 1984. *Teoría e Historia del Ensayísmo Hispánico*. Madrid: Alianza Editorial.

McNeillie, Andrew. 1988.*The Essays of Virginia Woolf*. New York: Harcourt Brace Jovanovich.

Negreiros, Almada. 1992. *Obras Completas*. Vol. 5. Lisboa: Imprensa Nacional - Casa da Moeda.

Nicol, Eduardo. 1961. *El Problema de la Filosofía Hispánica*. Madrid: Editorial Tecnos, S. A.

Pessoa, Fernando. 1991. *The Book of Disquietude*. Translated by Alfred Mac Adam. New York: Pantheon.

Popkins, Richard. 1979. *The History of Scepticism from Erasmus to Spinoza*. Berkeley: University of California Press.

Prado Coelho, Eduardo. 1984a. *A Mecânica dos Fluidos*. Lisboa: Imprensa Nacional - Casa da Moeda.

————. 1984b. "Ensaio". *Colóquio-Letras*, no. 78 (Março).

————. 1992. *Tudo o Que Não Escrevi*. Porto: Edições ASA.

Quental, Antero de. 1991. *Tendances Générales de la Philosophie dans la Seconde Moitié du XIX Siècle*. Paris: Éditions de la Différence.

Rebelo, Luís de Sousa. 1993. "O ensaio e a crítica de Jorge de Sena." *Anthropos* 150 (Noviembre): 50–53

Sanches, Francisco. 1988. *Quod nihil scitur—That Nothing Is Known*. Edited by Elaine Limbrick. Translated by Douglas F. S. Thompson. Cambridge: Cambridge University Press.

Sanjuan, Pilar A., ed. 1954. *El Ensayo Hispánico. Estudo y Antología*. Madrid: Editorial Gredos.

Saraiva, António José. 1980. *Filhos de Saturno*. Lisboa: Bertrand.

————. 1982, 1984. *A Cultura em Portugal*. Vol. 1. Lisboa: Livraria Bertrand.

————. 1984. *A Cultura em Portugal*. Vol. 2. Lisboa: Livraria Bertrand.

————. 1990a. *A Tertúlia Ocidental*. Lisboa: Gradiva.

————. 1990b. *Poesia e Drama*. Lisboa: Gradiva.

————. 1993. *Ser ou Não Ser Arte*. Lisboa: Gradiva.

Saraiva, Arnaldo. 1980. *Literatura Marginal/izada-Novos Ensaios*. Porto: Edições Árvore.

Schmitt, Charles B., and Quentin Skinner, eds. 1988. *The Cambridge History of Renaissance Philosophy*. Cambridge: Cambridge University Press.

Seabra, José Augusto. 1986. *Cultura e Política ou a Cidade e os Labirintos*. Lisboa: Vega.

Sena, Jorge de. 1985. *Sobre o Romance-Ingleses, Norte-Americanos e Outros*. Lisboa: Edições 70.

————. 1991. *Maquiavel, Marx e Outros Estudos*. Ensaio. Lisboa: Cotovia.

Serrão, Joel. 1989. *Temas de Cultura Portuguesa*. 2 vols. Lisboa: Livros Horizonte.

Silva, Agostinho da. 1988a. *Considerações e Outros Textos*. Lisboa: Assírio & Alvim.

————. *Dispersos*. Edited by Paulo Alexandre Esteves Borges. Lisboa: Instituto de Cultura e Língua Portuguesa, 1988b.

Sontag, Susan, ed. 1992. *The Best American Essays*. New York: Ticknor & Fields.

Torre, Guillermo de. 1956. *Las Metamorfosis de Proteo*. Buenos Aires: Editorial Losada, S.A.

Woolf, Virginia. 1990. "The Modern Essay." In *The Hutchinson Book of Essays*, edited by Frank Delaney, 31–50. London: Hutchinson.

3
Analyses

Challenging the Past/ Theorizing History: Postrevolutionary Portuguese Fiction

HELENA KAUFMAN
and JOSÉ ORNELAS

The revolution of 25 April 1974 presented literature with new space for the freedom of expression and textual and thematic experimentation. It also broke the power of two ideologies that had dominated Portuguese cultural and political life for almost half a century: the nationalist fascist discourse aligned with Catholicism and the Marxist oppositional discourse. This real and symbolic vacuum created a need and a challenge, as Lídia Jorge puts it, "to reinvent [anew] the Portuguese imagery" (1986, 58). In the case of Portugal, it is neither accidental nor surprising that writers would turn to history to reinvent the images, symbols, and metaphors that make up that collective imagination. This revisionist decoding and redefinition of the past—a confrontation of the writer with history—are as much a by-prod-uct of present sociocultural circumstances as they are a continuation of the traditional involvement of Portuguese intellectuals in the interpretation of national history.

Literary discourse about the historical past and the importance of that past in forming a national identity and national self-image have been stressed many times by intellectuals of different persuasions.[1] Portugal, one of the oldest nation-states in Europe, independent from neighboring Spain through-out almost its entire history, a pioneer of the Discoveries, and builder of a vast overseas empire, is also a nation that repeatedly has had to face its own mistakes in managing its destiny and has suffered periods of humiliation, weakness, and internal underdevelopment. The relationship of Portugal with its own history is, therefore, as ambivalent as it is strong. While it defines a Portuguese cultural uniqueness and is a source of national pride, it at the same time produces a castrating, inhibiting effect that brings an impossible match when compared with the present reality. It was romanticism that established the complex relationship between people and their history as a literary theme and as an ontological question. Two works come to mind: Almeida Garrett's *Frei Luís de Sousa* and Eça de Queirós's *A Ilustre Casa de Ramires*. In the twentieth century, the Salazar dictatorship used and abused the nation's historical mythology, especially its colonizing and missionary aspects, to justify its politics in Africa and eventually to enlist support for a bloody colonial war.

That long and exhausting chapter in Portuguese history provides the immediate reason why authors after the revolution of 1974 chose to publish novels that were "historical," i.e., set in a period historically distinct from their own. However, like most contemporary historical novels,[2] the importance accorded to history clearly goes beyond the role it played in nineteenth-century historical fiction. History ceases to function as mere background for the plot, providing dramatic or aesthetic decorum. It is no longer limited to the realistic description of forces that lead to a historical transformation of societies; nor does it simply offer the reader a popular, fictionalized version of selected historical event(s). By placing a historical theme at the center of the narrative, the contemporary writer's intention is to focus on the historical process as such and render it problematic. This technique invites the reader to contemplate the question of *how* history is made (produced) and *how* we come to know it. In other words, as the telos of official history is challenged by the complexity of present sociohistorical circumstances, the teleological characteristics of history are rejected altogether by contemporary Portuguese writers. Their narratives invite a philosophical and historiographic reflection about the past and problematize the relationship of history to reality and reality to language.

Lionel Gossman, who in "History and Literature: Reproduction or Signification" (1978, 3–39) addresses these issues, could easily be talking about the contemporary Portuguese literary scene, with its focus on a postmodern rethinking of the relationship between past reality and the writing of history. He claims that "Modern history and modern literature have both rejected the ideal of representation [the realistic model] that dominated them for so long. Both now conceive of their work as exploration, testing, and creation of new meanings, rather than as disclosure or revelation of meanings already in some sense 'there,' but not immediately perceptible" (38–39). Much of the rewriting of Portuguese history carried out by the postmodernist text involves an ideological unmasking that exposes the discursive construction of the ideas, beliefs, and symbols of the past.

A shift from validation to signification definitely has occurred. Many writers as well as historians are more interested in the meaning of a particular event than in the validation of its truth. Hayden White claims that contemporary "historical inquiry is born less of the necessity to establish that certain events occurred than of the desire to determine what certain events might mean for a given group, society, or culture's conception of its present" (1986, 487). Likewise, the historical inquiry taking place in contemporary Portuguese narrative is oriented toward an analysis of semiotic production and the reception of meaning. The historical documents that writers incorporate into their narratives serve as texts that rework historical reality and signification; they are rarely incorporated as mere sources for factual reality.

Portuguese writers' grappling with issues of history/reality/representation has been, needless to say, far from homogeneous. It is our intention to point out similarities and differences that a reader may encounter on the pages of the Portuguese novels written over the last two decades. At least three significant approaches can be identified: (1) defining and juxtaposing the "official" and "marginal" discourses within history, inspired by a clear desire to recover and reclaim the margins (Saramago, Jorge); (2) theorizing about history and the questioning of historical narrative and/or representation that blurs the lines between history and fiction (Saramago, Abelaira); and (3) a specific metatextual layering of historical facts, interpretations, fictions, and parodic parables (Antunes, Cardoso Pires, Saramago, Jorge, and Abelaira).

It is only logical to start with José Saramago. Not only is he the most widely read of all contemporary Portuguese writers, but also all his works since *Levantado do Chão* (1980) have history or the subject in history as their main subject. All of Saramago's texts, especially the ones that follow the publication of *Memorial do Convento* (1982, translated into English as *Baltasar and Blimunda* in 1987), incorporate a theoretical self-reflectivity of fiction and history as human constructs in order to rethink and reconstruct the forms and contents of the past. Moreover, Saramago's works have many affinities with the postmodernist text and/or historiographic metafiction that Linda Hutcheon theorizes in *A Poetics of Postmodernism: History, Theory, Fiction*. For example, Saramago's novels are representative of all three literary approaches identified above.

It is *Memorial do Convento*, the first of Saramago's novels to focus exclusively on a redefinition or rereading of history, that most relentlessly exposes a dominant power structure, which authorizes certain textual representations while prohibiting and invalidating others. The text narrates the eighteenth-century construction of the Mafra Convent, a monument that was built to satisfy the megalomaniac desires and the vanity of the nobility and clergy. It also describes the construction of an airborne vehicle by Father Bartolomeu Guzmão, with the help of Baltasar and Blimunda, the two main protagonists of *Memorial*. Preto-Rodas, in "A View of Eighteenth-Century Portugal," ascertains that

> For Saramago, as for other like-minded predecessors who have commented on Dom João's grandiose project [Mafra], the convent represents the triumph of obscurantism and its attendant forces of waste, ignorance, corruption, and religious fanaticism. No less persistent in Portuguese history, however, has been the kind of critical outlook and independence of spirit which account for a lesser known event of the period: the experiments of the Brazilian-born priest Bartolomeu Lourenço de Guzmão with the idea of an airborne vehicle. Saramago contrasts these two enterprises throughout his novel, so that the convent becomes the expression of the dead weight of reactionary absolutism while the flying machine embodies the aspirations of a few to soar above the limitations of their time. (1987, 27)

In his version of history, Saramago juxtaposes themes that are antithetic: religious fervor and sensuality; piety and sadomasochism; profane festivities and religious processions; bullfights and autos-da-fé; the poverty of the people and the ostentation and pomp of the clergy and nobility. The writer's descriptions and characterizations are based on a dichotomic vision of the period.

However, this version of history has long been hidden by official rhetoric. Historical representations of the eighteenth century, for the most part, used a wide range of tropes, images, and myths to convey an almost utopian vision of the period based on moral rectitude, idealism, virtue, religiosity, and grandiosity of principles. Saramago, with his presentation of contradictory and alternative evidence, exposes this distorted vision and shows how rhetorical strategies were used by certain social classes in a process of historical legitimation to maintain their power and privileges.

By stressing the extremes of privilege and poverty and extravagance and misery in the historical landscape of the eighteenth century, the novel reveals anxiety within the very discourse of the ruling classes. The clergy and nobility are well aware that they depend on the presence and consent of the people to maintain their authority. The people do obey, for the most part, the authority of the dominant discourse, but they do so under duress. What becomes clear in Saramago's text is the uneasiness and instability of the official discourse. Yet in spite of its weakness it cannot be criticized openly, as many people discover. The system has created institutions, such as the Inquisition, that maintain a constant vigilance for signs of resistance among the people and dissident members of the upper class. Blimunda's mother is exiled to Angola, Baltasar dies in an auto-da-fé, and an old man is killed with a club, all because they openly resisted the system with their actions and/or words. The old man, when rejected as a worker for the construction of the convent, declares openly that he is against the abandonment of agriculture and the depopulation of the kingdom because of the whims of a lunatic monarch. He also attacks the evils of greed and power, and claims that the king is infamous and the motherland unjust. His dissidence and resistance merit an immediate death at the hands of a soldier (Saramago 1982, 293). The old man is conceived in the image of another literary figure, the old man of Restelo in *Os Lusíadas*, who challenges fifteenth-century institutionalized discourse just prior to the departure of Vasco da Gama to India.

Clearly, Saramago is mainly interested in the voices of dissidence and, indeed, he has succeeded in producing an alternative discourse to displace the dominant system of historical knowledge associated with the eighteenth century. His text is the epic of the voiceless, those who have been forgotten either by history books or by literary productions. The novel can be viewed and understood as the consciousness of the differentiated and the marginal, and as an attempt to bring into the realm of representation that which has been omitted and left unspoken. In the process, Saramago redeems the lower classes, those who labored anonymously under difficult conditions but were never celebrated in official discourse. This redemption is accomplished through the biographical reconstruction of the lives of common people, among them Francisco Marques, José Pequeno, Joaquim da Rocha, Manuel Filho, Julião Mau-Tempo, João Anes, and the two protagonists, Baltasar and Blimunda. Not content with this reduced number of personages, Saramago mentions other names, always pluralizing them to indicate that there were many people with the same name, and finally he introduces a list of characters encompassing the whole range of the alphabet (242).

Above all else, it is Baltasar, Blimunda, and Father Bartolomeu, three individuals who represent respectively the pragmatism, spiritualism (human will), and idealism necessary to carry out the construction of the airborne vehicle, who establish an antithesis to the official and conventional rhetoric of the eighteenth century. Their dissidence and challenge to official discourse express the aspirations and desires of a whole social class. The airborne vehicle as a symbol of freedom and of the defeat of the forces of obscurantism indicates a striving toward knowledge and an openness to a plurality of historical representations. However, Saramago is well aware that dominant discourse can and will appropriate any marginal discourse for its own ends and purposes. That is exactly what happens when the airborne vehicle flies over the Mafra Convent. The would-be subversion of the flying vehicle is appropriated by the religious authorities to symbolize the Holy

Spirit descending to Earth to bless the convent and the religious zeal responsible for its construction. The rhetorical act of appropriation conceals the true nature of the event. Disguising it as a spiritual imperative is more appealing to the people, for it is tied to their salvation. By presenting the event as a postulate beyond contestation, official discourse affirms its moral authority. This appropriation only postpones the time when alternative representations of history will replace existing ones; it cannot really stop them altogether. Since the intended audience of *Memorial* is the twentieth-century public, the irony and the falsity of the appropriation are quite evident.

Another postrevolutionary narrative, Lídia Jorge's *A Costa dos Murmúrios* (1988), also attempts to reclaim the silenced or otherwise marginalized discourses (subjects) of history while introducing a new, particularly interesting angle—a female narrator's perspective through which the historical process becomes filtered. In the novel, the "official" dominant discourse is generated by a gender-specific power structure: the self-consciously masculine imperial ideology of the colonizer.

The novel recounts an episode from the relatively recent past—the colonial war in Mozambique—that provides a powerful commentary on the mechanisms of history. The text of the novel is divided in two parts. The first takes the form of a short story entitled "Os Gafanhotos" that describes in a very vague, metaphorical manner the African wedding of two *lisboetas*, Eva Lopo and a Portuguese soldier, *alferes* Luís Alex. It ends with the death of the groom and Eva's return to Portugal. The second part, the longer of the two, is made up of a dialogue between the author of "Os Gafanhotos" and the main protagonist of the events he describes, Eva Lopo. As Eva relives her past and fills the empty spaces left in the record, the reader learns more about the relationship between herself and Luís, marked by the alarming changes Eva discovers in her lover, obsessed with war and transformed into a cruel, ambitious, and primitive man who chooses as his best friend the ridiculously macho captain, Forza Leal. This personal theme is reflected in the general image of the colonial world as seen through the eyes of the Portuguese soldiers and their families who represent the status quo living in the luxurious hotel Stella Maris. Two episodes contribute to the understanding of the colonial reality: the mysterious poisoning of hundreds of Africans with methyl alcohol (a mystery that Eva Lopo and a local journalist try to uncover) and the first revolts of the local population against Portuguese occupation, resulting in serious military conflict.

The dialogue, established in the novel between these texts that constitute two very different versions of the same story and history, sustains a polemic view of the historical process, clearly dependent on the subject who constructs it, the prevalent ideology, and the type of narration. The short story "Os Gafanhotos" is written from the perspective of the colonizer, whose only attempt to understand the African world consists of imposing on it the values of the Western world. Moreover, by accepting the official ideological discourse of the Salazar state, the colonizer can justify the existence of the colonies and involvement in a colonial war. It is a discourse that depends heavily on historical symbols of conquest, Christian mission, and the glorious, virile, and warriorlike spirit of the Portuguese male throughout history.

Against this version of history Eva Lopo throws her own personal account of the events, filtered through the subjectivity of her emotions. Not only is her voice that of a woman, inherently marginalized amid all the symbology of war, virility, and power, but her narration purposely focuses on short personal stories, scattered episodes, and coincidental happenings that fragment and challenge the monolithic, recognized "official" history. The tragic labor of a soldier's wife, secretly told frontline tales of another, everyday life of women awaiting their soldier-husbands, and one woman's desperate narcissism and lesbianism—all form an alternative version of historical truth. This is the war's "backstage," unrelated, it seems, to military combat and other acknowledged historical "facts" and, consequently, absent from official accounts. However, this subjective and marginalized rendition of historical truth makes the concept of historical "fact" appear relative and transforms the perception of the historical process:

> [I]nto my concept of History fits the influence of invisible muscles that stretch and shrink the anus. If it were not for the accident with Zurique's wife's body, the [hotel] Stella would not have ignored the pianist's death, the gymkhana would not have been a surprise and the doors would not have been smashed. (Jorge 1988, 196)

Eva Lopo also literally *discovers* new facts that had been silenced or conveniently forgotten, and sarcastically exposes the ideological compromises of a history that glorifies an imperialist war. In fact, it is because of her ironic insistence on presenting the war through the plasticity of its massacres, fears, and pain, that any possibility of a positive depiction of violence, as attempted by Salazar's ideology, is undermined.

As in Saramago's novel, the blank spaces and silences are filled to communicate an alternative and differentiated view of history. Thus the official historical discourse can no longer be seen as absolute, objective, fixed, and totalizing. It is simply one among many discourses competing for the production of meaning. If Jorge's rereading and rewriting of history reinforce the necessity to reclaim the marginal and the minor, they also take the reader in two other directions. On the one hand, Jorge provides a metatextual, historiographic commentary on the construction of historical narrative. On the other, she reveals the potentialities of fictional/poetic language in the representation of historical (and other) reality, in both literature and history.

The dialogue between the two parts of *A Costa dos Murmúrios* develops the idea of an essential difference between truth and reality, between what appears to exist via representation and what actually happens. The short story seems "true," especially, as Eva Lopo observes, "in the matter of smell and sound" (Jorge 1988, 41), but in light of her own account, it is not real. In the second part of the novel, we clearly understand that the author of "Os Gafanhotos" aspired to achieve a literary representation of certain historical truths. Eva Lopo, however, considers the equation of reality/representation impossible: "[D]efinitely, truth is not real, even if they are twins" (1988, 85). Her advice to the author of the short story is that he should "tell the story for the story's sake," consider the truth as well as verisimilitude as impossible to reach, and concentrate on a concept of "correspondence" between the real and the representable. The world of "Os Gafanhotos," with its action and characters, represents a transfiguration of the real and should be seen as such. Through this self-reflexive commentary on the process of writing, Lídia Jorge seems to reject the idea that there exists an objective, "truthful" representation of reality. Rather, she proposes a multiplicity of such representations, which would include historical and fictional narrative alike.

Theorizing about the production of historical knowledge with its focus on historical representation, still relatively off-center in Jorge's novel, is transformed into a plot in Saramago's *História do Cerco de Lisboa*. The novel develops two parallel plots. One is a historically marked story of the siege of Lisbon and its conquest from the Moors with the help of the Crusaders. The other, set in contemporary Lisbon, tells the story of Raimundo, "a professional proofreader [who] corrects the galley proofs of a book about the history of the siege of Lisbon, and decides afterwards to write another history about the siege of the city and his love affair with Maria Sara" (Seixo 1989, 34). The "correction" becomes an "alteration" of the truth by Raimundo, who writes a *no* that should not have been included in the galley proofs. According to official historical documents the word *no* counters what really happened during the reign of the first Portuguese monarch: the Crusaders did cooperate in the conquest of Lisbon. With the correction, "what the book begins to tell is that the Crusaders will not help the Portuguese in their conquest of Lisbon, that is what is written and it has become the truth, even if different, what we call false has prevailed over what we call true, it took its place, someone had to write the new history" (Saramago 1989, 50). Thus Raimundo, by inserting a *no* in the revision, produces another text through transformation and subversion that is no less real than the original. It is just one more interpretation of a registered historical event.

The act of writing the word *no* should not be considered here as an attempt to correct or redefine the history of the Middle Ages. Although it allows for the articulation of an alternative version of the history of the period, its main purpose is to lead the writer to theorize about history, its rhetorical devices, and the concepts that are associated with it: truth, reality, referentiality, representation, and knowledge. Even if the main focus of the text is history as theory, it should not be forgotten that the way that Raimundo formulates and represents the past also influences his understanding of the present. It shapes and redirects his personal and emotional life: the word *no* leads to an encounter with Maria Sara and the two begin a love affair. Moreover, the love of the two protagonists parallels the love of Mogueime and Ouroana, two characters from the twelfth century. Many times the past and present overlap, and it is difficult to place the love stories historically. The two stories inform each other: changing the past transforms the present and the *no* of history becomes the *yes* of love.

The novel self-consciously assumes that it is a falsified version of the siege of Lisbon as represented in official documents. However, it also views its revisionist alteration of an established historical fact as a search for the real truth and as a way of questioning and pondering the essence of historical truth. The narrator of *História do Cerco* seems to suggest that there are multiple versions for every single historical event because history constantly selects from among many truths for its representation of the world. Thus, it can be inferred that history, just like literature, does not really deal with truth or the real but rather with *vraisemblance*, that is, the attempt made by the historical or literary text to convey to its readers the belief that its representations conform to reality *and* to truth at the same time. The epigraph of the novel—"As long as you do not reach the truth you cannot correct it. However, if you do not correct it you will never reach it. Meanwhile, do not give up" (1989, 9)—sets the tone for the interrelationship between literature and history and for the project that the proofreader wants to see through to the end: How is truth constructed, how does ideology affect the construction of it, how is truth naturalized, and what is the possibility of reaching a single, objective, and absolute truth?

Raimundo feels trapped between a bored and insignificant existence and the accuracy that he must maintain as a proofreader. Consequently, he decides to throw himself on the road of adventure (alteration of the original document) in order to reach the truth. Nevertheless, as the epigraph of the text indicates, the undertaking of the proofreader, his search for truth, is futile. The epigraph has a paradoxical and contradictory structure: only when you reach the truth may you correct it, but without correcting it you will never reach it. Thus, truth is an impossibility. The same can be said about the construction of truth in historical discourse. The fact that in *História do Cerco* history and literature are closely linked and almost undifferentiated lends even more credibility to the last statement. Raimundo claims that his book would be considered a history text according to the genre designation, and he believes that anything that is not life is literature. Thus when the proofreader places a *no* in the proofs he is not radically changing the truth of history; he is just creating another among a multiplicity of versions that historical discourse constructs to convey the contingency and the relativity of its many truths. As in Jorge's novel, truth in historical discourse is everywhere but can never be found. At the moment that history becomes discourse, it is already an interpretation and selection of facts and events to be narrated, subject to all the rules, codes, and conventions of discourse. Therefore, it can never be identical to reality, as Saramago suggests in his novel.

The proofreader (or the reviser, a word that better conveys the meaning of what Raimundo does), before he inserts a *no* in the manuscript, also accepts the theoretical postulates of traditional historiography and fiction. Nevertheless, as soon as he violates the "unwritten deontological code that governs the reviser's actions in his relationship with the ideas and opinions of authors" (50), he understands fully that words have the potential to transform reality and represent it differently. A simple alteration of words can lead to radical changes "and if people have any doubts about these new creations they have only to remind themselves that this was the way that the world was created, with words, some but not others, so that they remain so and not in some other way" (50). In other words, what the narrator conveys is that all systems of meanings and the whole production of ideas and images are strictly social constructs. Even the medium through which meaning is communicated—language—alters it: "If Raimundo could line up, in the exact order, everything that memory contains in loose sentences and words, it would suffice to dictate them, to file them in a tape recorder, and thus he would have, without the painful effort of writing, the history of the siege of Lisbon that he is still looking for, and the method being different, different would be the history, different the siege, different Lisbon, infinitely" (182).

When Raimundo contests the conventions and codes of all fictional and historical productions, and he problematizes the mimetic and realistic notions of referentiality in all types of narratives, he is accepting the idea of the textuality of fiction and history alike. However, by doing so he enters new, uncharted textual labyrinths that force him to admit that "his freedom began and ended at the exact moment that he wrote the word no" (253) and he can no longer return to the beginning to eliminate the *no* because that word has placed him in the presence of Maria Sara, his new lover, and she has changed his way of viewing and relating to the world. The word is also responsible for his acceptance of the insufficiency of any historical discourse to construct ontological and epistemological certainties. The revision accentuates that there is no authoritative past that legitimizes notions of knowledge. The textual past of *O Cerco* now has to take into account the *no* that questions and challenges its authority to represent the truth, because that word unmasks the ideological foundations used by all historical documents in their production of meaning. Raimundo's freedom begins with a *no* because the word makes him master the ways by which he can explore and create new meanings. The freedom also ends with the same word, because when he incorporates it into an official historical document, he is challenging the stability of historical facts, a stability that "must be continuously reinforced, shielded from accidents, subject to our losing the sense of our own actuality, and with a serious disturbance of the opinions that guide us and its derivative convictions" (79). It is Saramago's opinion that history should not be shielded or reinforced. On the contrary, it must be opened up, attacked, and forced from its referential foundation so that we can have differentiated and multiple historical representations.

Theorizing about history and representation, metatextual as well as intertextual commentary, to which Saramago's convergent past and present plots can be added, corresponds to similar projects carried out by two other contemporary authors. In the case of Augusto Abelaira's *O Bosque Harmonioso*, a contemporary narrator recounts the story of a sixteenth-century manuscript by one Cristóvão Borralho, which he found and decided to translate and edit. Embarking on a literary-historical investigation, the narrator discovers another text, a biography of Borralho written by Gaspar Barbosa, containing commentaries by a third author, an unknown commentator from eighteenth century. In a parallel plot, the reader learns about the narrator's romantic problems and about his political views on the subject of the 1980 presidential elections. *As Naus* by Lobo Antunes tells the story of *retornados*, Portuguese who returned to Portugal from African colonies after the 1974 revolution. They discover that the motherland is not ready to receive them. They will have to share a difficult political, social, and economic reality resulting from the years of prolonged dissolution of the overseas empire. They feel degraded, disillusioned, and alienated, and their stories compose a kind of disconcerting antiepic. In both novels, the historical period evoked in the text—the Discoveries—functions as a strong symbolic referent, since it draws on that part of collective historical consciousness which is of greatest importance to any "interpretation" of Portugal. While neither narrative consistently attempts to reconstruct or focus on the events of the period, they place, in different ways, history and its mechanisms at the center of their respective narrative structures.

Abelaira is very careful and historically aware when referring to the sixteenth-century manuscript and its supposed author. Here the author gets the closest to "historical fiction": a picaresque protagonist retells his adventures from travels around the Portuguese overseas empire. It is a mix of epic tales, allegorical fables, and dramatic instances. A comparison with the famous *Peregrinação* by Fernão Mendes Pinto becomes unavoidable and is even explicitly mentioned in the text.[3] But the main plotline develops through metatextual and historiographic digressions made by the contemporary narrator. The metatextual commentary involves the act of writing and producing a new "text," which not only must emerge from different texts (the manuscript, the biography, and the eighteenth-century commentary) but also must resolve the questions of anachronism, structure, and, generally, all the problems involved in transmitting/translating/editing a historically remote reality to a modern reader. On the other hand, history as such emerges from the text of the novel as a palimpsest constructed of different layers, different texts written on top of each other, in an attempt to constantly reinvent and rewrite both facts and ideas. The sixteenth century reflects, but is also mirrored by, other historical periods and contexts, including the present. The search for "historical truth," objective and conclusive, is bound to fail because it is the searching itself that constructs and defines history. As the narrator says, it is akin to "knowing that life has no meaning and still searching for it" (Abelaira 1982, 168). The more the narrator strives to "explain" and "clarify" history, the more convinced he becomes of its heterogeneous character, made up of interpretations and subjective, ideologically charged enunciations. Thus, at the end, his task becomes to "remake the History of Portugal, remake it against what it pretends to tell us" (113); he wants to "correct it" (129), "modify it" (141), and finally, "produce it" (147). The narrator's writing, supposedly committed to representing a historical reality and, in turn, searching for some kind of truth, becomes as paradoxical as the search of Saramago's Raimundo or Jorge's narrator/interviewer mocked by Eva Lopo in the second part of *A Costa dos Murmúrios*. All of them, although to a different degree, become increasingly more self-conscious and metatextual in their own narratives while realizing the need for openness and multiplicity.

Lobo Antunes is more intertextual than he is metatextual. His evocation of history operates on two levels. The first, more direct one consists of naming the novel's protagonists—the Portuguese who return from Africa—after famous discoverers: Pedro Alvares Cabral, Vasco da Gama, Fernão Mendes Pinto, Diogo Cão. The reader, while certainly recognizing the names as symbols of national heroism and fame, expects the characters in the novel to somehow mirror this historical greatness. Ironic intent becomes immediately clear when the expectation is not met and contemporary namesakes turn out to be a bunch of drunks, marginals, and pimps. It suggests that the Portuguese historical adventure in the outside world, directed from the fifteenth century on, comes full circle and, with the final end of the empire, returns home in 1974. That return is not glorious but miserable and tragic.

On the other hand, there is a more general, less consistent presence of historical themes and figures in the text, making it impossible to distinguish separate plots, as sometimes happens in historical fiction that deals with two different time frames. Not only are the main characters endowed with both a present life and a historical past (for example, Fernão Mendes Pinto, an owner of a bar-and-bordello network, tells his friends about his famous travels) but some paragraphs and even sentences display an almost phantasmagoric mixture of two realities, the historical and the contemporary:

> I managed to reach a line of stairs between two alleys from where one could see, at the same time, the monument, the trains to Cascais, and the lanterns of fishing boats on the river, and it was exactly then, esteemed readers, that the Carmo street was lit by a procession of torches and page's laughter . . . and King Sebastião appeared on a horse . . . followed by surprised policemen and night guards, on their way to Alcácer Quibir. (Lobo Antunes 1988, 166)

The narrative as a whole delivers a very bold, at times painful interpretation of national history, giving it a very specific tragicomical emplotment. It makes a very startling historical commentary because it manages to tell a story that in a meaningful way combines the postrevolutionary drama of decolonization with the newly awakened anguish about the historical past. History is approached here as a cultural intertext, which maintains a dialogic relation with literary narrative dealing, in fact, with contemporary reality.

In both history and literature, the rethinking of traditional concepts of history, fiction, and representation precipitates and is precipitated by the exploration of the role that poetic language and other, overtly fictional constructs play in the representation of reality. Saramago has been recognized as a creator of a new brand of magical realism. Fantastic, magical, or supernatural occurrences and characters appear in many of Saramago's novels, such as *Memorial do Convento* and *O Ano da Morte de Ricardo Reis*, and they are transformed into an important literary device that offers new insights into historical understanding. José Cardoso Pires in *A Balada da Praia dos Cães* (subtitled *Dissertação sobre um crime*) seems simultaneously attached to and detached from reality in formulating specific aesthetic and theoretical principles to govern the author's fictional representation of historical events. In both novels, it becomes clear that the language of imagination operating on factual reality provides yet another access to a multiplicity of discourses and leads to a better and fuller understanding of history.

In *O Ano da Morte de Ricardo Reis*, José Saramago recreates the sociopolitical climate of Lisbon in 1936, a year of complex changes throughout Europe: the Spanish civil war, the rise of fascism, and the strengthening of Salazar's "New State" in Portugal itself. Saramago's reconstruction of Lisbon's reality in its various aspects is so detailed and complete that it would provide a perfect script for a movie or serve as a literary map to walk the city's streets. And, going even further, the author includes newspaper articles and slogans from the period in the text of the novel. However, Saramago creates a protagonist of a different kind, whose status can be at best described as ambiguous, since he remains somewhere between absolute fiction and fictitious reality.

The title character, Ricardo Reis, a well-known heteronym of the poet Fernando Pessoa, is given the life of a physician, recently returned to Lisbon after sixteen years of exile in Brazil. His attempts to understand the new Portuguese sociopolitical reality and become an active participant in it are metaphorically compared to travel through a labyrinth of experiences, made of conversations, acquaintances, newspaper reports, police investigations, and discussions with another protagonist of the novel, Fernando Pessoa himself. In reality, Fernando Pessoa died in 1935, but Saramago magically brings him back from the dead for his novel, explaining to the reader that we all have nine months on Earth after we die and before we vanish into oblivion. Fernando Pessoa cannot intervene in the goings-on of the novel, but he proves to be a witty, cynical observer who frequently relies on the insights of his own poetry and functions as both Reis's consciousness and his *advocatus diaboli*. Conversations between the two include discussions of literature, philosophy, national history, and current events. They sharply see the contrast between the ecstatic news about Portugal's prosperity under

Salazar and the troubling bits of information about crime, poverty, and illiteracy, sometimes lost on the pages of the same newspaper. They are able to see (perhaps because they are poets) how words can be manipulated, especially words of those long dead, like the sixteenth-century poet, Luís de Camões, to suit the aims of the propaganda machine. Historical narration as well as fiction are constructed through language. Therefore, imagination, even at its most magical, can be called on to complement the factual record. An understanding of the given historical reality emerges from a variety of discourses, in which documents, poetry, and fiction are placed at the same level. Reis and Pessoa are both, to an extent, withdrawn from actual historical reality, but it is their examination as spectators, especially Reis's alienated yet penetrating examination,[4] that allows for the social structures, ideologies, and politically compromised discourse to be exposed and demythified.

Cardoso Pires's *Balada da Praia dos Cães* deals with a real historical event that took place in 1960, the murder of a dissident and antifascist major, Luís Dantas Castro, by three of his companions. The three assassins, just like the major, were members of the opposition and had taken refuge in a house in Vereda, a small village near Sintra. Major Castro, together with two other military men—an architect and a corporal—had escaped from the Graça Fortress in Elvas, where they had been awaiting trial for their involvement in an aborted military coup. Filomena or Mena, the major's lover, joined them after the escape. The four individuals were determined to carry out another attempt against the Salazar regime with the help of other dissidents, but the circumstances in which they found themselves thwarted their plans. Mena, the architect, and the corporal murdered the major in order to free themselves of the oppressive situation. After they murdered Major Castro, they buried him on Mastro Beach (Dogs' Beach in Cardoso Pires's novel).

It was from this real historical event that the writer constructed his narrative. However, as Cardoso Pires so succinctly puts it, "the fictionist aims at a later dimension of the facts. To be more precise, he does not have to restrict himself to the facts, although it is certain that he cannot live without them. The author does not want people to know for sure that the historical documentation of the novel is true or false or is truth or fiction. He would like them to think: this did not happen but he was there" (Ferreira 1982, 3). The novel's primary aim is, therefore, not to reconstruct objectively Portuguese history during the fascist period, and especially the reality of the early 1960s, or to report on a crime and a criminal investigation that took place in 1960–61. Its aim, on the contrary, is to redefine and to reformulate these events within their contextual circumstances in order to convey a more exact image of Portugal and its inhabitants at a time of terror, fear, surveillance, psychological and physical torture, and repression.

In an interview with *Jornal de Letras* regarding *Balada*, Cardoso Pires declares that the incorporation of many documents in the narrative adheres to literary conventions:

> In the novel, a reality is recreated. There are elements that I represent there, not because they really are part of the criminal proceedings, but because they define the social landscape, the period in which we were living. Certain clues are intentionally jumbled, because what did not really interest me, under any circumstances, was for the reader to be able to recognize in the narrative, step by step, the portrait of a real criminal proceeding. I insist: my method is not the one used by a Norman Mailer or a Truman Capote. The investigation is not the subject of my novel, but its starting point. (4)

The author claims further that "there were many things [documents] that I cut because they were so shocking that nobody would believe that they were true. And, nevertheless, they all are in the proceedings. . . . In order for the novel to reach its objectives, it was necessary that I eliminate everything, because it was too sensational and would bind me to the narrative of the criminal proceedings. I kept close only to the fiction. To a fiction of fears, of lies, of cages for wild animals, of bird-cages, of transparencies: of peacocks, of jays, of corrupt generals, of seals and merles, of fears and anxieties. Of dogs" (4).

Meaning, for the most part, is constructed in *Balada* through a metaphorical representation of reality, which includes a whole gallery of animals, especially dogs, that appear in the text as symbols of authority and possess many of the traits that are associated with the PIDE (Portuguese secret police). A lizard is kept in a cage and fed insects daily by Elias Santana, the principal investigator of the crime. Other images and events associated with a prisonlike existence are prevalent in the text. Images, actions, and ideas associated with surveillance, the gaze, and the intimidation of the other convey an atmosphere of terror and fear. In addition, the many structures of enclosure that permeate the text add to this atmosphere.

Cardoso Pires's language is also dominated by signs and images of social and moral decay, and debasement. There is a gallery of individuals, including Major Castro and Elias Santana, who are marked by a set of signs associated with degradation and moral pollution. Moreover, all these signs are coupled with eroticism and sadomasochism. Cardoso Pires creates the impression that Portugal is a spiritual and social wasteland. The imagery of debasement in *Balada* constitutes a kind of human pathology seemingly devoid of all recognizable humanity. More worrisome still is the fact that the pathological fabric of the narrative determines both the dominant discourse and the discourse associated with the opposition. There is really no difference between an Elias Santana who represents the established order and the major who is aligned with the opposition. The major gains satisfaction by making cigarette-burn marks on Mena's body and by lying to his companions about his activities apropos the attempted coup. Elias Santana, on the other hand, revels in the abuse of power; power becomes an aphrodisiac that intoxicates him.

Not unlike a historian who, according to Hayden White, "must include in his narrative an account of some event or complex of events for which the facts that would permit a plausible explanation of its occurrence are lacking," Cardoso Pires needs to fill the gaps in the official record. He does it, however, not on "inferential or speculative grounds" but by drawing upon the imaginary and the fictional (White 1985, 51). It is the imaginary that molds raw data and documents and gives them a literary form. However, the end result is the same. History and fiction are essentially interpretations of reality and/or historical processes, and thus are related.

In a final note to the novel, Cardoso Pires momentarily loses his bearings—he has a lapse of memory—and cannot confirm if what he is saying or writing belongs to the domain of the fictional or the historical. The lapse in memory occurs when the author recalls a conversation he had with the real (and not the fictional) architect Fontenova in 1980. During their meeting, Fontenova admittedly told Cardoso Pires that "fear is a dramatic form of solitude." (1983, 254) In the final note, the author, after reiterating Fontenova's words, makes the following observations: "Was he the one who said them? Are these his real words [the real Fontenova's] or do they belong to the one called here [in the text] architect Fontenova [the fictional character]? I wonder if I was not the one who said that and other things in an invented memory to make him more exact and real?" (1983, 256)

Certainly there is no need to answer these rhetorical questions. However, the questions posed by Cardoso Pires confirm a problematic relationship between fiction and history. In the same way that reality intervenes in the construction of the fictional text, fiction can constitute an essential structural component in the construction of the factual (historical) narrative. According to Hayden White, recent theories of discourse accept in principle the interrelationship between fiction and history. The critic claims that these theories "dissolve the distinction between realistic and fictional discourses based on the presumption of an ontological difference between their respective referents, real and imaginary, in favor of stressing their common aspect as semiological apparatuses that produce meanings by the systematic substitution of signifieds (conceptual contents) for the extra-discursive entities that serve as their referents" (1987, x). Cardoso Pires, in the novel's final note, seems to share these feelings. He states that "there are convergences and separations between fact and fiction at every step, and everything aims at an autonomous parallelism and conflictive confluence, at truth and at doubt that are not pure coincidence" (1983, 256).

The last novel to be discussed here, José Saramago's *A Jangada de Pedra*, is not a reinterpretation of history as already existing official discourse. Rather, it is a reading and interpretation of history and, particularly, of its impact on the present and future reality through the magic and fantastic representation of a hypothetical futuristic voyage. In it, all the aspects of contemporary fiction's contemplation of history find their places.

The text narrates the separation of the Iberian Peninsula from the rest of Europe. In the Pyrenees, on the frontier between France and Spain, a deep fissure occurs, which leads not only to the separation of the peninsula, but also to its ensuing voyage as a gigantic stone raft through the Atlantic in an aimless drift. After changing directions several times the peninsula ends up anchored in the South Atlantic, in a location that is exactly equidistant from Africa and South America. One must bear in mind that the novel was written at the same time that a bitter debate was taking place in Portugal between those who supported the union with the European Economic Community and those who staunchly opposed it. The official discourse of the period was already preparing the road for a union with the EEC countries, processing and codifying images that would rationalize its objectives. The economic, political, and cultural benefits that would derive from such a union were stressed. Even the future of Portugal was called into question; without the union there would be no future. Thus, an impression was created that the raison d'être of Portugal, the identity of its people, depended entirely on the formalization of the union.

A Jangada de Pedra is, to a great extent, a counterdiscourse; a discourse that seeks to project an alternative vision against the absorptive capacity of official history. Before certain aspects of Portuguese reality disappeared, with the established histories' ability to absorb difference and to suppress any underlying vestige of discourse opposed to full integration with the EEC, José Saramago began a process of definition and analysis of present social and historical conditions, so that facts and images connected with the discourse of the opposition would also be a part of Portuguese history. The raft voyage is the fictional production of a different history, but in no way is it less relevant or less crucial to the construction of official history.

It conveys, literally, the feelings and desires of a large segment of the Portuguese population. Thus in *Jangada*, through a narrative placed in a hypothetical future, Saramago battles against the imposition of a fixed and closed meaning by any future official representation of the period. The author, in an interview with the newspaper *Expresso*, stated that *Jangada* is

> a book against integration but it is not anti-European, nor could it be. Culture, language, institutions, everything comes to us from Europe. Now, we are talking about integration, which leads me to think that the connection has not been made yet. Incidentally, even Europe does not quite understand who she is or what it is, given that the preoccupation to construct Europe is evident in all fields including the cultural, when we see the multiplication of congresses, seminars, and meetings where the idea of Europe is discussed. I do not believe it is so unusual that, from this corner of Europe that was never entirely Europe, something is questioned that for Europeans is not very clear. Besides, I have the impression that, at the same time that the integration of the Peninsula into Europe begins, another idea is raised that is its opposite: the need for Portugal not to tie itself so much to Europe. It is not so much the fear for cultural identity but rather a need for a reorientation toward something from which we cut ourselves off: the countries of the Iberian-American and the Iberian-African areas. (1986, 36)

The symbolic voyage of the Iberian Peninsula and the interrelationship between the different Spanish and Portuguese fictional characters demonstrate that any historical representation, be it of the past or future, is always anchored in ideological motivations. It is in an ideological locus that the struggle for a definition and legitimization of culture takes place. In his counterhistorical discourse, Saramago conceals his ideological motives, just as official history would. The displacement of the writer's rhetoric takes the form of an idealization and fantasy of a stone raft navigating through the Atlantic, which brings forth images of the creation of an idealized and conflict-free space.

The image of an idealized island floating in the Atlantic suggests to Iberians that it would be in their best interest to accept the reality of a united Peninsula rather than join a union with a Europe that is still struggling to define itself and is full of problems and conflicts. The fundamental principle of the text is that Iberians will be morally, socially, and politically edified through active participation in the construction of an authentic Iberian space. This view is never expressed overtly in *Jangada*, but the reader is well aware that Saramago's ultimate goal is to manipulate people into identifying with the basic values and principles of his Iberian discourse.

By romanticizing the voyage, the author is appealing to an undivided Iberian cultural identity.

Jangada must counteract the integrative official discourse by using rhetorical methods of transference and displacement if it is to be successful in producing images and symbols that influence public opinion. The voyage stresses the communal characteristics of the Iberian Peninsula and brings Spaniards and Portuguese together. It forces the governments of two countries to work together in order to solve a crisis and hinder the development of chaotic conditions. It reveals that the cultural productions of the two countries are intertextually connected. The common pilgrimage of the Iberian Peninsula, that is, the cultural approximation between the two Iberian countries, has to be read as a conscious strategy of resistance to more powerful European cultural productions, which the author feels will impose themselves on Portugal and Spain if integration runs its full course. As Horácio Costa so appropriately explains,

> It is in this context that we can evaluate the insight of Saramago's metaphor: many of the arguments in favor of the integration of the Peninsula in the European Community seem to conceal under the gloss of reason the gesso of providence (in which an idealized Europe would mean salvation, and which seems deceitful according to the writer). If this is so, then the Peninsula has to be separated mysteriously from Europe, in an equally providential manner, and moved far away from it in the direction of those worlds that Portugal and Spain discovered and well or badly colonized, forming the plural but divided community of Portuguese- and Spanish-speaking countries. (1988, 33)

Official history may dislike the notion of an Iberian country and, in all likelihood, is formulating constructs that will create the proper postulates needed for all Portuguese to embrace the integrative discourse as an economic and political imperative. But this does not mean they are beyond contestation, as *Jangada* clearly and forcefully indicates. In "José Saramago: Viagens através do tempo," the author himself declares that "history when it remakes the referential always deletes many events and facts, that is, it produces changes that establish relationships with the events that are entirely new, and presents a totally different version of the original event" (1990, 17). Being aware that the future reader of history will have a distorted and incomplete vision of contemporary Portugal—in Saramago's opinion, that is what official discourses always convey—the author tries to anticipate these incompletions and distortions in his novel.

Postrevolutionary Portuguese literature experienced a true golden age in fiction: new authors, new narrative styles and themes, popularity among readers and critics alike, and an international recognition. As we have tried to demonstrate in this study, the fictional production of the last two decades in Portugal reveals a profound commitment to unraveling the complex new reality of the country as it emerges from almost fifty years of dictatorship and six centuries of colonial involvement. To comprehend this reality and to be able to make choices for the future entail an open discussion of the past that, in many respects, really seemed to have come to an end.

Can fiction challenge history? Can either fiction or history claim for itself the status of the true representation of reality, of objective truth? Can any narrative achieve that goal? How much does fiction contribute to the construction of historical discourse and vice versa? Does history contribute to the way the narrative is constructed? What are the links between fiction and history? Does the representation of the real belong to the exclusive domain of history and the imaginary belong to the domain of narrative? These questions may be examined from a new perception of both historical and literary narrative, analyzed as language constructs and dependent on the laws of discourse. There can be no historical truth without considering the subject, the narrator, the ideology that legitimizes it, and the rhetoric that constructs it. Even when these concepts are considered, the question of historical truth still remains problematic, as Saramago suggests in *História do Cerco*.

The Portuguese authors whose works have been discussed here attempted to deconstruct and demythify versions and concepts of history that were particularly abused and manipulated by the fallen Salazar regime. Most novels deal with the recent past: the beginnings of Portugal under the dictatorship *(O Ano da Morte de Ricardo Reis)*, its pathetic end *(Balada da Praia dos Cães)*; with the colonial war *(A Costa dos Murmúrios)*, and the difficult, postrevolutionary aftermath *(As Naus)*. Many authors use national history, especially pivotal moments such as the Discoveries and the Conquest, as a cultural intertext to inform a literary narrative about the present. Novels that belong to this category *(As Naus, Bosque Harmonioso*, or *História do Cerco de Lisboa)* tend to stress history as theory, becoming persistently metatextual and historiographic in their commentary. In two other novels, *Memorial do Convento*, dealing with eighteenth-century Portuguese history, and *A Jangada de Pedra*, dealing with a historicized future, José Saramago undertakes the task of (re)claiming the dissident or otherwise marginalized discourses and of confronting the official historical discourse. All of the novels analyzed, however, challenge established notions about both history and fiction and, on more specific grounds, stoke a debate about the past, present, and future of Portugal, and the self-image, identity, and role of its people in the contemporary world.

Notes

1. To name just a few: Lopes 1984; Lourenço 1988; Santos 1992.

2. Among these works are some of the most famous novels of the last twenty years: *Il Nome della Rosa* by Umberto Eco, *The French Lieutenant's Woman* by John Fowles, *Terra Nostra* by Carlos Fuentes, *Gravity's Rainbow* by Thomas Pynchon, *Midnight Children* by Salman Rushdie, *The Public Burning* by Robert Coover, *Ragtime* and *The Book of Daniel* by E. L. Doctorow, and many more.

3. The narrator refers to Mendes Pinto's work several times and compares it with Borralho's manuscript, suspecting that Pinto is the true author of the text (Abelaira 1982, 130). He also mentions another work and possible intertext for the novel, *Bosque Deleitoso* (1515). Comparing it to his own narrative, the narrator admits it is the object of a "more or less unfocused satire" (1982, 166).

4. Pessoa's heteronym, the poet Ricardo Reis, is a true "spectator of the world," a classicist, and a believer in the golden mean, always detached and refraining from emotional involvement in life's struggles.

References

Abelaira, Augusto. 1982. *O Bosque Harmonioso*. Lisbon: Sá da Costa.

Alves, Clara Ferreira, Francisco Bélard, and Augusto M. Seabra. 1986. "A Facilidade de Ser Ibérico." *Expresso/Revista*, 8 November, 36–39.

Costa, Horácio. 1986. "Memorial do Convento é também um Romance sobre a História da Língua." *O Diário/Cultural*, 21 December, 8–9.

Costa, Horácio. 1988. "Jangada de Pedra faz 'Arqueologia' do Caráter Nacional." *Folha de São Paulo*, 27 April, A-33.

Ferreira, António Mega. 1982. "Entrevista com José Cardoso Pires." *Jornal de Letras, Artes e Ideias* 47:3–4.

Garrett, Almeida. 1844. *Frei Luís de Sousa*. Lisbon.

Gossman, Lionel. 1978. "History and Literature: Reproduction and Signification." In *The Writing of History: Literary Form and Historical Understanding,* edited by Robert H. Canary and Henry Kozicki, 3–39. Madison: University of Wisconsin Press.

Hutcheon, Linda. 1988. *A Poetics of Postmodernism: History, Theory, Fiction.* New York: Routledge.

Jorge, Lídia. 1986. "Escrita e Emancipação." *Revista Crítica de Ciências Sociais* 18/19/20:57–63.

———. 1988. *A Costa dos Murmúrios*. Lisbon: Dom Quixote.

Lobo Antunes, António. 1988. *As Naus*. Lisbon: Dom Quixote.

Lopes, Óscar. 1984. "Seis Séculos à Procura da História." *Vértice* 44, no. 460:3–16

Lourenço, Eduardo. 1988. *Nós e a Europa*. Lisboa: Imprensa Nacional-Casa da Moeda.

Martins, Adriana Alves de Paula. 1994. *História e Ficção: Um Diálogo*. Lisboa: Fim de Século Edições.

Pires, José Cardoso. 1983. *Balada da Praia dos Cães*. Lisbon: Edições "O Jornal."

Preto-Rodas, Richard A. 1987. "A View of Eighteenth-Century Portugal: José Saramago's *Memorial do Convento*." *World Literature Today*, winter, 27-31.

Queirós, Eça de. 1900. *A Ilustre Casa de Ramires*. Lisbon.

Santos, Boaventura de Sousa. 1992. "Onze Teses por Ocasião de Mais uma Descoberta de Portugal."*Luso-Brazilian Review* 29, no. 1:97–113.

Saramago, José. 1982. *Memorial do Convento*. Lisbon: Editorial Caminho.

———. 1985a. *Levantado do Chão*. Lisbon: Editorial Caminho.

———. 1985b. *O Ano da Morte de Ricardo Reis*. Lisbon: Editorial Caminho.

———. 1986. *A Jangada de Pedra*. Lisbon, Editorial Caminho.

———. 1987. *Baltasar and Blimunda*. Translated by Giovanni Pontiero. New York: Harcourt Brace Jovanovich.

———. 1989. *História do Cerco de Lisboa*. Lisbon: Editorial Caminho.

———. 1990. "José Saramago: Viagens através do Tempo." *Jornal de Letras, Artes e Ideias* 400:17.

Seixo, Maria Alzira. 1986. "Narrativa e Romance: Esboço de uma Articulação Teórica." In *A Palavra do Romance: Ensaios de Genologia e Análise*. Lisbon: Livros Horizonte.

———. 1989. "História do Cerco de Lisboa ou a Respiração da Sombra." *Colóquio/Letras* 109:33–48.

White, Hayden. 1985. *Tropics of Discourse: Essays in Cultural Criticism*. Baltimore: The Johns Hopkins University Press.

———. 1986. "Historical Pluralism." *Critical Inquiry* 12, no. 3:480–93.

———. 1900. *The Content of the Form: Narrative Discourse and Historical Representation*. Baltimore: The Johns Hopkins University Press.

No Longer Alone and Proud:
Notes on the Rediscovery of the Nation
in Contemporary Portuguese Fiction

ELLEN SAPEGA

The 25 de Abril and the Transformation
of Portuguese National Identity

When asked to consider the question of national identity in contemporary Portuguese literature, the critic must take into account many unique events in the nation's recent history, most of which are direct consequences of the 1974 revolution. The demographic changes that accompanied the end of Portugal's imperial stronghold in Africa, the nationalization (and subsequent denationalization) of the country's principal modes of production, and the gradual reintroduction of a democratically elected government after more than forty years of authoritarian rule have forced the citizens of contemporary Portugal to reconsider a number of ideological assumptions that informed the representational codes previously employed in national discourses of identity formation. Given the abrupt and decisive nature of the events that followed the revolution, several of the symbols and discourses traditionally used to refer to the Portuguese nation were naturally discredited. As Portugal ended its five-hundred-year policy of overseas expansion, the nation sought new political and economic alliances; over the past decade, Portugal's ties to the European Economic Community have come to play a crucial role in shaping the horizons of its future.

Inaugurating a new era of political, social, and economic experience, the revolution would seem, therefore, to have contributed to a national "explosion of shared values." Indeed, the magnitude of this change is succinctly conveyed by the explicit rejection of the old regime's official slogan of *orgulhosamente sós* (We are alone and proud). Used to justify the

168

Estado Novo's intransigent position in regard to any negotiated settlement of the colonial wars, this slogan sought to reassure the Portuguese that their government was dedicated to upholding a unique and noble national heritage. By the 1980s, however, a recently elected socialist government was optimistically proclaiming that the nation had forged new alliances, assuring the populace that they were living a situation described as *a Europa connosco* (Europe is with us). These two diametrically opposed slogans reflect the political relationships assumed by the Portuguese government in regard to its European neighbors; as such, they constitute the separate poles around which many official discourses of identity were constructed before and after the revolution.

While serving as good general indicators of the governments' official political positioning before and after April 1974, the guiding attitudes behind these slogans certainly are much more complex than the two positions that they simply state. When juxtaposed, however, they neatly capture the most basic aspects of an ongoing debate as to the necessity and the means of restructuring of national goals. To date, the events surrounding the 25 de Abril and the question of its impact on the future of the Portuguese nation have generated many lengthy bibliographies in which political scientists, historians, and social scientists attempt to assess the importance of that moment and to address the question of the nation's future.[1] Given this large-scale outpouring of writing about Portugal's past, present, and future, it is hardly surprising to find many contemporary novelists also choosing to explore the field of Portuguese national identity. As Benedict Anderson has shown, the rise of "print capitalism" in the late eighteenth century directly contributed to the construction of modern national consciousness. Through the creation of "print languages," readers "became capable of comprehending one another via print and paper" (1983, 47). By the mid-nineteenth century, the novel became a primary vehicle for representing the aspirations of the nation, admitting the reader into an "imagined community" that served as a metaphoric repository for the values and goals of the nation-state.

In the present case, it would appear that the Portuguese novel has once again become a site for imagining the nation, for many critics of contemporary Portuguese literature agree that this genre's resurgence comes as a direct response to the socioeconomic changes brought about by the revolution. Indeed, it seems that contemporary Portuguese novelists are presently engaged in an activity that Anderson describes as "re-presenting the *kind* of imagined community that is the nation" (30), or in the cultivation of a type of narrative that Fredric Jameson has defined as national allegories: "[T]he story of the private individual destiny is always an allegory of the embattled situation of the public third-world culture and society" (1986, 69).

Jameson's comments on the national allegory seek to differentiate between the political role currently played by writers of fiction in the developed world and that of writers working in the developing world. Although not specifically directed toward the question of Portuguese literary production, they do, nonetheless, provide us with a useful introduction to a discussion of national representation in contemporary Portuguese fiction. Following on Benedict Anderson's line of thought regarding the centrality of fiction in the creation of national consciousness, Jameson argues that the work of contemporary third-world writers, invested with a mix of the political and the personal, necessitates their being read and interpreted as national allegories. In his view, the literature of advanced capitalist societies no longer fulfills Anderson's signifying function of providing the reader with representations of belonging (Tomlinson 1991, 81). Instead, this literature registers a separation of the public and the private spheres of experience that reflects the postmodern condition.

In his lucid response to Jameson's essay, Aijaz Ahmad notes that "the binary opposition that Jameson constructs between a capitalist first world and a presumably pre- or non-capitalist third world is empirically ungrounded in any facts" (1992, 101). While providing a handy typology of differing literary practices, Ahmad observes that Jameson's distinction between first- and third-world literatures is simplistic, at best, for it fails to recognize the heterogeneity of noncanonic or non-Western literature. Among the many facets of Jameson's argument he critiques is the assertion that the "'third-world' is *constituted* by the singular 'experience of colonialism and imperialism'" (102). This dichotomy is clearly problematic for the student of Portuguese literature for, if accepted at face value, we are left wondering how one should approach the contemporary novel, which is ostensibly the product of a nation whose ambiguous situation has been described as the "pioneer of the first world [and] the partner of the third" (Macedo 1990, 101).

As this observation by Helder Macedo indicates, the contemporary Portuguese novel presents a good, and often overlooked, example of the complex realities that underlie the first- and third-world (or canonic and noncanonic) dichotomies that Jameson makes use of in the elaboration of his theory. In the present essay, which seeks to evaluate the novelist's role in contemporary debates on the status of the modern Portuguese nation, I will attempt to situate the novel in its wider context by describing the historic role of the intellectual in the formation of discourses of Portuguese national identity. In the second part of this study, I will map out some of the new thematic concerns that have appeared in recent Portuguese fiction, assessing these themes in light of Anderson's concept of the "imagined community," as well as applying to them Ahmad's comments regarding the importance of the collectivity: "[O]ne may indeed connect one's personal experience to a 'collectivity'—in terms of class, gender, caste, religious community, trade union, political party, village, prison—combining the private and public, and in some sense 'allegorizing' the individual experience, without involving the category of the nation" (1992, 109–10).

The Role of the Intellectual in Determining the Structures of Portuguese National Identity

As a starting point in the analysis of the images of national identity that appear in postrevolutionary Portuguese literature, one must first pose the question as to whether there have occurred any recent and significant internal or external challenges to a sustaining, centralized notion of Portugal as an "imagined community." Unlike many European nations (among them Spain, which is Portugal's closest neighbor and its logical cultural counterpart), the problem of a national language that asserts its hegemony over other distinct languages spoken within the national borders has no relevance in the Portuguese case. Although dialectal differences between various regions certainly exist, the nation is marked by a linguistic conformity that must be recognized as constituting one of several unifying elements in discourses of Portuguese national identity. In much the same fashion, nearly all the citizens of present-day Portugal share the same religion (Roman Catholicism) and identify with a common ideal of national sovereignty that dates to the Middle Ages. Due to the unifying characteristics evidenced in Portugal's linguistic, religious, and ethnic homogeneity, no significant regional oppositions or political resistances to the centralized concept of the nation-state have appeared in postrevolutionary Portugal. In addition, it would seem equally unlikely that such challenges will appear in the near future.

As there have occurred few, if any, internal struggles that seek to challenge or redefine the representational structures of the nation-state, Portugal could be characterized as possessing a "mature cultural identity" (Tomlinson 1991, 74). In turn, this absence of coherently organized oppositional groups has led many to conclude that the basic tenets of Portuguese identity have not been seriously modified by the events following the revolution. A good example of this perspective can be found in the work of Eduardo Lourenço, one of the nation's most respected commentators on contemporary Portuguese literature and culture.[2] In several of his most recent essays, Lourenço repeatedly notes that Portugal's ontological sense of security has remained largely intact, in spite of the radical change in governments that forced a restructuring of national goals:

> The end of a regime that seemed to fit Portuguese reality perfectly led neither to a reappraisal nor to any critical examination of our self-image, although undeniable changes overtook the latter. Present-day Portugal is not identical to what it was in 1974: its political and historical situation is still undergoing one of the most radical changes in its history (a movement it shares with the whole West), but in its essence the image cultivated for years remains untouched. We may even say, however shocking it may seem, that such an image has even strengthened itself. (1990, 116-117)

By making a clear distinction between the conscious effort toward national self-examination and the unavoidable realities that have modified Portugal's image of itself, Lourenço recognizes that new elements central to the reshaping of Portuguese national identity have most certainly had an effect on daily experience. It is curious, however, that these elements are portrayed as having appeared independently of any organized effort to reappraise or critically examine the discourses of national identity. Lourenço asserts that "the image cultivated for years remains untouched," and he reassures his readers that his nation's identity is the product of a seemingly historical continuity, thereby resulting in a situation in which he can confidently state that "The new image of Portugal did not change the structure of 'hyperidentity' that has characterized us since the sixteenth century" (117).

Hoping to provide a concrete example of the uniquely Portuguese phenomenon of "hyperidentity," Lourenço cites the surprising lack of effect that the end of the five-centuries-long history of overseas expansion and empire had on his fellow citizens. In what he considers a characteristically Portuguese response to these historical events, the author observes that this potentially traumatic development was accepted by his fellow citizens with "a mix of unawareness and realism that is probably unique in the history of European colonization" (117). Here, by stressing the uniqueness of Portugal's response to the loss of its colonies, Lourenço's thought illustrates, perhaps unwittingly, one of the central precepts of his theory of Portuguese "hyperidentity," a condition that he describes in another essay as based upon the presupposition of difference from other models of European development:

[O]ur problem . . . is not a problem of *identity*, if one takes it as a question to our status as a nation, or a preoccupation with the sense and purpose of the profound adherence with which we feel and know ourselves to be Portuguese, a people inscribed in a certain physical and cultural space, but of hyperidentity, of almost morbid fixation on the contemplation and the pleasure of the difference that characterizes us or that we imagine such in the context of other peoples, nations, and cultures. (1988, 10)

Before addressing the question of whether or not Lourenço's theory of "hyperidentity" can be applied successfully in an analysis of the discourses of national identity in contemporary Portuguese fiction, I would like to emphasize the manner in which his thought illustrates what has, until recently, been a general tendency of many analyses of the question of national identity. It is evident here that Lourenço believes in the possibility of cultivating a centralized and centralizing discourse of identity that is capable of encompassing all elements of his society. He stakes out an intellectual position for himself as the "legitimate representative of a universal subject" and implicitly endorses the traditional or "legislating role" of the intellectual within his society (Ribeiro 1993, 485). Moreover, it would seem that Lourenço's reasons for emphasizing his mission as both universal and disinterested are abundantly clear. By arguing that few, if any, significant changes have occurred and that the bases of Portuguese national identity have not been altered over the past two decades, Lourenço is able to assure a place for himself in his nation's ongoing process of self-affirmation.

The author's extensive bibliography and his international prestige have undoubtedly assured Lourenço the role in the formation of the discourses of national identity that he clearly desires. In addition, his assertion of an underlying continuity of Portuguese national identity seems relatively easy to accept. As I have noted, the citizens of contemporary Portugal have not had to confront any internal or external challenges to the authority of the nation-state. Lourenço's approach, however, steadfastly refuses to take into account many new factors that have shaped Portuguese national experience over the past two decades. In addition to consigning the consequences of the loss of empire to a merely imaginary plane ("only in terms of the *imaginary* . . . was [Portuguese] *national identity* tied to the existence of the overseas territories" [1988, 12]), Lourenço, with a skillful use of parentheses, acknowledges that Portugal is presently sharing a movement of radical historical and political change with the Western world. Although these changes are neither enumerated nor described, one may assume that he is alluding to Portugal's entry in the European Community as well to the less quantifiable effect that the experience of late-capitalist modernity has had on ontological approaches to defining both individual and national identities.

However, by recognizing the existence of change in an aside and relegating Portugal's similarities with the West to a mere parenthesis, Lourenço makes use of his legislating authority to divert attention from these new factors. In effect, by opting to stress the "exacerbated" qualities of the Portuguese self-image, he is able to deny both the feasibility and the necessity of attempting to identify new perspectivęs in recent discourses on national identity. I would argue that this attitude—the unwillingness or inability to recognize that "the reality of that country, and not the image, is the new frontier to be explored" (Macedo 1990, 106)—represents one of the basic structures of hyperidentity. In this sense, one may conclude that Lourenço's own work provides the reader with an excellent example of the rhetorical structures and the ideological content of the discourse of hyperidentity.

It should be noted that Lourenço is not alone in his view of the Portuguese nation as a coherent entity whose self-image may be described or analyzed. Like him, many scholars have contributed to current debates on the question of Portuguese national identity and his comments deserve to be situated in the wider context of a long literary and intellectual tradition that has defined itself by alternately lamenting the weaknesses or praising the strengths of the Portuguese national character. This tradition, which continues to the present, constitutes a corpus that, in many respects, may be termed the "bibliography of hyperidentity." In a recent article that presents an overview of the question of national identity in contemporary Portuguese literature, Onésimo T. Almeida observes that the national fixation with Portuguese identity has become exacerbated since 1974. In introducing the general thematic unity of this corpus, Almeida agrees with Lourenço's observations regarding the ease with which Portugal ended its five-centuries long policy of colonial expansion. In his view, the most acute national trauma presently suffered by the Portuguese remains grounded in the centuries-old lament that their country's historical contributions to the formation of modern Europe have been overlooked, underestimated, or forgotten (1991, 492).

In addition to citing several novelists, whose work I will treat in the second part of this study, Almeida correctly identifies a general characteristic in the field. Like Eduardo Lourenço, many other highly respected Portuguese literary critics have sought to assume an active role in selecting (and rejecting) the images used to structure the discourses of Portuguese national identity. Almeida explains this tendency in the following terms: "They approach this thematic from a literary standpoint because, only in literature do they find data about something intuited as constitutiı ▾ ı theme worthy that reflection—Portuguese behavior" (495). Here it would appear that Almeida's observation regarding the participation of Portuguese intellectuals in the discourses of identity formation corroborates Jameson's position regarding the importance of literature during the moments when a nation is actively involved in debating the contours of its national identity. It is curious, however, that both Lourenço and Almeida assert that Portugal is not presently involved in such a process; on the contrary, they repeatedly stress that Portugal's image of itself has remained relatively secure.

This apparent contradiction may be resolved in historical terms by examining the role of the Portuguese intellectual over the past two centuries. The tendency for Portuguese literary critics to assume an active role in the debate on national identity draws on a long history of discussion regarding the "fate" and the "mission" of the modern Portuguese nation. Since at least the beginning of the nineteenth century, the theoretical question of national identity has constituted no less than an obsession for the Portuguese cultural elite. With the generation of the romantics, a concern for such issues was often accompanied by concrete interventions in the political sphere aimed at reshaping the material course of the nation. In the years that followed, however, many authors' continued fixation with the problem of national identity attained mythic, rather than practical, proportions. As Boaventura de Sousa Santos has observed, most critiques of the Portuguese national subject originated in the ranks of the country's intellectual elite. At the same time, this group found itself progressively lacking in or denied access to a strong philosophical or scientific tradition:

> The mythic excess of interpretations of Portuguese society is explained, to a great extent, by the prolonged and narrow reproduction of cultural elites with literary backgrounds, who were very reduced in number and almost always distant from the areas of political, educational, or cultural decision making. They tended, thus, to function in a closed circuit, suspended between an unlettered populace, who had nothing to say to them, and a self-convinced political power, who refused to say anything to them. They never had a bourgeoisie or a middle class that tried to "bring them to reality," they could never compare or verify their ideas, nor were they ever held responsible for the eventual social impact of their ideas. (1992, 97–98)

While Sousa Santos sees the intellectual's obsession with the question of national character as resulting from the political and economic marginalization of the nation's cultural elites, he also openly identifies Salazarist Portugal ("almost fifty years of Salazarist censorship" [97]) as the last manifestation of this centuries-long policy of marginalization. In effect, he is of the opinion that a more realistic assessment of Portugal's present situation requires new methods of analysis that only the social sciences can provide. This, in turn, implies that the 25 de Abril created new opportunities for the cultural elite, who would seem to have been "freed" from the obligation of defining the national character in order to create a viable or meaningful space for themselves within a repressive society.[3] In this respect, Lourenço's theory of hyperidentity may be taken as constituting a final response to Salazarist discourse rather than as proposing a new approach to the question of national identity. Taking into account the intellectual's historical obsession with the question of national identity, Lourenço's theory serves as a late example of the intellectual elite's desire to occupy a central role in legislating the images that Portugal holds of itself.

Finally, one must add that Lourenço's theory is put to the service of defending a position that is very common in many current debates on Portuguese national identity. He employs the rhetoric of hyperidentity in order to attribute to the nation an active and unique role in present-day configurations of European identity: "We now face the so-called European challenge, a challenge that, deep down, the Portuguese experience is neither a challenge nor a threat. We are superlative Europeans because we have long been a mediating element in world history" (1990, 117). We are forced to reconsider the two slogans that I mentioned in the introduction to this essay (*orgulhosamente sós* and *a Europa connosco*). While apparently embracing opposing viewpoints, these two slogans actually present very similar perspectives. In an article on the relationship of literature and the rhetoric of the Portuguese fascist state, Ronald Sousa demonstrates how the authors most closely identified with the rhetoric of the Estado Novo cultivated a "glorious-past-glorious-future thematic" that used a mythology of the Discoveries and the empire to link the spiritual to the physical and to subordinate the latter to the former (1985, 132). In the present case, it would appear that critics like Lourenço, while affirming Portugal's new role within Europe, continue to view these two aspects of Portuguese history as the principal constitutive elements of Portuguese national character. Still dominant in the postrevolutionary period, this discourse based on the "uniqueness" of the Portuguese historical situation is now being used as a sort of currency that will help the nation in negotiating a new role for itself in the European Community.

We may conclude, therefore, that Lourenço's theory of hyperidentity continues, for the most part, to make use of the glorified moments, monuments, and texts of a national tradition that dates from the romantic period.

Like him, many intellectuals and critics of Portuguese literature have continued to base their theories on historical analyses of the national situation.[4] As such, they must be viewed as essentially continuist in their strategies, for they have not aimed to challenge or rewrite the "pedagogical" (dominant, historicist, and historicizing) function of the narrative of the national subject. Homi Bhabha characterizes the pedagogical as a dominant or master discourse, against which he situates the "performative," which seeks to renegotiate the "times, terms, and traditions through which we turn our uncertain passing contemporaneity into the signs of history" (1990, 297). Lourenço's theory of hyperidentity, based as it is upon the mythic and utopian qualities of the Portuguese as historically privileged "others," belongs to, and implicitly reinforces, a long tradition of intellectuals striving to participate in the formation of pedagogical discourses of Portuguese national identity.

The Question of National Identity in the Contemporary Portuguese Novel

The problem of reaffirming Portugal's role in the formation of Western Europe is undoubtedly the most common thread in the discourses of national identity that recently have appeared in the ranks of the nation's cultural elite. Moreover, most of these discourses have been grounded on a shared sense of national fragility stemming from a shared sense of Portugal's backwardness vis-à-vis the other nations of Western Europe. By choosing to emphasize Portugal's historical contributions to the formation of modern Europe, these critics have tended to regard the nation's problem in strictly temporal terms. However, as they choose to foreground the nation's glorious past, the question of Portugal's failure to keep up with the pace of European development is handily relegated to the margins of their arguments.

In this section, I will comment briefly on the narrative strategies employed by four well-known authors who have used the novel to respond to contemporary debates on the Portuguese national subject. It is my contention that, while the question of modernity is also central to the thematic of the contemporary Portuguese novel, the "problem" of Portugal's past recently has been posed in much different terms by several of the nation's best-known writers. Most notably, references to Portuguese history (both recent and remote) often appear in a critical light, which bespeaks a lack of confidence in the traditional or pedagogical discourses of identity. In addition, a renewed desire to regard the nation in spatial terms has come to the

fore. As I will demonstrate in my examination of the narrative strategies
employed by José Cardoso Pires, José Saramago, António Lobo Antunes,
and Lídia Jorge, the novel has become the site of the performative or the
supplementary, for it is in this genre that one finds the voices that antago-
nize "the implicit power to generalize, to produce the sociological solid-
ity" (Bhabha 1990, 306).

Both José Cardoso Pires (1925–) and José Saramago (1922–) began to
publish before 1974, during the period of the Estado Novo, and their early
work was marked by a confidence in the material progress of history, typical of the neorealist movement in Portugal. In the postrevolutionary period,
however, their fiction took a new turn, as it began to openly question and
problematize the cultural discourses of the Estado Novo. Cardoso Pires,
whose literary reputation was firmly established at the time of the revolution, is well known as the author of several novels and collections of short
stories that were highly critical of the values and discourses of the fascist
regime. Since 1974, he has published two novels that continue in the same
vein and expand upon his explorations into the workings of contemporary
Portuguese society.

In 1982, Cardoso Pires published the *Balada da Praia dos Cães* (Ballad of Dog's Beach, 1986), a best-selling novel whose appearance inaugu-
rated a new cycle in contemporary Portuguese fiction. The overwhelming
success of this book attests to the novel's renewed vigor and its capacity to
reach a wide reading audience. As Helder Macedo observes:

> The novel *Balada da Praia dos Cães* . . . has had twelve printings in
> Portugal in just over four years, representing around a hundred thousand
> copies. Stylistically, this is a difficult book, and Cardoso Pires is a writer
> who would be considered "highbrow" in an Anglo-Saxon context. Bear-
> ing in mind that Portugal's population is slightly over 10 million and that
> the United States has a population of about 240 million, an American
> novel of a comparable level of sophistication would have to sell 2.4 mil-
> lion copies in hardback to match the performance of this Portuguese best-
> seller. (1990, 104)

I would argue that the interest generated by *Balada da Praia dos Cães* is
due, in part, to the author's explicit borrowing from history in order to
comment, fictionally, on his nation's collective experience. The same may
also be said of José Saramago, whose two best-known novels, *Memorial
do Convento* (1982) and *O Ano da Morte de Ricardo Reis* (1984), have also
gone through more than the equivalent of twelve printings. Although they
pursue very different courses in their critiques of Portuguese society, one

can identify several similarities in the literary projects of José Cardoso Pires and José Saramago, especially in regard to the novels *Balada da Praia dos Cães* and *O Ano da Morte de Ricardo Reis*. In both cases, the authors situate their plots at times that are prior to the revolution in order to seek an understanding of contemporary Portuguese society in light of its recent Salazarist past. At the same time, however, they openly indicate to their readers that their narratives originated in a historical moment that is posterior to the change in governments, thereby creating a double-edged temporal perspective that allows them to effectively expose and deconstruct the symbols and discourses that were closely associated with the political ideology of Salazar's Estado Novo.

In *Balada da Praia dos Cães*, the author reworks the format of the traditional detective novel in order to recreate the climate of terror that was collectively experienced by the nation during the some of the most repressive years of Salazar's *Estado Novo*. Choosing to recount the motivations behind a seemingly political crime that captured the public's imagination in the spring of 1960, Cardoso Pires presents a complex meditation on the apparatus of state terror and succeeds in evoking the collective paranoia that resulted from the isolation imposed on the nation. Although it turns out that the crime depicted in the novel was not directly tied to political motivations, its victim is metaphorically associated with the regime and its leaders, all of whom, like the victim himself, were intent on hiding their weakness and impotence behind a facade of control and domination.

As was the case in his earlier novel, *Memorial do Convento,* Saramago in *O Ano da Morte de Ricardo Reis* questions the premises of conventional historiography by demonstrating the relativity of the discourses that have traditionally been used to create narratives of the national subject. In *O Ano da Morte de Ricardo Reis*, Saramago's propensity to insert fictional plots and fantastic characters in a historical framework results in the selection of a protagonist who is drawn from the national literary tradition; Ricardo Reis, one of the poet Fernando Pessoa's heteronyms, is returned to Lisbon in January of 1936, a month and a half after his creator's death. In what appears to be an exercise in the historical contextualization of Pessoa's work, Saramago uses this premise to explore the events in a key year in the consolidation of Salazar's political power. Moving between the worlds of the bourgeoisie and the working classes of the Portuguese capital, Reis comes face to face with such issues as widespread hunger, emigration, and inadequate health care.

In both novels, the authors return to the years of the dictatorship and expand upon the historical specificity of their fictional projects by incorporating a wide variety of documentary sources. Cardoso Pires opens his novel with a reference to an advertisement for TAP, the Portuguese National Airline, that proclaims the country to be "Europe's Best Kept Secret." At other points in his narrative, he includes police reports and witnesses' depositions, as well as summarizing the contents of contemporary newspaper reports on the crime. In a similar vein, Ricardo Reis's own poetry works its way into Saramago's text, as do myriad press reports from throughout Europe that are regularly filtered through the protagonist's thoughts.

This appropriation of sources extrinsic to the novels' plots, most importantly those arising in the official press, helps to clarify both the openly propagandistic character and the repressive nature of these discourses. As the characters are denied access to a balanced view of their national situation, it becomes progressively clear that their government is striving to limit or to "sanitize" its citizens' universe. This technique is reminiscent, of course, of Benedict Anderson's observations concerning the importance (and the possible dangers) of the "print media" in the establishment of a sense of national community. At the same time, the incorporation of daily news reports serves to thicken the novelistic portrayal of time and space, for the reader is reminded of events that are taking place outside Lisbon— in the provinces, in Spain, in Europe, or in the colonies. This second element, in conjunction with the historical distance afforded the reader of these novels, allows for a revisionist view of Portuguese society and demonstrates that the characters' lived reality had little or nothing in common with the official versions that the Estado Novo sought to impose upon its citizens.

While these and other similar historical novels are certainly oriented toward supplementing the historical information so often included in the pedagogical discourses of Portuguese national identity, they refrain from an analysis of the present conditions of postrevolutionary Portugal. While the present exists as an implicit point of reference, the challenges currently facing the nation cannot easily be addressed in such novelistic revisitations of the Salazarist past as *Balada da Praia dos Cães* or *O Ano da Morte de Ricardo Reis*. In contrast, António Lobo Antunes (1942–) and Lídia Jorge (1946–) belong to a generation that came of age during the years of the colonial wars and began their careers as writers after the revolution with the publication of a series of novels that refer directly to the turbulent events of the early 1970s. In their work, one encounters a more complex problematization of the before-after dialectic that marks much of Pires's and Saramago's fiction. As they make use of radically decentered narrative voices in which Portugal's past images of itself overflow into contemporary constructions of the national subject, Antunes and Jorge explore the new spatial configurations of the nation and comment ironically on

Portugal's postrevolutionary desire to be recognized among the developed nations of Western Europe.

While a metaphoric return to the land, patent in Portugal's loss of its African colonies, is registered in António Lobo Antunes's *Os Cus de Judas* (1978) and in Lídia Jorge's *A Costa dos Murmúrios* (1988), an almost simultaneous departure from the limits of the country's physical borders is alluded to in *O Cais das Merendas*, published by Jorge in 1982. Although the tendencies of reterritorialization and deterritorialization (Santos 1992, 101) are apparently contradictory, I believe that the spatial metaphors implicit in these novels register a common desire to comment on the abrupt changes and discontinuities that have characterized recent Portuguese national experience.

In *Os Cus de Judas* and *A Costa dos Murmúrios*, the question of national reterritorialization is addressed through the problematic of the protagonists' divided sense of spatial relationships. In both novels, competing images of national space are presented by means of a similar narrative technique—that of a first-person narrator who, while physically situated in Portugal, reveals the imaginary pull still exercised by the colonial spaces in Africa (Angola and Mozambique, respectively). These protagonists share a dual apprehension of space as they are consistently divided between the lived and the imagined. This is not to say, however, that the narrators maintain similar views as to the meaning of this former colonial space which, at the time of narration, can only exist in the speaker's memory or imagination.

The protagonist of *Os Cus de Judas*, a soldier returned from military service in Angola, is unable to free himself of his memories associated with the war. The story he has to tell is an unqualified denunciation of the events of that war and yet his inability to maintain an articulate coherency with his present surroundings reveals an extremely schizophrenic sense of spatial relations. This protagonist's narrative act does not result from choice; rather, its telling is manifested as an unavoidable necessity. Equally important is the fact that no one has wanted to hear this story and that its teller has thus been forced to seek out interlocutors in the late hours of barroom conversation. These elements would seem to indicate that the protagonist's attempts to return to the *pátria* have been unsuccessful, and the particular violence with which the two narrative spaces clash may be interpreted as metaphoric references to the traumas of the colonial wars and of the abrupt shock of repatriation suffered by many in the years immediately following decolonization.

Published ten years after *Os Cus de Judas*, Lídia Jorge's *A Costa dos Murmúrios* presents radically different reasons for revisiting the colonial spaces of prerevolutionary Portugal. Although the structure and thematic of this novel are somewhat reminiscent of Lobo Antunes's, Eva Lopo, the narrator of Lídia Jorge's novel, *chooses* to narrate the experience of the war in Mozambique, consciously returning to a place described as "a place that grows darker week by week, day by day, with the velocity of the years" (1988, 41). As the protagonist seeks to reorganize and to reinterpret the information communicated in the short, third-person narrative entitled "Os Gafanhotos," Eva Lopo demonstrates that she has succeeded in separating the past from the present and, as such, the novel's overall narrative structure registers the protagonist's acquisition of a new sense of space.

While revealing atrocities similar to those witnessed by Lobo Antunes's protagonist, *A Costa dos Murmúrios* juxtaposes past colonial space with an ironic awareness that this past has been effectively reduced to a series of murmurs. Thus, the conscious use of a divided narrative space speaks to the fact that the protagonist's apprehension of her past has been definitively changed by her present experience. A period of more than ten years has gone by since the events recollected by Eva Lopo occurred and an even vaster psychological distance separates the two narrative spaces of the novel. This distance is communicated, above all, through Eva's attempts to contextualize her story in terms of a wider European experience through references to contemporaneous events, such as the war in Vietnam and the Prague Spring of 1968. In this manner, the reader is treated to a perspective on Portugal's colonial past that is fundamentally rooted in the knowledge that national experience must be understood in light of the present, that is, as related to the complicated interplay of international forces that characterize the contemporary global community.

Finally, an important difference in Lobo Antunes's and Lídia Jorge's narrative approaches to the question of repatriation lies in the gender identifications of their respective protagonists. While both make use of psychologically divided first-person narrators, Lobo Antunes's male protagonist is both literally and figuratively repressed and he is unable to come to terms with the traumatic events of his past. When read as a commentary on the experience of the national collective, his narrative affords an ironic view of the dysfunctional elements associated with the "deep horizontal comradeship" that Benedict Anderson has identified as central to constructions of national consciousness (1983, 16). In contrast, Lídia Jorge's novel must be taken as a sort of narrative response to the patterns of homosocial male bonding that are relentlessly depicted in Lobo Antunes's fiction. While focusing thematically on the same historical events, Jorge's narrative representation of the colonial wars is marked by an acute awareness of the long-standing exclusion of the feminine from the historical events that ground pedagogical discourses of Portuguese national identity. Thus, while registering Portugal's awakening to the realization that its present position in the world has dramatically changed, this novel also is able to incorporate perspectives that previously had been excluded from descriptions of the national character. By voicing a concern that is transnational—that of the suppression of female perspectives in the construction of narratives of national identity—Jorge widens the scope of the debate and introduces an aspect that is not particular to the Portuguese situation. Implicitly posing the question of who speaks for the nation, Jorge recognizes that Portugal, like most modern nations, is comprised of a variety of collective entities or groups.

Eva Lopo's war narrative includes implicit references to new cultural identifications that began to be voiced in Portugal in the years since 1974, and it presents a picture of Portuguese national identity that is not based on stressing the historical uniqueness of Portuguese national experience. In Jorge's earlier novel, *O Cais das Merendas,* even more explicit recourse is made to an image of Portugal as a nation that is no longer able to believe in or depend on an image of itself as "unique" among European nations. When Jorge, in the title of the novel, ironically substitutes Portugal's traditional image as a *jardim à beira mar plantado* with that of a seaside picnic zone, she alludes to the new cultural forces of internationalization that have come to characterize Portuguese national experience. In an Algarve mostly populated by foreign tourists, the story of a young girl's suicide is told through the use of a narrative technique that draws together bits and pieces of the conversations, memories, and internal monologues of a group of working-class Portuguese. However, as they inhabit a world increasingly characterized by such transnational cultural institutions as tourism, emigration, television, and the movies, these characters' lives are shaped, for better or worse, by their deep fascination with European and American popular culture. Taken to its extreme, this fascination eventually results in a collective loss of memory on the part of the novel's characters.

This symbolic loss of cultural memory can once again be attributed to the character's divided sense of space, for I believe that this scene evokes the extremes that can result when a nation's citizens lose their traditional ties to the community. Indeed, *O Cais das Merendas* seems to pose a new problematic of national space by recognizing and drawing attention to the fact that contemporary Portugal constitutes an extremely contradictory and heterogeneous space where premodernity, modernity, and postmodernity can easily coexist and often overlap. It is in this sense that, although *O Cais das Merendas*, in contrast with *Os Cus de Judas* and *A Costa dos Murmúrios*, does not rely upon the juxtaposition of two geographically distinct places, the characters' struggle with an ongoing process of social and economic deterritorialization attests to a similar, if not identical, process of cultural renegotiation that can be traced to Portugal's recent demographic and geographic ruptures.

Conclusion: "Europe is with us"

To conclude this necessarily brief overview of the contemporary Portuguese novel and its renewed importance in the formation of discourses of national identity, I would like to return, once more, to Eduardo Lourenço's description of the Portuguese as suffering from a "hyperidentity crisis." In light of the changing metaphors of time and space contained in the novels under discussion, I believe that it is safe to say that many contemporary novelists in Portugal are presently involved in a heated debate in regard to Portuguese national identity, implicitly asking the question of what it means to be Portuguese and exploring how this "condition" should be represented in their fiction. At the same time, however, they reject the sensibility of continuing to subscribe to any historical, mythic, or utopian discourse of identity similar to that propounded by Eduardo Lourenço. In fact, the novels that I have mentioned in this study seem to contradict Lourenço's assertion that Portugal's image of itself has not changed in the years since the revolution, and one may conclude that their various questionings of the concept of hyperidentity are tantamount to a desire to recognize and call attention to the complex process of cultural renegotiation currently taking place in Portugal.

As the authors propose various ways of reconciling the national allegory with modernist or postmodernist narrative strategies, their work serves to expose the complex realities that underlie the first- and third-world dichotomies employed by Fredric Jameson in his observations regarding the role of the national allegory in third-world literary practice. In effect, a national self-image based on an exclusively "colonialist" or "colonized" historical experience is particularly problematic in the Portuguese case. In addition, the act of proclaiming that "Europe is with us" does not necessarily grant to all the citizens of Portugal the status and privileges implicit in this affirmation. As I have shown, the contemporary Portuguese novel often voices specific subject positions that must be taken as representative of groups existing within contemporary Portuguese society rather than of the "nation" as a whole. Speaking either of (or to) those who directly experienced the repression of the Estado Novo, those who lived or fought in Africa, or those who had previously been denied an active role in the project of defining Portuguese national identity, this body of writing registers a heterogeneity of spaces and positions that must be taken into account in future attempts to characterize Portuguese national experience in the late-twentieth century. It is to these spaces and perspectives that we must look when seeking to evaluate the changing contours of Portuguese identity.

Notes

1. For an overview of the number and variety of titles published before 1987, see Chilcote 1987.

2. Best known for his astute philosophical observations on works of the poet Fernando Pessoa and the poets of the neorealist group, Lourenço, after the revolution, began to publish analyses of contemporary Portuguese society with great frequency in the daily and weekly press. In 1978, he published *O Labirinto da Saudade*, a volume of essays subtitled, in English translation, "A Mythic Psychoanalysis of the Portuguese Destiny." It has since come to be considered a classic text on the question of Portuguese national identity. I have taken the two essays that I cite in the following pages from his more recent collection, *Nós e a Europa ou As Duas Razões*. A translation of the second of these essays, "Portugal-Identidade e Imagem," also appeared as the conclusion to *Portugal: Ancient Country, Young Democracy* (Kenneth Maxwell and Michael H. Haltzel, eds.) under the title "Portugal's Identity." When citing this essay, I have relied on the editors' translated version; the translations of passages from "Identidade e Memória—O Caso Português" are my own.

3. See Ribeiro 1993. He looks specifically at the intervention of Portuguese literary figures in politics during the period 25 April 1974–25 November 1975. He concludes that the relation of literature to Portuguese society was significantly redefined by many writers who sought to avoid both populist and paternalistic approaches to the question of national identity, thereby contributing to a new, more "critical" concept of intellectual "responsibility" (511).

4. Among the many literary critics who have written on the subject, the most notable are probably António José Saraiva and António Quadros. In *A Cultura em Portugal: Teoria e História*, Saraiva acknowledges the risk of "arbitrary impressionism" (1981, 81) in his task of describing the Portuguese cultural personality; he goes on, however, to conclude that his nation's historical comportment demonstrates "a certain liberty in relation to cultural frontiers, a certain promiscuity between Self and Other, a certain lack of cultural prejudice, [and] the absence of the sense of superiority that generally characterizes the peoples of the Western world." Quadros's theories based on the concept of the *paideia*, which he sees as the "civilizing and civilizational potential [*devir*] of a community" (1992, 16), have most recently been summarized in a collection of essays published in 1992, under the title *Memórias das Origens, Saudades do Futuro*.

References

Ahmad, Aijaz. 1992. *In Theory: Classes, Nations, Literatures*. London and New York: Verso.

Almeida, Onésimo Teotónio. 1991. "A Questão da Identidade Nacional na Escrita Portuguesa Contemporânea." *Hispania* 74:492–500.

186 ELLEN SAPEGA

Anderson, Benedict. 1983. *Imagined Communities: Reflections on the Origin and Spread of Nationalism*. London and New York: Verso.

Antunes, António Lobo. 1979. *Os Cus de Judas*. Lisboa: Dom Quixote. Translated by Elizabeth Lowe under the title *South of Nowhere* (New York: Random House, 1983).

Bhabha, Homi K. 1990. "Dissemination." In *Nation and Narration*, edited by Homi K. Bhabha, 291–322. London and New York: Routledge.

Chilcote, Ronald H. 1987. *The Portuguese Revolution of 25 April 1974: Annotated bibliography on the Antecedents and Aftermath*. Coimbra: Centro de Documentação 25 de Abril—Universidade de Coimbra.

Jameson, Fredric. 1986. "Third-World Literature in the Era of Multi-National Capitalism." *Social Text* 15:65–88.

Jorge, Lídia. 1988. *A Costa dos Murmúrios*. Lisboa: Dom Quixote.

———. 1992. *O Cais das Merendas*. Lisboa: Europa-América.

Lourenço, Eduardo. 1978. *O Labirinto da Saudade*. Lisboa: Dom Quixote.

———. 1988. *Nós e a Europa ou As Duas Razões*. Lisboa: Imprensa Nacional—Casa da Moeda.

———. 1990. "Portugal's Identity." In *Portugal: Ancient Country, Young Democracy*, edited by Kenneth Maxwell and Michael H. Haltzel, 113–18. Washington D.C.: The Wilson Center Press.

Macedo, Helder. 1990. "Portuguese Culture Today." In *Portugal: Ancient Country, Young Democracy*, edited by Kenneth Maxwell and Michael H. Haltzel, 101–6. Washington, D.C.: The Wilson Center Press.

Pires, José Cardoso. 1982. *Balada da Praia dos Cães*. Lisboa: O Jornal. Translated by Mary Fitton under the title *Ballad of Dog's Beach* (London: J. M. Dent & Sons, 1986).

Quadros, António. 1992. *Memórias das Origens, Saudades do Futuro*. Lisboa: Europa-América.

Ribeiro, António Sousa. 1993. "Configurações do Campo Intelectual Português no Pós-25 de Abril: O Campo Literário." In *Portugal: Um Retrato Singular*, edited by Boaventura de Sousa Santos, 483–512. Porto: Afrontamento.

Santos, Boaventura de Sousa. 1992. "11/92 (Onze Teses por Razão de Mais uma Descoberta de Portugal)." *Luso-Brazilian Review* 29, no. 1: 97–113.

Saraiva, António José. 1981. *A Cultura em Portugal: Teoria e História*. Lisboa: Bertrand.

Saramago, José. 1982. *Memorial do Convento*. Lisboa: Caminho. Translated by Giovanni Pontiero under the title *Baltasar and Blimunda* (San Diego: Harcourt, 1987).

———. 1984. *O Ano da Morte de Ricardo Reis*. Lisboa: Caminho. Translated by Giovanni Pontiero under the title *The Year of the Death of Ricardo Reis* (San Diego: Harcourt, 1991).

Sousa, Ronald. 1985. "Literature and Portuguese Fascism: The Face of the Salazarist State, Preceded by Two Pre-Faces." In *Fascismo y experiencia literaria : reflexiones para una recanonización*, edited by Hernán Vidal, 95–141. Minneapolis, Minn.: Society for the Study of Contemporary Hispanic and Lusophone Revolutionary Literatures.

Tomlinson, John. 1991. *Cultural Imperialism*. Baltimore: Johns Hopkins University Press.

Love and Imagination among the Ruins of Empire: António Lobo Antunes's *Os Cus de Judas* and *O Fado Alexandrino*

PHYLLIS PERES

Reconstructing Portugal: Empire and Postempire

English national identity, in other words, cannot be understood outside of England's colonial dependencies. Jamaica, a small island in the Caribbean, may never have been seen by the majority of the English population yet it occupied a place in their imaginary. Their ethnic identity as *English* was rooted in a series of assumptions about others.

—Catherine Hall

It cannot be said of the Portuguese what Nietzsche said of the Germans (in a query potentially extensible to several other peoples), that they were a people that spent their lives asking themselves "What does being a German mean?" All Portuguese are, or feel themselves to be, so to speak, "Hyper-Portuguese."

—Eduardo Lourenço

This essay on love and imagination among the ruins of empire is put forth as both an interpolative and interpellative exercise on constructs of Portuguese identity in two texts by António Lobo Antunes. By interpolative, I mean the manner in which one reads to alter and corrupt. Interpellative, likewise, is understood as interruptive and questioning, a reading back, so to speak, of the discursive constructions and reconstructions of empire and postempire in contemporary Portuguese fiction.[1]

I frame the first part of this interpolative/interpellative reading with two provocative quotes, the first from Catherine Hall's essay on Baptist

missionary stories.[2] Hall's rather painstaking text is based not on the reconstitution of Englishness, but rather on the disclosure of what is hidden
in the construction of white English ethnicity—namely, that national identity is always recognized in relation to others. In the historically specific
conditions of England in the 1830s and 1840s, certain colonizing subjects
empowered themselves as narrators with the authority to speak for others.
As Hall succinctly writes, those others, as a result, "were partially silenced"
(1992, 245).

    As I read Hall's text, I invariably turned to the question of what I have
elsewhere described as "the crisis of the Portuguese master narrative."[3]
This, of course, was unavoidable, as was the appearance of nineteenth-
century missionary stories in an essay ostensibly about contemporary Portuguese fiction. If Hall is engaged in a project of disclosure, that project is
above all antithetical to the closuring of national identity set off against
peripheries and others. It is a project of revealing a specific privileged subjectivity that actually obscured more than closed, that really oppressed and
silenced differences in the name of giving them voice. That Hall's project
of disclosure resonates against the current remappings and questionings of
national identities in Europe speaks directly to the present Portuguese crisis of national identity.

    It is in this interpolated dialogue between readings of nineteenth-cen-
tury missionary stories and two texts by António Lobo Antunes that the
interpellative sense of this present essay begins to take shape, particularly
within the positioning of national subject articulated in Eduardo Lourenço's
1990 text on Portuguese national identity.[4] Lourenço's essay is breathtaking in the leaps of fate —indeed, a true *fado* —that it takes through a gloss-
ing of Portuguese national identity across the centuries. Lourenço spurns
an Iberian identity not on the basis of linguistic, religious or cultural differences, but rather through the specific version of a *"colonial adventure"*
(italics added), which although "parallel to that of Spain, left us nevertheless with a different memory thereof, and a different identity" (1990, 114).

    Undoubtedly, this defense of Portuguese identity only underscores the
contestability of national subjectivity, so that, as Hall convincingly argues,
"Portugueseness" just like "Englishness" is not a category simply bestowed
with meaning, but discursively constructed and reconstructed within historically specific conditions. These discursive reconstructions are precisely
what interest Lourenço; the imaginations of nation, of a Portugal both small
and colonizing.

    The paradoxes of what Lourenço terms the "colonial adventure" are
well documented and too numerous to detail in the confines of this essay.[5]

What is essential here, however, is his own reelaboration of nation, an imagining of postimperial space still imbued with hyperidentity. In what can only be described as the quickest (post)colonial recovery on record, Lourenço contends that since the independence of Angola and Mozambique, "politically conscious Portuguese may not have been happy with the disastrous economic situation of their former colonies (and, paradoxically, this means that we think of them now more than we used to), but they are fully resigned to the end of the imperial adventure and even feel somewhat relieved" (1990, 117). The "disastrous economic situation" is not, of course, given human dimensions, so that the "them" that "we" think about is so "othered" as to refer only to former colonies, not even to former colonized subjects.

In Lourenço's de-problematized version of postcoloniality, Portugal's relief from the adventure of empire has actually rebestowed some meaning and truth to Portugal's always doubled identity, that of a "nonhegemonic European people and a people of widespread global dispersion" (117). Thus, Lourenço can argue that if the use of colonial ideology got out of hand over the centuries, it really was always nonhegemonic in nature, since the "practical, lived ecumenism" of the rural Portuguese people at home in the tropics always mediated the excesses of colonialism. Indeed, it is precisely this essential Portuguese subject positioning, that of a "mediating, European people with a universal calling," that Lourenço reconstructs in an age of what he refers to as that of the "European challenge" or the dilemma of all Western peoples whose "imagination is gradually [being] unified" (118). Portuguese hyperidentity is here willfully positioned as "superlative" Europeans, as if to make mockery in the face of the current anecdote that Europe is the last continent to be discovered by Portugal. It is an imagining of postcoloniality, indeed a conjecturing of postnational identity among the ruins of empire. Lourenço's reconstruction, moreover, ultimately plays off the imagined center of Portuguese identity, always based on exaltations of difference.

In his recent article on Lobo Antunes, Luís Madureira critiques what he terms the "persisting seductiveness of the empire for contemporary Portuguese (historiographic) discourses" (1995, 19). Madureira pays special attention to how these postmodern discourses on difference reconstruct a common (post)colonizing ground that is quintessentially European—an admission, not necessarily by open invitation, into the dining room of the (post)imperial family.[6] In these present disseminations of Portuguese identity, Europe, as Madureira stresses, "figures still as the agent of human history, inseminating the world's tropical places with meaning and historicity" (21). It is precisely this privileged positioning, this reconstruction of (post)national agency that Lourenço poses as the center of a Portuguese hyperidentity that has remained unchanged during the centuries of maritime and colonial adventure.

In this sense, one might propose—and not necessarily in jest—that the motto of Portuguese national positionality has always been and remains Nothing Adventured Nothing Gained, though, of course, that measure of gain has never been made adequately accountable in human terms. Ultimately, what Lourenço deems a European "challenge" is, of course, actually a European "crisis" of all possible imaginations of space. Paradoxically, Lourenço is correct, inasmuch as the Portuguese are, indeed, superlative players in this hypercrisis. However, they finally get to sit down and eat at the European family dinner table—albeit as second cousins twice removed—only to find that the table has already been cleared. The question now, of course, in these terms, is that of the next sitting: who gets served, who does the serving and, most important, what (or who, as the case should be) gets eaten.

Into this crisis of imaginations of space and the reconstructions thereof, I would interpolate as a means of interpellation, one more European voice—that of Michel Foucault's historical tracing of space in his "Of Other Spaces." There is, perhaps, no better way to end this first section of my essay than with a bridge to the next and the seductive eloquence of Eurocentricity, so elegantly reconstructed by Foucault:

> [A]nd if we think, after all, that the boat is a floating piece of space, a place without a place, that exists by itself, that it is closed in on itself and at the same time is given over to the infinity of the sea and that, from port to port, from tack to tack, from brothel to brothel, it goes as far as the colonies in search of the most precious treasures they conceal in their gardens, you will understand why the boat has not only been for our civilization, from the sixteenth century until the present, the great instrument of economic development . . . but has been simultaneously the greatest reserve of the imagination. The ship is the heterotopia *par excellence*. In civilizations without boats, dreams dry up, espionage takes the place of adventure, and the police take the place of pirates. (1986, 27)[7]

Os Cus de Judas: And the Rest Is Silence

> When I embarked for Angola, on a ship full of troops, finally to become a man, my tribe, grateful to the government for giving me the opportu-

nity for metamorphosis, appeared en masse at the docks, consenting, in a transport of patriotic fervor, to be elbowed by a restless crowd that came there impotently to witness its own death.

—Lobo Antunes

Everywhere in the world where we drop anchor, we announce our adventurous presence with Manueline standards and empty preserves cans. I have always thought that we Portuguese should erect a monument to spit in—a spit-bust, a spit-marshal, a spit-poet, a spit-tomb of the unknown soldier, a spit-equestrian—something in honor of the perfect Portuguese male who boasts of his most recent fornication and then spits.

—Lobo Antunes

Foucault's memorial to European colonialism—"in civilizations without boats, dreams dry up"—resonates against the crisis of European imaginations of space, an attempted remapping, so to speak, of territories that were really always contested. Eduardo Lourenço's reconstruction of Portuguese identity is no less a positing of Portugal as a boat, a reserve of the imagination upon which the nation is continually regenerated through centuries of crisis. Reasonably, however, one might argue with Foucault that the expansionist motif goes hand in hand with the imaginary topoi well before the sixteenth century, should we care to take *The Odyssey*, for example, as an instance of the aesthetic of colonial traveling.

What is essential here, however, is the present crisis of Portuguese space and, in particular, its discursive imaginings. Of course, it might easily be conjectured that there has always been a Portuguese discursive crisis. *Os Lusíadas* came wrapped in critical controversy, but remains the most resilient articulation of the master narration of the nation circa the age of discoveries. However, if the epic, as the discourse of collectivity, glorified the divinely chosen Portuguese race, as well as the violence of Counter Reformation empire-building, then the *Peregrinaçam* held up the mirror of the encountered others to the Portuguese heroic image and reflected back "devils in the flesh."[8] Fernão Mendes Pinto's narrative, long misread as another tale of expansionist and Counter Reformation adventure, ultimately trumps the venture with the view of the Portuguese as the other, an imperial version, so to speak, of the empire writing back.

Strangely, the present crisis is both radically different and the same. The epistemological crisis, not thrust upon but eagerly cultivated by the Portuguese (and, of course, European) imagination in the age of Camões and Mendes Pinto, was, above all, a crisis of (imaginable) space.[9] The discursive resolutions (always imaginary, always ideological) of historiography and fiction were not of accommodated space—for, to quote Fredric Jameson, "The only way through a crisis of space is to create a new space" (Stephenson 1988, 18)—but rather of appropriated space. Of course, these five hundred years of spatial cannibalism are also marked by continuing crises: the loss of independence, the loss of king, the loss of Brazil, the loss of a transcontinental *mapa cor-de-rosa,* the loss of monarchy, the loss of republic, the loss of India, the loss of Africa. Until the present, however, the imaginary resolutions had found their bases in discursive regenerations of Portuguese imperialism that reconstructed a gloried moment of discovery, that after all these centuries was just that, a moment.[10]

The present crisis is, above all, a crisis of space, whether that of political space, economic space, transnational space, geographical space, or, of course, the imaginations of space. The creative subject of Portuguese modernism, however much fueled by the European consumption of an imagined cultural primitive, eventually set off to sea. Destination: Africa. Not just any Africa, but a white man's Africa, the rediscovered colonial space of the exoticized imaginary. The de-centered subject of Portuguese postmodernism—still Portugal itself—also casts off on a *jangada,* that reconstructed reserve of imagination, floating in the Atlantic, lost at sea, so to speak.[11] Perhaps the text par excellence of Portugal's European challenge is the Amoreiras shopping center in downtown Lisbon, the megastructure of ex-centricity, of loss of national agency in transnational, postimperial Europe.

During the protracted liberation wars in Angola, Mozambique, and Guinea-Bissau, the Portuguese struggle to maintain appropriated space was illustrated by the placard placed in buses, trains and billboards. Superimposed on a map of Europe were maps of the Portuguese "territories," as they were known (keep in mind that Angola alone is fourteen times the size of Portugal), accompanied by the slogan: *As verdadeiras dimensões de Portugal.*[12] The map of postcolonial Portugal is still being drawn amid the crisis of national space. For the subject of Portuguese fiction of the postempire, the crisis becomes one of not hyperidentity, but rather of hypersubjectivity—the inability to be situated in postcolonial space, or to even recognize that space as somehow Portuguese. And in the particular relation of national space, identity, and subjectivity, the crisis of narrative positioning and agency is nowhere else more felt in such profusion than in two narratives by António Lobo Antunes, *Os Cus de Judas* (1979), translated into English as *South of Nowhere* (1983) and *Fado Alexandrino* (1983), published in English with the same title in 1990.

As I began my interpolative reading of Lobo Antunes, I was struck by the lack of critical reception of his narratives. This relative critical silence toward an author whose texts have enjoyed multiple printings in Portugal can only lead one to ponder why, an endeavor, however, which I will not engage in at the present. I would only conjecture that, at least in the two works in question, and certainly in *As Naus* (1988), Lobo Antunes constructs the Portuguese postcolonial adventure, and that in so doing plays against the reconjuring grain of centered national identity and ethos, even amid the ruins of empire. More importantly, in the discursive construction of postimperial adventure (and of course, I could have easily have written "misadventure"), Lobo Antunes reimagines, in true Manueline style, no less, the dangers of colonial enterprise, only here without the saving grace of practical ecumenicism.

Elizabeth Lowe's translation of *Os Cus de Judas* into *South of Nowhere* no doubt reflects the pitfalls of translation, as the English title lacks the resonance of the original. Yes, *Os cus de Judas* does signify "south of nowhere," but Lowe's obviously difficult task was to similarly evoke the Christian and anatomical soundings of the original Portuguese expression. The unfortunate resolution, however, was to totally embrace the geophysical unpositivity of the original title and to enforce a reading that identifies the Gago Coutinho Outpost, three hundred kilometers to the south of Luso, as the respective south and nowhere of the title. Even as a geophysical option the English title choice ignores that in the original Gago Coutinho is described as "este cu de Judas de pó vermelho e de areia" (Antunes 1983b, 48–49), leaving open the possibility of other *cus de Judas* as well.

The English title, however, does capture one significant reading of the Portuguese original—*os cus de Judas* as the end of the line, an image that resounds against the risks of the medieval maritime enterprise and the perceived dangers of sailing off the edge of the world. This image is purposefully cultivated, since if Lobo Antunes is engaged in imaginings of end of empire, this discursive construction evokes the empire's beginnings. However, the first quote from *South of Nowhere* that begins this section of my essay narrates a gathering of the Portuguese tribe—so reminiscent of the gathering in *Os Lusíadas*, as the nation sailed off from the banks of the Tejo in Belém to find its imperial identity—that reflects the seeming unraveling of colonial imagination. Here the crowd is not witnessing the heroic birth of nationhood, however tempered by the famous diatribe of Camões' "old man of Restelo," but rather, its own death. This is not the epic passage from nation to nationhood, but rather the failed rites of a decadent imagining of empire and manhood that leave impotent both nation and narrator.

Os Cus de Judas assumes the form of a first-person narration, an associative discourse that begins in a Lisbon bar and follows the events of a one-night stand between an ex-army doctor and a woman whose voice never appears in the narrative.[13] Her silence, indeed her unnaming, sets off the narrative as one of seeming seduction, a repeated bit of oral history told to a woman who is most likely one of a series of women on one of a series of nights. Luís Madureira emphasizes, however, that this continual retelling of the story—a sabotaging of textual closure reinforced by the seeming interpolations of orality and dialogue—is countered by the layout of the twenty-three lettered chapters which he describes as being as "self-contained as the drawers of an archive, as static as pictures at an exhibition" (1995, 9).[14]

Madureira further describes *Os Cus de Judas* as a "traveling travel narrative" marked by displacement. Here, however, the displacement is not dispersion, and while the alphabetical chapters arrange the narrative sections like so many static museum pieces, the artificial order is ultimately that of the breakdown of imagination. These are the ABCs of ex-centricity, the postcolonial epic deconstruction of empire in which reinvention takes the place of imagination. The reserve of imagination has been drained; the nation-boat has lost its moorings (both in the physical and spiritual senses) and is beached in the space of postempire (although it imagines itself to be running on empty).

As postcolonial epic, the narrative loses its sense of shared meaning in a community that, in effect, has witnessed its own death by colonialism. The fitting monument to that death (and here I refer to the second quote which begins this section) is one dedicated to the oral ejaculations of Portuguese homoeroticism—the boasts of conquests and fornications, in other words, the colonial adventure par excellence. In this sense, *Os Cus de Judas* is the impotence of travel narrative, the failure to seduce and excite the European imagination among the ruins of empire. The climax of the narration, both sexual and textual, is not really, as Luís Madureira sees it, a possible anticlimax. Rather, it is a nonclimax; not orgasm, not turning point, not rhetorical forcefulness, not community. There is no narrative revelation here, no astonishing disclosure, no enlightenment made possible through travel.

Thus the narrator recounts his travel to Africa, through the "unimaginable landscape in Angola," where the enemy is invisible, to fight a "hallucinatory war" (Antunes 1983b, 23, 27). His reconstruction of the other is no more than an elaboration of European inventions of Africanness, played out against the repetition of jazz motifs, which, as Luís Madureira points out, underscores the presupposition that "to listen to jazz is to have already glimpsed the African" (1995, 27). On arrival in Luanda, the doctor compares the expression of the blacks with that of John Coltrane, "eyes turned inward as he blew sweet bitterness into the saxophone, drunken angel"

(Antunes 1983b, 15). While he feels himself to be "the melancholy heir of an old awkward and dying country, of a decaying Europe," the Luchazi tribesmen confront him with an "inexhaustible vitality [he] had first sensed years before, in the Promethean solos of Louis Armstrong" (35–36). In Gago Coutinho, the African soldiers in the colonial army speak a language that the narrator cannot comprehend, but in which he "heard Charlie Parker's swing" (120). And finally, back in Lisbon, as he reinvents his African travels, there is the possibility of "sudden proud free laughter of the Luchazis sounding like Dizzy Gillespie's trumpet" (147).

The return to Lisbon is not an end to the travel narrative, but rather, a continuation of journey through invented space:

> . . . Lisbon, understand, is an amusement park, a traveling circus set up beside a river, an invention of tiles that repeat each other, approach and recede, their indecisive colors paling in rectangles on the sidewalks. No, seriously, we live in a land that does not exist, it is absolutely useless to look for it on maps because it does not exist, it is only an eye, a name, not our country. Lisbon begins to take shape, believe me, only from a distance, to acquire depth and vitality. (77)

Lisbon here is the invention of colonial space, an imaginary land that only acquires meaning and vision from a distance. The impossibility of narrative closure is the impotence of narration, the failure of narrative agency to partake in a postimperial reinvention of nation.

Thus, the silence of the woman—who, as Luís Madureira so correctly asserts, is unoccupied territory "who acquires meaning insofar as she is written, troped, penetrated" (1995, 22)—is the failure of Manueline resonance. I would amend that the troping is more the interpolative embellishment to the impotent narration whose meaning cannot be shared and can only be matched by the sterility of silence. Her voice is not reproduced as there is no impregnation, only penetration that is not interpenetration.

Luís Madureira reads *Os Cus de Judas* as the dis/closure of gendered colonial space with its substitution of colonial impregnation as colonial sodomy: "'Os cus de Judas' are, in effect, self-referential toponyms. They are meant to reflect (?) not an endearing fiction but the self-destructive 'narcissism' of Portugal's metaphoric (and constitutional) marriage to its colonies" (1995, 25). What Madureira misreads, however, is that Portugal is married to its colonies, most particularly in the case of Africa. Portuguese hyperidentity was always tied to its relationship with others, but this was never a marriage of convenience. Following Madureira's reading of sodomy as the trope for African colonization, the colonies then were at

best mistresses, for in the chivalric code of Portuguese masculinity, anal
penetration of one's wife is forbidden.[15]

Here, of course, the term "colonial adventure" gains added significance
if *aventura* is used instead. It becomes not only (as if that were not enough)
the imperial venturing into the unknown in search of the precious treasures
hidden in colonial gardens, but also the masculine invention of the gendered
other and the homoerotic discourse of colonial dissemination. Thus, Sofia,
the African woman with whom the narrator does not exchange words, is
the other upon which he was nurtured in fascist Portugal, ultimately the
colonial woman with whom he might reenact his childhood. His reinvention of Sofia is the stuff upon which colonial masculine dreams are made:

> I could have sworn that the hollow in the straw mattress was the shape of
> my body, as if you had been waiting for me forever; that your vagina was
> perfectly fitted to my penis . . . I could have sworn that the mulatto boy
> had features resembling mine. . . . (Antunes 1983b, 123)

Indeed, after Sofia's arrest by PIDE, the brigade chief, in another one of
those grandiose Manueline gestures of fornication and spit, assesses Sofia
as "a nice piece of ass" to be shared among the heroic adventurer-soldiers
(126).

In the ruins of empire, the textual impotence is also sexual, as the passage to manhood, like the rites of shared narration of nation, is really an act
of coitus interruptus, a nonclimax without closure where even the possibility of reinvention rests on national silence and forgetting:

> Everything is real except the war that never was; there were never colo-
> nies, or fascism, or Salazar, or the Tarrafal prison camp, or the PIDE, or
> the revolution, none of that ever existed, you understand, none of it, time
> in this country stopped so long ago we have forgotten about Marches and
> Aprils and Sundays. Luanda is an invented city I take my leave of, and in
> Mutamba invented people take invented cars, to invented places where
> the MPLA subtly insinuated invented political commissioners. (152)

And love among the ruins of empire is ultimately not the one-night stand
with the silent woman with whom there can be no climax. Rather, the narrator returns to bed to reimagine Tia Theresa, "a fat black woman, maternal
and wise, receiving me on her straw mattress with matronly indulgence"
(123). If he closes his eyes, he just might conjure up Theresa's shack whose
walls are covered with pious images and picture postcards, the remnants of
a traveling nation reinventing itself—albeit here not through fornication

and spit, but rather through self-referential masturbation—among the ruins of empire.

Alexandrine Fate/*Fado Alexandrino*

António Lobo Antunes's 1983 narrative, *Fado Alexandrino* is, indeed, just as the title announces, an alexandrine *fado* of empire and postempire. Actually, it is a three part *fado*, as the text's three sections—"Before the Revolution," "The Revolution," and "After the Revolution"—each are divided in true alexandrine fashion in twelve chapters.

The main narrative event that ties the *fado* together is a reunion dinner (and its aftermath) among five army comrades who were in the same battalion in Mozambique—the soldier, the communications office (a lieutenant), the second lieutenant, the lieutenant colonel, and the captain. They are representative of the Portuguese class structure, and the interweaving of their voices sets a chronological narrative, of sorts, that begins with their return from Mozambique and culminates with the murder of one of their group. The result, however, is not even an attempted historical or narrative closure, but rather, within the ex-centricity of postempire, a narrative that reverberates with ruptures, fragmentations, maskings, and discontinuities.

In *Fado Alexandrino* the subjective displacement of *Os Cus de Judas* is multiplied through the disjointed conversational voices of four of the army comrades. The captain, ostensibly the listener, becomes the narrator whose own displaced subjectivity marks the text in rare instances of overt questioning:

> And I thought, looking around me at the bald heads, the gray hair, the worn out faces that were smiling and chewing and talking. We got old for nothing, or is it still possible, can anything be possible? Because for me that was the worst part of it, that we'd screwed ourselves in vain, that we'd worn ourselves out for no reason. (Antunes 1990, 19–20)

As in *Os Cus de Judas* the reconstruction of colonial adventure and its aftermath is permeated with possibilities of homoerotica, especially given the narrative setting. And as was the case with Lobo Antunes's earlier novel, *Fado Alexandrino* ejaculates the promise of homoerotic narration in a tale of nonclimax.

Fado Alexandrino's discursive reconstruction begins with the return from Africa to Lisbon and conveys the overlapping of colonial and metropolitan space: "I'm in Lisbon and in Mozambique. I can see the houses in the lower middle class neighborhood and the trees in the jungle at the same time" (3); "We're still in Africa, we're still following the remains of trails . . ." (7). The meshing of these spaces is displacement, and also commentary on the socioeconomic conditions of colony and metropolis: "The way dogs and small boys look alike in this country . . . is the way they look alike in Africa: the same begging expression, the same dull hair, the same slack-lily limbs" (8). The experiences in Mozambique are repeatedly reimagined within the context of a Lisbon made strange and unknown. The soldier explains to his captain that he should have stayed in Africa, since he returned like a stroke victim and had to relearn everything syllable by syllable. What is displaced here, as in *Os Cus de Judas,* is an empire invented on difference, when after all, as the soldier comments when asked about Africa, it's "pretty much like here."

The collapse of empire is reiterated in the strangeness of Lisbon, in terms of both geographical and invented space, as well as in the nonheroic welcome home for the members of the group. The soldier is unwelcome at his sister's house and moves in with his uncle's family. He works for the uncle's moving company, but moonlights as a male prostitute. The second lieutenant searches in vain for something familiar in his wife's topography, and the colonel arrives in Lisbon the day after his wife's death from cancer. Only the communications officer returns home to his supposed elderly aunt and godmother who live behind the Feira Popular, an amusement park world—The Pit of Death, "The World of Illusion"—which by now we know is really a trope of the ruins of empire.

The end of empire is reconstructed around the dinner table by the five increasingly inebriated army comrades. The events, of course, are viewed through both personalized and drunken lenses, but this is ultimately the reconstruction of collective revolutionary farce; the ineptness of the Portuguese opposition, the failure of the revolution, and the crisis of national identity. Thus, the same Captain Mendes who has a command role in the revolution of 1974 later turns up as a glorified smuggler in Cabo Ruivo. The colonel, in another grand gesture of dying colonial impotence, refuses to support either the captains' revolt or Caetano's government. After the revolution, he is given the job (complete with revolutionary cubicle) of reviewing the cases of high-ranking officers and is informed that the more brigadier generals are discredited, the better his chances for promotion. The communications officer, part of the Portuguese Marxist-Leninist-Maoist Organization, is left to rot in Caxias while his comrades act out slapstick bank robberies.

The prevailing postimperial displacement sets the tone for the narration—

a confused intermingling of voices—that is taken to yet another degree as countless characters, who are seemingly different actors in supposedly different plays, actually have multiple identities and roles. The soldier's wife Odete (the daughter of his uncle's wife) is also Dália, the communication officer's contact from his opposition cell, as well as the object of his unrequited desire. The second lieutenant's ex-wife becomes the love of the colonel's daughter, after an anguishing—for the then-husband, that is—affair with the purple-haired lady. The second lieutenant seeks revenge, but not love, in the arms of the midget, secure in his imagining that no one else could possibly want her. The concierge has been the lover of both the colonel and the soldier. The colonel's second wife—"the cloud of perfume"—is also the lover of the communications officer.

This masquerade of characters is truly the dismantled World of Illusions, an alexandrine *fado* of dying empire performed in the Pit of Death. Thus, what should be the climatic narrative event, the murder of the communications officer, is the shock of nonshock—again, the nonclimax, the expected nonexpected, within the fragmentation of collective imagination and narrative. Was he murdered as revenge for his affair with the "cloud of perfume?" Was it payback for desiring Dália/Odete? Or is this merely the mercy killing of the impotent Portuguese Left? In the nonsafety of displacement, the soldier's truck is smashed against the viaduct and in his imagination the violence of impact meshes with the violence of the war in Mozambique. He imagines his death—does he die in the crash or during a heroic suicide mission, grenade in hand, running toward a Mozambican village? The second lieutenant loses his car, his lunch, and his freedom in the postimperial Lisbon sea of concrete.

The glue that remains to patch together nation and ethos in a reinvention of Portugal is still the grandiloquent discourse of empire (the Crusades, the navigators, Magellan, da Gama, etc., etc.) but in the ruins of empire it resonates against the "parade of countless little organ-grinder monkeys with rifles on their shoulders" (Antunes 1990, 345). The articulation of nation has become disarticulation, as even regeneration cannot bring about the reinvention of the nation. The narrator in *Os Cus de Judas* is left to masturbate among photos of his military ancestors frowning down on him from the mantle—meaningless showcase images from the discursively constructed past. In *Fado Alexandrino*, the narrative ends with a nonsunset, a smuggler's seaplane slowly rising "through the empty degrees of evening on the way to the sea" (1990, 497). The reinvented nation again takes to the sea, as pirates of an impossible postcolonial traveling aesthetic, in search of gardens with concealed treasures where imperial dreams never dry up.

Notes

1. I have limited my reading here to *Os Cus de Judas* and *Fado Alexandrino*, although other texts by António Lobo Antunes—including *As Naus* (1988) and *Ordem Natural das Coisas* (1991)—are also critically open to such a reading. In an effort to be inclusionary in regard to audience, I am restricting the reading to the first two mentioned texts as both are available in English versions. The first appears as *South of Nowhere*, in a somewhat problematic translation by Elizabeth Lowe. The second, translated by Gregory Rabassa, retains the title of the Portuguese original, as well as its breathtaking alexandrine complexity.

2. I am grateful to the participants of an informal cultural studies reading group—José Rabasa, Sangeeta Ray, Peter Hulme, and Henry Schwartz—for sharing their readings of Catherine Hall's text and questions of national identities.

3. See Butler 1991. Sections from that paper have been rewritten and are included in this present essay.

4. My reading of Lobo Antunes is informed by Luís Madureira's wonderful essay, "The Discreet Seductiveness of the Crumbling Empire: Sex, Violence and Colonialism in the Fiction of António Lobo Antunes," to which I refer on numerous occasions throughout this essay. Madureira sets his own reading against redefinitions of Portuguese national identity in the post-revolutionary period. He cites Eduardo Lourenço's 1978 work, *O Labirinto da Saudade: Psicanálise Mítica do Destino Português,* as well as his later "Camões et l'Europe" (1988), but unfortunately does not refer to Lourenço's 1990 text.

5. I will make special mention of Perry Anderson's long-ignored essay, "Portugal and the End of Ultra-Colonialism" written at the beginning of the protracted liberation struggles in Portugal's former African colonies. Anderson analyzes the Portugal's self-proclaimed civilizing mission and the distortions of colonial ideology.

6. I have placed these "posts" in parentheses to draw attention to them as highly contestable signifiers that continue to privilege empire and colony as the central space of reference.

7. Foucault contrasts heterotopias to utopias, as types of "counter-sites" in which "all the other real sites that can be found within the culture, are simultaneously represented, contested and inverted" (1986, 24).

8. In 1989 Rebecca Catz published a remarkable translation and critical edition of *The Travels of Fernão Mendes Pinto*.

9. I insert "European" in parentheses and call attention to Da Gama's announcement in *The Lusiads* as he greets the governor of the island of Mozambique in the first canto: "We come from Europe, the home of strong and warlike peoples, and are bound for India" (Camões 1952, 49).

10. The terms "regeneration" and "regeneratism" are used in this context by Sousa 1981.

11. The reference, of course, is to José Saramago's novel *Jangada de Pedra*.

12. For the description of the detailed maps depicting "the true dimension of Portugal," see Hamilton 1981.

13. In fact, her jingling bracelets speak more than she does.

14. The twenty-three lettered chapters in the original represent the letters of the Portuguese alphabet. The English version contains twenty-six, the three additional chapters being illustrations not in the Portuguese text.

15. Here, one only need think of all the meanings of the Portuguese interjection *Vai tomar no cu.*

References

Anderson, Perry. 1962. "Portugal and the End of Ultra-Colonialism." *New Left Review* 15:83–102, 16:88–123, 17:85–114.

Antunes, António Lobo. 1979. *Os Cus de Judas.* Lisbon: Dom Quixote.

———. 1983a. *Fado Alexandrino.* Lisbon: Dom Quixote.

———. 1983b. *South of Nowhere.* Translated by Elizabeth Lowe. New York: Random House.

———. 1988. *As Naus.* Lisbon: Dom Quixote.

———. 1990. *Fado Alexandrino.* Translated by Gregory Rabassa. New York: Grove Weidenfeld.

———. 1991. *Ordem Natural das Coisas.* Lisbon: Dom Quixote.

Butler, Phyllis Reisman. 1991. "The View From the Metropolis: Africa Revisited in Portuguese Post-Colonial/Modern Literature." Paper Presented at the Annual Conference of the Midwest Modern Language Association, Chicago, 3–5 November.

Camões, Luís Vaz. 1952. *The Lusiads.* London: Penguin Books.

Foucault, Michel. 1986. "Of Other Spaces." *Diacritics,* spring, 22–27.

Hall, Catherine. 1992. "Missionary Stories: Gender and Ethnicity in England in the 1830s and 1840s." In *Cultural Studies,* edited by Lawrence Grossbery, Cary Nelson, and Paula Treichler, 240–76. New York and London: Routledge.

Hamilton, Russell. 1981. *Literatura Africana, Literatura Necessária I-Angola.* Lisbon: Edições 70.

Lourenço, Eduardo. 1988. "Camões et l'Europe." *Critique,* August/September, 664–75.

———. 1990. "Conclusion: Portugal's Identity." In *Portugal: Ancient Country, Young Democracy,* edited by Kenneth Maxwell and Michael Haltzel, 107–11. Washington, D.C.: The Wilson Center Press.

Madureira, Luís. 1995. "The Discreet Seductiveness of the Crumbling Empire: Sex, Violence and Colonialism in the Fiction of António Lobo Antunes."*Luso-Brazilian Review* 32, no. 1:17–29.

Mendes Pinto, Fernão. 1989. *The Travels of Fernão Mendes Pinto.* Edited and translated by Rebecca Catz. Chicago: University of Chicago Press.

Sousa, Ronald. 1981. *The Rediscoverers.* University Park: Pennsylvania State University Press.

Stephenson, Anders. "A Conversation with Fredric Jameson." In *Universal Abandon?* edited by Andrew Ross, 3–30. Minneapolis: University of Minnesota Press, 1988.

Women's Writing in Contemporary Portugal

ISABEL ALLEGRO DE MAGALHÃES
Translated by Hanna Götz and Anna Klobucka

Examining the works of fiction written by Portuguese women authors in the last decades we notice the nonexistence of a *feminist writing*. Differently from what can be observed in several European countries and in North America in the second half of the twentieth century in Portugal we come across only *one* outstanding work that is clearly feminist in perspective: the *Novas Cartas Portuguesas* (New Portuguese letters). Under the patriarchal and dictatorial regime that governed us at the time of its publication, this book by Maria Velho da Costa, Maria Isabel Barreno, and Maria Teresa Horta had a predictable fate: it was immediately withdrawn from circulation and a lawsuit was filed against its authors. Its international acceptance, however, especially among women writers and critics of various countries, surpassed all expectations: the work was translated into some ten languages, a theatrical version of it was staged in Paris, and it has often been referred to by feminist writers and critics in Europe as well as in the United States. The text's great originality is apparent at various levels. On the one hand, the "three Marias" assume simultaneously the roles of subjects and objects of their narrative and give no explicit credit to the individual authorship of various parts of the book. On the other hand, the *New Portuguese Letters* display a trait rarely found in the fabric of other feminist literary texts: the association of an indictment against the oppression of women's bodies in the private sphere and the oppression discernible in women's relationships in the public sphere. As Maria de Lourdes Pintasilgo has noted, "[T]he body works as a metaphor for all hidden and not yet overcome forms of oppression" (1980, 10). And, above all, it is a text of great literary quality. In the absence of other feminist literary works in Portugal, this one alone suffices to include Portugal in any historical mapping of international feminist discourse.

Indeed, it is impossible to locate any other work of similar proportions, before or after *Novas Cartas*. There are, however, some literary texts with a feminist slant, or written from a female point of view, and engaged in an articulation of specifically feminine values. These include *Mestre*, by Ana Hatherly (1961), a number of works by Natália Correia, by Maria Velho da Costa, by Maria Isabel Barreno, and by Natália Nunes, and almost entire body of writing—with but a small share of narrative fiction—by Maria Teresa Horta.

While speaking of "feminine values" and features peculiar to women's writing, I do not do so with the intent to define a specificity restricted to female authors. In such a case, one would immediately be forced to recall texts of male authorship presenting similar features. What does interest me, however, is to distinguish characteristics that may be recognized as *predominantly* feminine inasmuch as they are attuned to prevailing traits in the lives of women. That is, I intend to identify indicators of another sensibility, of another way of perceiving the real, of another logic that is expressed in literary texts as being more closely tied to female experiences: experiences related to women's bodies and inner awareness, as well as to their social and cultural existence. But these traits are not exclusive to women: many men share them too.

This is surely what led Julia Kristeva to talk about Joyce and Proust, along with Virginia Woolf, as authors whose writing displays marks of an *écriture féminine*; or what caused Hélène Cixous to mention Jean Genet's works, along with those by Colette and Marguerite Duras, as examples of feminine writing. This may also mean that it is impossible to divide the waters with clarity; that there are no two distinct poles defined by the gender of whoever writes. We may be able to speak of the "gender of the text," that is, of its prevailing tendencies. We realize that the dominant "symbolic order" did not completely repress, in most women, and in some men, what Kristeva has called "semiotic elements," that is, elements that, despite the fact that they are not expressed in the logocentric discourse, are visible in the rhythm, the structure, the tone, the silences, or other such aspects of the text. And it is only natural for these marks to be more manifest in women's writing than in men's, since the established symbolic order is, in its origin and in its substance, a masculine order.

Let us examine a number of works, published after the "25 de Abril"—the date used here as an inescapable landmark, both real and mythical, for any area of Portuguese life. Speaking in a panoramic fashion rather than offering exhaustive proof, I will examine three aspects of these works which exhibit some "feminine" characteristics. Their number includes about forty novels, or novellas, by sixteen women writers (see the bibliography). It is important to note that, in the last decades, a large number of women writers—many of indisputable stature—have appeared in Portugal, along with a vast body of works of narrative fiction. This fact becomes particularly meaningful in a country where there have been no significant feminist movements and where practically no consistent theoretical reflection has been developed on questions of gender.

It is important to consider the following aspects of those works in three distinct stages:

1. The themes developed; the worlds and the social environments brought into existence.

2. The viewpoints of female narrators/authors and the creation of their female characters.

3. Finally, the characteristics of style and narrative construction.

Themes, Worlds, Societies

The subjects and themes approached by the writers do not give, in and of themselves, any indication of the author's gender. However, there are aspects related either to the point of view or to an emphasis on specific nuances, which impart a particular hue to the texts and reveal their feminine provenance. Let us take a look at some examples: the colonial war is a theme developed by several male but also by three female authors: Joana Ruas, Wanda Ramos, and Lídia Jorge, respectively, in *Corpo Colonial* (Colonial body), *Percursos* (Journeys), and *A Costa dos Murmúrios* (The Coast of Murmurs), novels whose actions take place in Timor, Angola, and Mozambique.

The personal and collective experiences of the 25 April 1974, the effects of 25 April on the lives and minds of the Portuguese, all constitute fertile material for novels by Lídia Jorge, Maria Velho da Costa, Teolinda Gersão, Agustina Bessa Luís, Olga Gonçalves, and Luísa Costa Gomes. *O Dia dos Prodígios* (The day of wonders), *Lúcialima, Paisagem com Mulher e Mar ao Fundo* (Landscape with a woman and the sea in the background), *Pessoas Felizes* (Happy people), *Ora esguardae* (Behold now), *Pequeno Mundo* (Small world), and *Retrato dum Amigo enquanto Falo* (Portrait of a friend while I speak) are all texts in which the so-called April revolution emerges in specific contexts and with very different purposes but always as a highly charged fact of collective or individual life. Clearly, this theme also plays an important role in various literary works written by men.

Similarly, historical themes that are so dominant in contemporary fiction can be found in works by both male and female Portuguese authors. Many of Agustina Bessa Luís's novels rely on historical subjects: such is the case with *Fanny Owen*, *A Corte do Norte* (The northern court), *A Monja de Lisboa* (The Lisbon nun), and *O Vale de Abraão* (The Valley of Abraham), among others. Fictionalized biography also serves as a literary formula through which history is approached, as in Bessa Luís's *Florbela Espanca* and *Sebastião José*, or in Vieira da Silva's *Longos Dias Têm Cem Anos* (Long days are a hundred years old), or in the most recent novel by Luísa Costa Gomes: *Vida de Ramón* (Life of Ramón). A related theme found in some literary works is a questioning of recent aspects of Portuguese history as a means to better understand the country's present or the identity of its people. Isabel Barreno's recent novel, *Crónica do Tempo* (Chronicle of time), is an example of this.

Within this group of novels, we find yet two other social themes, developed in three books by Olga Gonçalves: prostitution in the Lisbon night life (*Armandina e Luciano, o Traficante de Canários* [Armandina and Luciano the Canary Dealer]) and Portuguese emigration to Northern Europe (*A Floresta em Bremerhaven* [The forest in Bremerhaven], and *Este Verão o Emigrante Là-bas* [This summer the emigrant Là-bas]). The two latter novels constitute an excellent account of the emigrants' lives in France and Germany and of their returns to their villages in Portugal.

The social environments that provide the narrative contexts for these women's novels are also relevant, since they relate closely to the topics developed. Here, as in novels written by men, we find a great diversity of social and ethnic environments. While the capital city of Lisbon (particularly its intellectual, artistic, political, and professional circles) still seems to provide the most popular setting, there are also representations of working-class environments; of urban and suburban life; of new and old rural bourgeoisie (Bessa Luís, Correia); and of popular rural environments (Jorge, Correia).

There is also a considerable ethnic mixture that reflects the cross-breeding of cultures that has always shaped Portuguese reality: these include characters of Jewish origin, Muslims, Brazilians, the French, the English, and so on.

And if it is true that the places of action are usually geographically defined (for instance, Lisbon, the North, the Algarve, the Alentejo, Beiras, the Madeira Islands; the former colonial lands in Africa and in Timor; emigrant communities in France and Germany; countries such as Belgium, Germany, and Brazil), there also are atopic and anonymous spaces, locales without any specific geographic identity.

Another feature found in women's narratives is the creation of fantastic or "magical realist" fictional worlds, in which the supernatural interweaves with daily life. In Lídia Jorge's *O Dia dos Prodígios* people are more inclined to believe that a flying serpent crossed the sky above their village than that a revolution has occurred; and a woman fears that the dragon she is embroidering on a bedspread may fly off. In Hélia Correia's works, *Montedemo* and *A Casa Eterna* (The eternal house), there are "blue women with their mouths half-open," characters with "fish eyes," "bird eyes," "yellow eyes," "porcine eyes," or "caprine mouths," and dogs that "the night has dyed purplish." Other worlds also appear, where religious or biblical references are of fundamental importance. We see this in Hélia Correia; almost all her book titles and epigraphs—which function as stars guiding the texts—evoke biblical references. Maria Velho da Costa's most recent novel, *Missa in Albis*, has the formal structure of a Catholic mass, suggesting a plurality of meanings. We also find satiric, burlesque, and humorous narratives (unusual among women writers), such as Yvette Centeno's novella, *As Muralhas* (The walls), as well as ironic narratives, as in *Festa em Casa de Flores* (Party in Flores's house), by Fernanda Botelho.

This variety of subjects, themes, and settings does not reveal, in general terms, any traits specific to feminine fiction. Many of these themes can be found in contemporary narratives written by men. However, while apparently gender-neutral, these narratives do betray certain dominant traces and slants that impart to them an identity of their own. Let us consider what happens in the narratives of the colonial war. In the three female-authored novels mentioned above, the memory that evokes the events—a fictionalized and inventive memory, either overtly or covertly autobiographical, insistent upon recalling the position and the individual or collective suffering of both the Portuguese and the indigenous people—has a great deal to do with the female condition in a country where men went to war with wife and family, so that women, too, experienced the war. Their female narrators and characters possess an indisputably distinctive angle of vision. They are women who reveal another manner of viewing the lived reality, and this, undoubtedly, as a consequence of the place—a different place—from which they have experienced the same event. As we contrast these narratives with those written by male authors, we are almost prompted to ask whether they refer to the same war.

Another example may be taken from novels dealing with the "historical" subjects, be they from recent or ancient history. Agustina Bessa Luís's masterly exploration of minute facts, of little coincidences, and veiled feelings distinguishes her novels from those written by men. The prolonged and intricate meanderings of her analyses of situations, sentiments, and attitudes (as, for example, in *Eugénia e Silvina*), reveal a clearly feminine attention and patience.

With regard to the social environments, one observes in these novels the inclusion of a greater variety of settings. The female narrators pay much attention to people of social classes other than their own: the humiliated and suffering members of society's lower strata are endowed with great human richness and their strong presence in the narrative indicates that they are not subservient to the main characters (for instance, servants in the provincial or urban homesteads, emigrants, or prostitutes, who are scrutinized with painstaking affection).

As far as the anonymous places are concerned, these atopic and above all utopian locales may have something to do with the women's projecting themselves into spaces beyond the real and the concrete, in the direction of "elsewhere" of desire in which they are ready to take off. Curiously, this element is also a constant presence in women's narratives from other countries.

Viewpoints and Techniques of Female Narrators/Authors and the Creation of Female Characters

We have seen that the novels' themes, considered in themselves, do not generally betray female authorship, but that the angle from which they are approached frequently unveils a different attitude with regard to the events narrated. Let us now consider certain aspects of writing that have to do with the situations and the attitudes of the narrators[1] and with the creation of female characters. This includes aspects such as the perception of reality, the telluric dimension, relationship with time, relationship with rationality, self-referentiality, and treatment of intersubjective relations, all of which confer a unique character on the narratives.

We observe in these texts an incarnation of the idea of writing produced by the body, a "body writing," as the Americans have called it. Such writing has to do with an inner perception, in which the body is expressed from within instead of being looked upon from the outside. For example, Yvette Centeno says that in the voice of the female narrator in *Matriz* (Matrix) "[W]riting is an adventure; it is she from the inside" (1988, 73); or that "I write only that which insists on me, [. . .] which infiltrates my blood, so to speak, and which won't let me live if I don't write it down" (102). And the external view of the body is brought into descriptions of what is not the body, such as descriptions of objects. Bessa Luís speaks of a house in which two new flights of stairs will serve the construction's body "as a kind of a pannier on its smooth belly" (1989, 106). In *O Cavalo de Sol* (The sun horse) by Teolinda Gersão, there is mention of a "smooth belly of the water." On the other hand, this body writing also creates its own relationship with the world: with nature and objects, with people and events.

At the level of *perception* we find a new, rounded, rather than linear, way of capturing reality. If, throughout western history, the sight has been the dominant sense involved in apprehending the world—and literature and art display undeniable signs of this—here, in many of the authors, we encounter a widening of perception to a variety of senses: the smell, the hearing, the touch, and the taste reveal themselves as equally important and sharp antennas tuned to a plural awareness of life. The language bears witness to this: aromatic nouns, tactile adjectives, and sensitive verbs all render new flavors to the texts.

The novels by Teolinda Gersão are an excellent example of this: all of them are permeated by a semantics of sensuality. Works by Hélia Correia, Teresa Salema, Maria Velho da Costa, and Agustina Bessa Luís also provide many similar examples. In many of these authors there is a kind of diffuse eroticism related to this dispersed form of feminine sensuality.

In addition, it is possible to notice a special quality of *attention*, so often originating in time spent listening and being silent, a quality that infuses these texts with a unique intensity directed at diminutive facts and objects, at their details, and at rudimentary traces captured by intuition. An example can be found in Lídia Jorge's novel *A Costa dos Murmúrios*, where intricate relations between the public and the private sphere are dissected by the female narrator observing the colonial war. The narration establishes an almost causal relationship between one of the war's tragic moments and an everyday distraction of the officers' wives awaiting the end of a battle at their hotel; or between the reception following the narrator's marriage to an officer and a massacre taking place nearby at that same moment. In such a manner, the narrator discovers how apparently insignificant facts become vivid signs unmasking the colonial ideology. Hers is an affective (and effective) attention geared to subtle connections that a generalized vision—in this case the military/masculine vision—leaves undetected. And this is because women, who have been forced by life's normal course to be keenly aware of their surroundings, and who possess an inclusive and multiple sensuality, express also in their writing characteristics that are in profound harmony with their lives and their own bodies.

The expression of a special connection with the earth, with nature and its rhythms, also presents a constant feature of their writing: it is a bodily, earthly relation with life, its sources, and spaces. These penetrating earthly forces, tuned to the rhythms of nature and to the breathing of the universe itself, are patent in characters such as Bessa Luís's "Sibyl" (*Sibila*), and many others created by Lídia Jorge and Hélia Correia. This harmony with the cosmic rhythms may be detected even in the structure of a novel like Velho da Costa's *Lúcialima*.

The centrality of spaces such as the *house* is common to most of these writers. On the one hand, the house as a place conforms to nature, its configuration changing with the rhythms of the seasons (open in the spring and closed in the winter, as in Gersão's *O Silêncio*); or it is an empty house to be filled by an expansive affluence of words. On the other hand, the house is a place of passage, filled with memories, a secret, warm, and intimate place, almost uterine, where the present goes by and where the past remains alive in things that tell its story, which bring it back with a wishing rod of any smell, or touch (the houses of Bessa Luís and Velho da Costa, and those of Hélia Correia, so strong that her last novel is entitled *A Casa Eterna* [The eternal house]). The house is also the pivot of the universe, a fixed place from which women constantly depart on journeys through time (while men leave it to "cross continents," as in *Lúcialima*). The house also functions as a metonymic and metaphoric space, as the place of writing and of women's bodies.

The radiant presence of things also becomes the object of special attention (furniture, drawers, a chair, a table); for example, Gabriela Llansol, in *Um Beijo Dado Mais Tarde* (A kiss given later), speaks about a "presence enveloping objects" and a "fulminating awareness that objects exist who are people"; or about a "cupboard that has a high-pitched voice" (1990, 32). These objects constitute, for her, a kind of "inanimate community" (34). The inanimate things acquire particular importance in descriptions, in the unfolding of sentiments, or as an inspiring point of departure for the creation of new narrative levels, as in the novels by Bessa Luís, Lídia Jorge, Hélia Correia, and Maria Velho da Costa.

The creation of female characters, which at times also encompasses the female narrator, constitutes a novelty in itself, given their variety and complexity. This diversity of feminine ways of being-in-the-world alone suffices to reveal at its origin a knowledge about women acquired from the *inside*. Among the protagonists we find the strong, earthly, solitary, and mysterious women of Bessa Luís or Lídia Jorge; the divided, restless women, reflecting on themselves and on the past, portrayed by Maria Velho da Costa and Fernanda Botelho; women presented as dreamers, always searching for something else, for a meaningful "elsewhere," like the characters of Teolinda Gersão and a few of Lídia Jorge; those passively and patiently awaiting for a different time (in Lídia Jorge and Maria Velho da Costa); those who travel through time in a continuous flashback, without envisioning any meaning for the present, like some characters of Bessa Luís, Velho da Costa, Luísa Gomes, and Maria Isabel Barreno; and finally women who savor with delight the past, which occupies their present, as in the novels by Olga Gonçalves, Velho da Costa, and Bessa Luís, to give but a few examples.

But what really makes these characters "special," what basically makes them live a different life, is their relation to the flowing of time, that is, their living experience of time. The female characters are placed in a present that they almost never consider meaningful. It is always a frustrated kind of present, and always overtaken in their affections by the past or by a utopian time to come. Time is therefore, in itself, the ever present, heavy, essential stuff of their lives (witness the titles of Wanda Ramos's novels: *As Incontáveis Vésperas* [The countless eves], *Os Dias, Depois . . .* [The days, after . . .]; or Isabel Barreno's *Crónica do Tempo* [Chronicle of time]). Time is never lived "unidirectionally." In the construction of these characters we encounter a kind of break from a "linear" experience, understood as a simple succession of "nows." This linearity, if one may call it so, is replaced by a circular movement or by a constant back-and-forth oscillation between different moments in time: past, present, future. It is supplanted by a permanent, emotional inward journey between what once *was,* what now *is,* and what *may* someday *be.* In a certain way, this reflects a specifically feminine tradition, in which time takes the shape of a circle, or of a spiral—a tradition still alive, despite all the social transformations of the late-twentieth century.

The experience of time from within, the intratemporality—Heidegger's *Innerzeitlichkeit* —is what brings about this change in women. That is to say, the chronological time, *kronos*, with its relentless and indifferent flow, seems not to weigh on them; we do not find in them any anxiety caused by life's fugacity.

This happens because, rather than the *kronos*, women live the *kairos* and the *aion;* that is, instead of the irreversible flowing of time they experience the opportune time, that moment of exact coincidence between themselves and life, be it through memory and reminiscence of past experiences, or through dreams or anticipation of the future. Or else, they experience such frustration with the present, and are so possessed by something exterior to the moment in which they exist (be it through imagination or fantasy, be it through memories and their *anamnesis*), that the feeling of time, of temporal transition and irreversibility, is practically abolished or dissipated. This magic power to manipulate the temporal dimension allows them to become transported to all times simultaneously, thus escaping the anguished consciousness of its unstoppable flow.

Another sphere into which various authors venture is that of self-referentiality and self-reflection. It is an intimate reflection, often combined with an analysis of the writing process and its sources. For example, the hypothetical writing of a book that is inscribed in the text side by side with the narrative, engaging in a kind of game between reality and fantasy, can be found in *Esta Noite Sonhei com Brueghel* (Last night I dreamt about Brueghel) by Fernanda Botelho, in *Jardim das Nogueiras* (Walnut garden) by Yvette Centeno, and in *Os Dias, Depois* by Wanda Ramos. And a number of women narrators/authors bear witness to a curious experience of an almost symbiotic union with their texts, between writing and life, where the aesthetic distance between themselves and their writing is abolished, inasmuch as their own lives are transfigured by the power of the poetic word. The lexical field of the body becomes a central axis uniting the body's breathing with the breathing of the writing itself.

This might be the reason for the marked attraction of several of these authors toward personal forms of expression, for their choice of a quasi-confessional register, perhaps but not necessarily in the form of a diary, which points to the effects of a life experienced as art and an art experienced as a form of life. (The insistence on treating the domestic reality as an artistic reality, which we find vividly represented in various texts, is a clear sign of this.) Despite their differences, it is possible to include in this category almost all of Maria Gabriela Llansol's works, as well as several by Yvette Centeno, Maria Velho da Costa, Wanda Ramos, Fernanda Botelho, and Isabel Barreno.

The intersubjective relations are also accorded a prominent place in most of these novels. These include both relations between men and women that are problematized and reflected upon, presented through silences and words either blocking or attempting to build bridges of dialogue (in Gersão, Centeno, Velho da Costa, among others) and new relationships woven between women who seek networks of another solidarity and an anticipated harmony which unites them. What emerges in this context is the women's connection to the figure of the *mother*—an always difficult and stormy relationship in all feminist literature. Texts by Maria Velho da Costa, Isabel Barreno, Teolinda Gersão, Teresa Salema, and Agustina Bessa Luís give undeniable emphasis to this complex fabric of relations.

Language and Discourse Construction

Let us now see what elements expressing a feminine way of being in the world can be found in the narrative construction, structure, syntax, semantics, or rhythm of a literary work.[2]

We frequently encounter a discourse that, however literary it might be, incorporates traits bringing it close to the *spoken language*. Elements such as unfinished sentences, interrogative forms, noun clauses, a fluid syntax with interrupted sentences or dialogues—suspended by pauses, ellipsis points, blank spaces—give the text its own rhythm and are manifested in many novels (for example in Ramos's *Percursos* or in Centeno's *No Jardim das Nogueiras* and *Matriz*, as well as in a number of Bessa Luís's works). Yvette Centeno, in fact, draws directly from the oral word, endowing the short, ruptured sentences of her dialogues and/or monologues with particularly suggestive power. Wanda Ramos intersperses her syntagmatic construction with pauses and gaps that make the reader slip into the unspoken hiding in the cracks of memory. Bessa Luís's stories also contain sentences that do not always follow their thread, but get lost in the web of word associations, yet in the end fulfill their destiny.

The impression caused by many of these texts is that of a constant back-and-forth movement between multiple points at the same time. This kind of writing is analogous to the polycentric feminine way of life. It no doubt parallels women's daily lives, in which they answer countless simultaneous requests. In their fragmentation, in their wanderings, and in their apparent disorder, these narratives display constant interlocking of various semantic networks that fit no hierarchy in the memory. It is important to establish a connection between this fragmentation and (dis)order of women's narratives, their oscillation in time and space, and their existential *souci*. Women's writing performs a surreptitious break with the calendar symbol and also with the time of social reality that mutilates their interior time, in the end breaking away from the dominant symbolic order. If the tendency to "de-chronologize" the narrative seems to be general nowadays in both men's and women's writings, it is more clear in feminine prose. The relations created and lived by women in their writing are *achronic* systemic relations, as Paul Ricoeur called them in a different context.

As witness to that, Bessa Luís uses constant departures and deviations from the story line, or the absence of structural coherence; Hélia Correia, Wanda Ramos, and Maria Velho da Costa jump from one narrative level to another, jump between spaces, times, and different characters, which are not aleatory but rather metaphorical, originating in a deeply felt unity of all things; and Teolinda Gersão uses the verbal modes with the infinitive and the conditional as vehicles of a suspended time in a kind of nebulous outside of all time. Yvette Centeno inserts numerous interruptions in her narrative, which, in their constant back-and-forth movement, do not, however, distract the reader from the main thread of the story: a search for meaning in the narrated, fictionalized, and contemplated daily life. Witness, in *Matriz*, this intratextual reflection on the text itself: "For the people this is not a novel. [. . . it is] a jumble of sentences and disarranged situations. It has no order. One doesn't know where it leads." But, significantly, we read in the same novel that "all language tells lies as it brings itself to order" (1988, 81, 154).

The fact that many of these feminine narratives do not have "closure," that they are in some way open-ended, is similar to what happens in writings from other cultures and certainly is analogous to the way in which women go through life: in multiple directions, without *one single* orientation, without a *one*-and-only goal. What Marguerite Duras has to say on the subject is symptomatic. When asked: "Mais, vous parlez de quoi?" she answers: "Je parle . . ."

There are novels by Bessa Luís that, in their last words, declare themselves incomplete and without an ending, something the author herself confirms: "[M]y novels never end," she says in an interview.

The last page of Yvette Centeno's *O Jardim das Nogueiras* also explicitly declares: "To be continued," and in *Matriz* we read: "It was written in the book: the end. But then the woman amended: it still goes on" (182). And, in truth, even when they formally end, many of these novels close in a spiral-like, open fashion.

Another related aspect is the combination of rationality with an emotional and affective attitude. The kind of rational thought that operates independently from emotion and feelings is clearly absent. Instead we find an affective intelligence, concerned more with the strength of correlations and analogies than with structures of coherence, with a synthesis, or with the necessity to arrive at some conclusions. The *logos* appears to be inseparable from the *pathos*, in a perhaps unconscious conviction that feeling is also a valid epistemological instrument: "[E]motional involvement, even love, is an intellectual resource for the understanding, not an impediment to its operators" (Perry 1989, 300).

Bessa Luís's novel *Eugénia e Silvina*, ostensibly designed as a thriller, is prevented from fulfilling its design precisely because the affective logic does not allow for the elimination of successively raised hypotheses in order to come to a conclusion (in this case the decision as to who committed the crime). The absorption in the complexity of feelings makes it impossible to arrive at any definite conclusion. The novel leaves the reader only more aware of the complexity of human sentiments. Bessa Luís confronts us with a sort of emotional involvement that, so to speak, superimposes itself over the always cold logic of pure rationality. Albeit in a different fashion, Velho da Costa not only does not seek, but clearly avoids, any clarification of narrative situations in *Missa in Albis*, any elucidation as to who is given the word and made to narrate: "[T]o confuse is the only suitable rule, according to your own understanding" (1988, 125).

The creation of a new vocabulary is one of the traits generally mentioned as characteristic of feminine writing. In Portugal, differently from France, there have been no cases of creation of "feminist" vocabulary or attempts to "feminize" language. In a playful gesture of protest against male domination over language, some French writers have changed the grammatical gender of words, giving them new meanings and unmasking the suppression of femininity; or reinscribed the silenced female body through a modified spelling of common words (for example, "le casserôle" instead of "la casserole"; "la ciel" instead of "le ciel"; "peaussibilité" [*peau* = skin] and "seintillation" [*sein* = breast]).

Among the Portuguese writers, however, another, more relevant phenomenon has occurred at the level of semantic creativity. We find, in a number of narratives, a plastic use of language, leading to the invention of new words or to their modification through various processes.[3] Perhaps the most important examples are those in Velho da Costa's works, particularly in *Casas Pardas* (Gray houses) and in her most recent novel *Missa in Albis*. Her texts testify to an intense working of words, almost a craftsmanship that uses language as its material.

We also find in her texts parody based on intertextual appropriation of alien elements (considered typical of postmodern fiction), revelatory of a long process of cultural sedimentation. In the text of *Casas Pardas*, for example, there are traces of Virgil, Camões, or Pessoa, guiding presences that permeate the rhythm, syntax, or semantics of segments of discourse ("Arma virumque Cão"); and in *Missa in Albis* quotations from contemporary authors are filtered through playful assimilation of signifiers (for instance, "torre sem barbela" (1988, 440), parodically evoking Ruben A.'s novel *Torre de Barbela*).

As these processes make clear, the intention here is to rupture the habitual verbal fabric (a goal similar to that of modernism and of the experimental literary currents of the sixties), to perform an intentional transgression in order to both induce a playful disposition in writer and reader and bring more resonance, rhythm, and "information" into the language in a Jakobsonian sense, in order to increase its poetic value.[4] Evidently, this is not a feminine trait, but it certainly reflects the desire to transform the "normal" state of the language, a desire women writers of various countries have expressed in the last decades. On another level, some texts make frequent use of vocabulary that is clearly derived from the feminine *qué hacer*, that is, from activities traditionally attributed to women, such as cooking, sewing, or other manual chores.

In the narrative voice of *Os Dias, Depois* . . . , Wanda Ramos refers to "our quiescent nonchalance [. . .] seasoned with a pinch of smells and flavors" (1990, 58) and pictures the narrative construction itself as "growing like bobbin lace" (88). She also refers to the tasks of "tidying up" that occupy women's daily life. In the narrative, these tasks are applied to "compartments of memory" (88) and are also reflected in an almost excessive numbering and arranging of paragraphs of her text. In Centeno's *Matriz*, the narrator says of the act of writing novels that it "seems like a sewing job" (92). There are many other examples of this kind to be found in almost all of the novels under discussion.

In conclusion, I would like to call attention to two points that, given my framework of analysis, seem of particular interest. In the first place, two factors occur simultaneously: on the one hand these women writers have dedicated themselves so consistently to society-oriented themes, to topics dealing with lives and problems other than their own, which is a relatively rare phenomenon in the writings of women from other countries. This may be explained by the impact that the events of the "25 de Abril" have had upon Portuguese society. On the other hand, there is the undeniable presence of elements that go deep into the core of questions related to feminine identity, an aspect paralleling what we observe in women's literature of other countries.[5]

This connection between life's public sphere and the private sphere of women's experience represents originality, even though it is more of a juxtaposition than an interrelation. Obviously, in saying this, I do not forget yet another, previously described, facet, which coexists with the above and which consists in a deep, courageous, and healthy narcissism found in many of these literary works.

In the second place, Portuguese women writers not only *do not intend to be* different as women (as no artist intends to be different: s/he either is or is not), but also a majority of them say that they *are not* different as women in their writing. All the same, their literary works seem to reveal a tangible *difference* in relation to works by male authors.

Probably *à son insu*, or *malgré elles*, these women's writings contain particles of *another* identity under various guises: residual mythical elements of women's millenary culture, to which I referred previously, surviving even in this century; aspects of a different sensibility, of another logic, another perception and *souci,* of another expression of the reality that has to do with their own way of being and living in this world; also, trangressive strategies operating at various levels of the real and symbolic "status quo."

This allows us to think that the nature of the questions raised by feminists is, after all, so intrinsic to women's existence, that it manifests itself even when women are unaware of it, even when they approach the same subjects that male writers do. Does that imply, in some way, that there is an irrepressible unconscious force, let loose now in the aftermath of all the struggles for sexual and political liberation of women and of all the contemporary anthropological, philosophical, and cultural discussions of the feminine identity—whether or not we are aware of it?

Notes

1. While it is true that the narrative voices do not always appear clearly identified as female characters, it is equally true that, *in most cases,* they allow themselves to be perceived as such, even revealing themselves, be it openly or in a veiled fashion, as identical with the authors. Therefore, I shall refer to them here simply as female narrators/authors.

2. My analysis was influenced by García 1981, 197–353.

3. Examples from Velho da Costa's works: *falajar, palmeirar, dessaber, furiável, amantemente, doutrora,* etc.

4. See, for example, the formations of lexemes through their splitting; associations established through phonological or etymological proximity; cases of the dissemination of phonemes and graphemes derived from a theme word; and anagrams, to mention but a few examples. In the end, as we read in *Casas Pardas* and in *Lúcialima,* "os significados entram em variância até a insignificância" [the signifieds vary into insignificance] and we experience a "predomínio do significante, e esta dividida percepção, emanação dos sentidos" [predominance of the signifier, and this divided perception emanating from the senses], testifying to an intention to invent a new reality with the power of language. On this subject, see Menezes 1987.

5. A curious exception is constituted by Luísa Costa Gomes, whose two novels do not seem to contain any of the elements identified here as indicators of "feminine writing."

References

Barreno, Maria Isabel. 1979. *A Morte da Mãe.* Lisboa: Moraes.

———. 1982. *Inventário de Ana.* Lisboa: Rolim.

———. 1990. *Crónica do Tempo.* Lisboa: Caminho.

Bessa-Luís, Augustina. 1975. *As Pessoas Felizes.* Lisboa: Guimarães.

———. 1977. *As Fúrias.* Lisboa: Guimarães.

———. 1979a. *Fanny Owen.* Lisboa: Guimarães.

————. 1979b. *Florbela Espanca*. Lisboa: Arcádia.

————. 1981. *Sebastião José*. Lisboa: Imprensa Nacional/Casa da Moeda.

————. 1982. *Longos Dias Tem Cem Anos- Presença de Vieira da Silva*. Lisboa: Imprensa Nacional/Casa da Moeda.

————. 1985. *A Monja de Lisboa*. Lisboa: Guimarães.

————. 1987. *A Corte do Norte*. Lisboa: Guimarães.

————. 1989. *Eugénia e Silvina*. Lisboa: Guimarães.

————. 1991. *O Vale Abrãao*. Lisboa: Guimarães.

Botelho, Fernanda. 1987. *Esta Noite Sonhei com Brueghel*. Lisboa: Contexto.

————. 1990. *Festa em Casa de Flores*. Lisboa: Contexto.

Centeno, Yvette. *No Jardim das Nogueiras*. Lisboa: Bertrand, 1983.

————. 1988. *Matriz*. Lisboa: Presença.

Correia, Hélia. 1993. *Montedemo*. Lisboa: Ulmeiro.

————. 1991. *A Casa Eterna*. Lisboa: Dom Quixote.

Dionísio, Eduarda. 1979. *Retrato dum Amigo enquanto Falo*. Lisboa: Armazém das Letras.

Escrava, Bárbara. 1986. *As Muralhas*. Lisboa: & etc.

García, Irma. 1981. *Promenade femmelière: recherches sur l'écriture féminine*. Paris: Éditions des Femmes.

Gersão, Teolinda. 1981. *O Silêncio*. Lisboa: Bertrand.

————. 1982. *Paisagem com Mulher e Mar ao Fundo*. Lisboa: O Jornal.

————. 1990. *O Cavalo de Sol*. Lisboa: Dom Quixote.

Gomes, Luísa Costa. 1988. *O Pequeno Mundo*. Lisboa: Quetzal.

————. 1991. *Vida de Ramón*. Lisboa: Dom Quixote.

Gonçalves, Olga. 1975. *A Floresta em Bremerhaven*. Lisboa: Bertrand.

————. 1978. *Este Verão o Emigrante là-bas*. Lisboa: Moraes.

————. 1982. *Ora Esguardae*. Lisboa: Bertrand.

————. 1988. *Armandina e Luciano, o Traficante de Canários*. Lisboa: Caminho.

Jorge, Lídia. 1981. *O Dia dos Prodígios*. Lisboa: Europa-Améroca.

————. 1988. *A Costa dos Murmúrios*. Lisboa: Dom Quixote.

Llansol, Maria Gabriela. 1987. *Finita*. Lisboa: Rolim.

————. 1990. *Um Beijo Dado Mais Tarde*. Lisboa: Rolim.

Menezes, Manuel Tojal de. 1987. "Maria Velho da Costa: Un atelier d'écriture." Vol. 2. Ph.D. diss., University of Toulouse-le-Mirail.

Perry, Donna. 1989. "Procne's Song: The Task of Feminist Literary Criticism." In *Gender, Body and Knowledge: Feminist Reconstructions of Being and Knowing*, edited by Alison M. Jaggar and Susan R. Bordo, 293–308. New Brunswick, N.J.: Rutgers University Press.

Pintasilgo, M. L. 1980. Preface to *Novas Cartas Portuguesas*. 3d ed. Lisboa: Moraes.

Ramos, Wanda. 1981. *Percursos (Do Luandino ao Luena)*. Lisboa: Presença.

————. 1983. *As Incontáveis Vésperas*. Lisboa: Ulmeiro.

————. 1990. *Os Dias, Depois . . .* Lisboa: Caminho.

Ruas, Joana. 1981. *Corpo Colonial*. Lisboa: Centelha.

Salema, Teresa. 1991. *O Lugar Ausente*. Lisboa: Dom Quixote.

Velho da Costa, Maria. 1079. *Casas Pardas*. Lisboa: Moraes.

———. 1983. *Lúcialima*. Lisboa: O Jornal.

———. 1988. *Missa in Albis*. Lisboa: Dom Quixote.

Reengendering History: Women's Fictions of the Portuguese Revolution

ANA PAULA FERREIRA

> Perhaps woman does not have a history, not so much because of any notion of the 'Eternal Feminine' but because all alone she can resist and step back from a certain history (precisely in order to dance) in which revolution, or at least the "concept" of revolution, is generally inscribed. That history is one of continuous progress. . . .
>
> —Jacques Derrida

Revolutions, not unlike love, are ideally to be lived beyond all forms of symbolization: suicidal leaps that suspend the split between language and reality; "feminine acts" pointing to the abyss of the Real, rather than performances of word and deed aiming to constitute a new order.[1] As a result, during the aftermath of the Portuguese revolution of 25 April 1974, the compulsion to represent what appeared to be a "real" experience of social communion was doomed to expose, if not properly enact, the contradiction inherent in the attempt to (re)construct linguistically a plenitude—be it erotic or historical—belonging properly in the order of dream and fantasy. Nevertheless, fascinated with the newly repossessed pleasure of a seemingly free, transparent language, which censorship had increasingly stifled since 1926, writers did strive to capture for posterity the ambivalent, "miraculous" moment, as seen from the perspective of normalcy into which revolutionary demonstrative gestures soon degenerated. It is important to note that among those fictional works bearing the so-called Revolution of Carnations as their explicit or implied referent many have been written by women authors. Therefore, my rhetorical juxtaposition of revolution and sex—two apparently disconnected phenomena: one associated with a public, local, and temporally specific event, the other with an intimate, and supposedly ahistorical, universal one—was not meant so much to evoke

219

the (once) cherished feminist motto "personal is political" as to emphasize the need to conceptualize the interconnectedness of politics and sexuality, given precisely the considerable artistic and ideological import of this body of textual evidence.[2] Published during the late seventies and early eighties by established writers such as, for example, Agustina Bessa-Luís, Natália Correia, Maria Teresa Horta, and Maria Velho da Costa, and by less-known ones, such as Olga Gonçalves, Lídia Jorge, Eduarda Dionísio, and Teolinda Gersão, these texts constitute a non-negligible corpus of historical revisionism that simultaneously inscribes and internally questions the representation of the revolution as a transformative new beginning, a collective love affair commanded by a seemingly unmoveable patriarchal order. By doing so, they deconstruct the narrative of a "new" April in Portugal, while reconfiguring the traditionally silent wombs of history as the empowered subjects of a revolution yet-to-be.[3]

On the Critical Dyad "Literature and Revolution"

In the first and still only systematic assessment of how the military coup affected Portuguese literature, the renowned critic and intellectual Eduardo Lourenço suggests that the revolution belonged from the start, and even before its effective occurrence, to the imaginary order of dream or miracle. The creative investment of writers from the forties and sixties on the revolution as utopia would have been curtailed by the revolution as historical event. As such, it was predestined to become much more "the 'empty' place of a writing worthy of its name than its dream source" (1984, 7; my translation). While, according to this view, writers such as Fernando Namora, Vergílio Ferreira, Cardoso Pires, Augusto Abelaira, Almeida Faria, Agustina Bessa Luís, and Maria Velho da Costa do eventually reconstruct the memory of the formerly unspoken (and unspeakable) past leading to 25 April, their individual writing styles remain virtually untouched by what was perceived as a belated and unfulfilling "accident" of history. Only the new generation of writers who emerged after the revolution, most notably Eduarda Dionísio, Lídia Jorge, and Olga Gonçalves, were to chronicle in new mythic, symbolic, and non-naturalist literary modes what for them represented an open horizon of historical, personal and creative discovery (Lourenço 1984, 13-15).

Inspired by "the explanatory imperative" that, according to Ronald Sousa, characterizes cultural production in post-revolutionary Portugal (1984–85, 358),[4] Eduardo Lourenço's pronouncements on the fate of literature and revolution are as well-informed and thought-provoking as they may be disconcerting, particularly by virtue of some resilient blind spots of traditional literary history. One of these concerns the tendency to group writers according to generational parameters; the other is related to the presumably neutral concept of gender that rules canon formation (Winders 1991, 11–23). João Camilo dos Santos's own account of the story may be said to epitomize this critical predicament.

Although not essentially differing from Lourenço's notion of the revolution as a long-standing cultural myth, Santos argues that this myth was already deeply fragmented by the ideological crisis that assailed European thinkers and writers before the Portuguese revolution actually occurred (1992, 169–70). Notwithstanding what, to my mind, is an indisputable point, the critic discusses exclusively works that may be said to continue the tradition of a particular generation of politically committed, "discontented" *male* writers (163).[5] Lídia Jorge's name is thrown in among them, without as much as a publication reference (171); "[c]ertain early feminist tendencies in Portuguese literature [i.e., *The New Portuguese Letters*]" are said to have begun "to develop more vigorously after the revolution" (172), but neither names nor titles seem to be worthy of mention. It is paradoxical that Santos criticizes the literary portrayal of the revolution, which "tends to forget that in reality some victories were attained, preferring to dwell instead on what was *not* achieved" (179; original emphasis), when he too chooses to ignore at least one of these possible achievements: the unprecedented upsurge of fiction by women writers during the late seventies and eighties.

Despite the broader crisis of all narratives of legitimation that, for Lyotard, defines "the postmodern condition" (and of which the general confusion, not to say disillusion, that set in shortly after 25 April was a virtually graphic illustration), the revolution could not fail to open up "a new cultural space" (Lourenço 1984, 13, 16). Perhaps the most inclusive description of this space has to do with the consequences ensuing from what an informed participant characterizes as "the revolution not of the gun, but of the word" (Riegelhaupt 1983, 3). Even if social, economic and institutional transformations were not readily visible, language, especially the social status and use of language, did in fact change (6).[6] It should not be surprising that precisely women have become prominent figures in "*the literary generation of the Revolution*" identified by Lourenço (13). Nonetheless, the critic refrains from pointing it out, just as he refrains from making any gender-biased distinction among the writers comprising the "older generation." This may be regarded as a positive critical strategy aimed to prevent the "ghettoization" of literary works signed by women. On the other hand, however, it fails to make what is still a necessary political case for the undeniable fact that never before had there been "at least as many women as men publishing books in Portugal" (Sadlier 1989, xiii).[7] Unfortunately, only one Portuguese critic, Isabel Allegro de Magalhães, has consistently attended to the writings of these women authors (see bibliography).

If the category of gender is to integrate, not to say redirect, any attempt to map out the effects of the revolution on the Portuguese literary imagination, it cannot, however, be simply deduced from the sheer number of titles by female authors, nor from immanent readings of texts, extrapolated from the context in which they were written. For it is this context—call it the new cultural space made possible by the revolution—that at least in part explains those numbers, as well as the self-consciously woman-centered representations of recent history evinced in a number of fictional works published both by women who began their literary careers before 25 April and by some who emerged after it.

The period from 1975 to the early eighties witnessed the advent of Portuguese women, if not as highly visible political subjects, at least as talked about social entities or objects of study. In her informative overview of feminism in Portugal, Darlene Sadlier asserts that "[a]lthough military men overthrew the regime in 1974, women were responsible for much of the activity that ensued" (124). If, indeed, women not only joined in the Feast of Carnations but also subsequently took hold of factories, led strikes, seized vacant homes and demanded the reform of institutions of public service, nevertheless such enthusiastic revolutionary gestures did not necessarily improve their lot. The establishment in 1975 of the government-affiliated Commission on the Status of Women was instrumental for the passing of new legislation on behalf of women's rights and for supporting public, scholarly, and editorial activities concerned with understanding and changing the social status of Portuguese women. By 1976, the new Constitution declared men and women to be equal, and amended the Civil Code to give wives the same rights as husbands in all aspects of family life (125). Yet regardless of democratic laws and the efforts of recently formed women's groups to raise public consciousness, deeply rooted beliefs and cultural practices prevented any effective changes from taking place, whether in the so-called private or public spheres.

It is no wonder then that women's issues or "the female condition" became new topics of debate and scholarly research between the late seventies and early eighties. The impressive bibliography on the topic, constituted by reports, statistics and studies, mostly by social scientists and journalists, points out to what an extent the postrevolutionary cultural scene has been marked by a generalized tension between the demand for political expression and representation on the part of women (or on their behalf) and the realization that, in effect, women continued to have no real political or, for that matter, historical voice.[8] Mention need only be made of the fact that during the years immediately following the revolution, only three women occupied government posts—Magalhães Colaço, Maria de Lurdes Pintasilgo, and Maria de Lurdes Belchior (Salgado 1978, 83). This perhaps explains why historical overviews of the revolution and of post-1974 Portugal omit any discussion of women's activities and organizations, or even of individual public figures such as Pintasilgo.[9]

The proliferation of published women authors during this period can thus be correlated to, on the one hand, institutional interest in making women's rights part of democratic agendas and, on the other, the continuing suppression of women as articulate, self-representative political subjects. This basic tension is most likely to have hit home, both figuratively and literally speaking, in a form resembling the statement reportedly issued by the Swiss Women's Liberation Movement: "The 25th of April abolished political fascism but not 'macho' fascism" (86; my translation). Women's fictional rewritings of the revolution not only denounce the seemingly unbendable symbolic structure on which "fascist" or, more properly, authoritarian patriarchal politics are founded; they also offer complex, in-depth historical analysis of how such a possibly (trans)cultural phenomenon accounts for what Phil Mailer has called "the impossible [Portuguese] revolution."

Women and Revolution: Toward Another (Love) Story

A 1977 poem by Maria Teresa Horta aptly points out to what an extent the enthusiasm for the promise of a new beginning for women as autonomous subjects compelled the celebration of the revolution as a narrative of historical accomplishment. The Marxist persuasion of this narrative inevitably collapses women into indistinct masses:

>Deu-nos Abril
>o gesto e a palavra
>fala de nós
>por dentro da raiz
>
>. . . . . .
>
>O povo somos:
>mulheres do meu país

[April gave us
the gesture and the word
it speaks about us
from inside the root

.   .   .   .   .   .

We are the people:
women of my country.][10]

(1977, 106)

If the very prominence of published female authors cannot but attest to their complicitous partaking of the military's "gift" of speech, their works tend to undermine the democratic ideal of free expression for all.

In spite of Horta's optimism, her verses bluntly acknowledge that the voice of April speaks through a feminized people, through their very "interior root," thereby keeping them from representing themselves outside of that discursive construct. In the present, as in the past, women are in this way reduced to being the bearers of a male-made version of history:

Mulheres—companheiras
ombro a ombro
o ventre a crescer-nos de coragem

.   .   .   .

Mulheres—companheiras
hoje—aqui

.   .   .   .

em trabalho de parto de um país

[Women—companions
shoulder to shoulder
womb growing with courage

.   .   .   .

Women—companions
today—here

.   .   .   .

in labor for the birth of a country]

(109–10)

The great ideological as well as formal challenge that women writers have faced is, understandably, the following: how to avoid becoming the mouthpieces of a historical fiction that continues to silence women, along with the traditional "silent minorities," precisely at the conflicting juncture of revolution and sexuality as reproduction.[11]

As early as 1976, Maria Velho da Costa had already perceived the necessity for women to engage in maneuvers of historiographic/representational bracketing if they were to "fly" all on their own with the language "stolen" from the (male) rhetoricians of April.[12] The amorphous, discontinuous fragments included in her *Cravo* (*Carnation*) constitute a pioneering example of a writing that defies the temptation to recount a story of historical progress under the patriarchal sign of the carnation: "Flor sublinhada, macha, única flor de serrilha e hirsuta" [Underlined, male flower, the only serrated and hairy flower] (1976, 12).

As declared in its opening lines, the book presents instead what may be considered portraits or, better yet, still lifes conjuring up the tissue of life that remains unnoticed between the "acts" of history: "Entre actos, coisa curta, de afogadilha, fôlego preso. De entre gestos, dejectos melhor seria, pequenos jactos. Fogueiro preso e mais, imagens, imagens não retidas" [Between acts, something short, rushed, withheld breath. From between gestures, dejects would be better, little jacts. Lit blaze and more, images, images not retained]. This constitutes a program of nonrepresentational writing that not only recalls Virginia Woolf's highly experimental, historical novel *Between the Acts* (1941) but is also in line with contemporary feminist understanding of the "trick[s] of history" (see Forrester 1979).[13] However difficult her writing turns out to be, Costa deliberately refuses the containing, hegemonic ruse of traditional historical narratives in order to be "with" the anonymous, voiceless masses: "Aprendi acaso a carecer mais de explicar-me por causa destes actos', destes tempos em que este escrever no tosco esteve perto de quem nem sabe 'esse' dizer" [Perhaps I learned the need to explain myself more due to these acts, to these times when this writing on rough was near those who do not even know "such" a saying] (1976, 11).

It is thus not incidental that the centerpiece of the collection, titled "Women and Revolution," calls forth the everyday activities of peasant women—in the fields, in the home, in bed—a labor not sung by the revolution's hailing of the proletariat. These women are shown to have become the instruments of a revolutionary process they hardly understand: "Elas gritaram muito. Elas encheram as ruas de cravos. . . . Elas ouviram falar de uma grande mudança que ia entrar pelas casas. . . . Elas iam e não sabiam para onde, mas que iam" [They screamed a lot. They filled the streets with carnations. . . . They heard that a big change was going to enter the homes. . . . They went and they did not know where, but that they went]. In the end, they find themselves still repeating the same nonverbal, vital gestures, as though untouched by the event in question. It can be said that their reproductive labor passes through the system of the dominant order only to be expelled as its excrement or surplus. But, by virtue of their status as *dejectos*, the numerous small "between-acts" that constitute women's history may be a source of continued resistance, the link to what in Lacanian terms one could envision as the disruptive potential of the real within the symbolic structure of law (Zizek 1992, 45–46). Perhaps for this reason, Costa does not single out any one woman as an exemplary figure able to rise above or break with established cultural roles as a result of the revolution. This tactical refusal to represent what must remain outside of representation, if it is ever to make a political difference, can be considered a most effective form of feminist literary resistance. The dyad "Women and Revolution" fulfills, therefore, a reflective or theoretical function rather than an unproblematic "reflexive" one. As it juxtaposes two dissimilar conceptual categories, it suggests the unresolved tension between the performative or "historical time" of the revolution and the "monumental time" of women that cuts across it diagonally in the spatial form characteristic of sexual and symbolic practices of reproduction (Kristeva 1986, 190–95). As such, the two terms point to the need to continually rethink in what ways women as necessarily historical but also as transcultural social entities might relate to, might be affected by, and might ultimately erode masculinist revolutionary pretensions. Since this fundamentally analytical goal appears to be shared by all the texts under study, it can be considered—apart from being or not a distinctive mark of "feminine writing"[14]—an ideologically invested form of circumventing the appeal to silence, brought about by the recognition that, after all, "women and revolution" are not a smoothly matched pair.

In what constitutes the first full-fledged novelistic account of the equivocal alliances made under the spell of April, Eduarda Dionísio calls out for the need to believe in the continuing transforming potential of love, above and beyond any historical disillusion. Written as a long letter addressed to a male friend who remains politically aloof during the increasing dissolution of long-sedimented revolutionary promises, *Retrato de um Amigo Enquanto Falo* (1979) is one such demonstration of love. In an effort to simultaneously explain and avert the reactionary consequences of the turn towards "normalcy" during the late seventies, the narrator insistently demands that the *amigo* take note of her version of past history with an amorous, if not forgiving, gaze. Questions such as "Can you see?" "Do you understand?" "Do you remember?" "Doesn't it bother you?" lend the narrative a personal immediacy as they mark the rhythm of a confession that is as much of the "I" as of the social group to which she, albeit uncomfortably, belongs: "Tens que compreender o que se passou comigo, porque foi o que se passou com muita gente" [You have to understand what happened to me, because it is what happened to many people] (1979, 64).

Described as a professor of mathematics who enjoys poetic paradoxes, leads a secluded married life, and has occasional escapades with the narrator since the days of the "miracle," the addressee remains a distant "other," the narrative being the only bridge that might reunite those who persist in believing in the all-encompassing love affair of revolution—another revolution, to be sure—and those who have given up all hope. For this reason, the novel reconstructs the history of a whole generation of intellectuals who, already skeptical of the utopian beliefs that guided their parents, mistook forbidden readings and, above all, catchphrases for real militancy founded not upon elitist cultural practices but upon experiential knowledge of social and political realities: "Estás a ver, enquanto dormias no mato, nós, na capital, passávamos o Verão" [Do you see, while you slept in the jungle, we, in the capital, were spending the Summer] (39); "Estávamos cada vez mais longe da História. . . . éramos a vanguarda da decadência" [We were farther and farther away from History. . . . we were the vanguard of decadence] (57). Rather than a mere naturalist denouncement or a literary pretext for a collective mea culpa, Dionísio's novel may be thus seen as a generous "proof of love" (71) offered to those who no longer care to speak about, much less act toward, the creation of politically effective modes of social communion.

As with the authors of the "old generation," one of whom happens to be Eduarda Dionísio's father (Mário Dionísio), writing is still a mode of political resistance, but a resistance that, in this case, is self-consciously woman-centered. Following a literary tradition that is considered to be a feminine one par excellence—from the Galician-Portuguese medieval women's songs and subsequent ventriloquist appropriations of women's voices (as, for example, in the *Lettres Portugaises*), to the feminist reinventing of this tradition by the authors of *New Portuguese Letters* (1972)— *Retrato de um Amigo Enquanto Falo* constructs a gendered, specifically female position vis-à-vis an absent male lover. Yet, contrary to other literary images of women suffering from unrequited love, Dionísio's confessional narrator inscribes herself as a desiring, scriptural subject for and of a history that encompasses the political and the erotic.

It is not incidental that the text ends precisely by confronting and thereby negating the formal separation between what would be the "feminine" genre of the love letter and the "masculine" one of historiography. Whereas the epilogue begins with the statement "I do not speak to you of love" (115), a short appendage titled "History" recounts from an apparently neutral perspective the story of a peasant boy who goes to study in Lisbon and, in the early sixties, exchanges a relationship with an older woman for politically subversive activities. Though the story of the apparently gratuitous love affair of the narrator is enmeshed in a long history of oppositional politics, the "History" of the would-be revolutionary ends up as a narrative of a search for objects of love. What the novel calls for, in the last instance, is that the Portuguese revolution and the writing thereof not be conceived apart from the always overdetermined individual acts of loving that went into its making. However futile seem to have been the "affairs" between people who espoused different individual as well as historical commitments, only by inventing "new forms of organization" (115), reinventing transgressive forms of loving and social communing—as Maria Velho da Costa's *Lúcialima* (1983) will show—could there be any hope for truly revolutionary change.

Like Dionísio, Teolinda Gersão also explores the confessional mode in order to outline the portrait of the generation who spoke, read, and wrote about (while some also died for) a transformative project that, in the end, they were merely allowed to witness with confusion and dismay. Centered on the character of a mother who contemplates suicide, having lost her son to the colonial war before the revolution, *Paisagem com mulher e mar ao fundo* (1982) presents, however, a story of survival through the deliberate recollection of the specters from the past that continue to haunt the (postrevolutionary) present. Although seemingly personal, the fragments of memories that coalesce into the narrative are framed by a testimonial appeal signed by the author in the form of a prefatorial statement : "O resto do texto também não é meu. De diversos modos foi dito, gritado, sonhado, vivido por muitas pessoas, e por isso o devolvo, apenas um pouco mais organizado debaixo desta capa de papel, a quem o reconheça como coisa sua" [The rest of the text is not mine either. In different ways it was said, yelled, dreamed, lived by many people, and for that reason I return it, only a bit more organized underneath this paper cover, to those who may recognize it as their own]. In a more subtle way than *Retrato de um Amigo Enquanto Falo*, Gersão's novel assumes thus a simultaneously intimate and collective cathartic function that, again, draws upon the connection between what went on "out there" and the small, invisible, but nonetheless political acts that all the while occurred "in here," particularly those performed by mothers.[15] The eminently discursive character of these acts—be they consenting or resisting acts—constitutes the main focus of the text, the thread that pieces together its discontinuous fragments into the "landscape" referred to in the book's title. While on what could be conceived of as a first plane, the suicidal woman undertakes a self-regenerating, deconstructive analysis of the language that inhabits her (as it inhabits those whose voices she echoes); on the broader, second plane, the woman's life emerges as one of permanent struggle against the containing, virtually alienating function of that language. This lends the novel a metafictional, theoretical dimension, which suggests the extent to which individual historical consciousnesses are thoroughly overwritten by the words that speak them; no revolution has succeeded in smoothly replacing these words with putatively more truthful, liberating ones. Which is not to say that the protagonist's voyage through the text of memory does not move toward, and provide a model for achieving, this very goal.

By positioning the main character between the choice of silence and complete self-annulment offered by an overdose of Valium and the choice to survive and speak through recollection, Gersão emblematizes a broader collective impasse that is essentially one of language as both an instrument of control, of the "death" of the subject, and the necessary locus of its existence as such (Lacan 1977, 300, 308–9). Only by deliberately fleeing the easy death prepackaged in the language of hegemonic representational injunctions (learned since grade school), can the woman hope to survive as a subject while carving for herself an alternative, "real" place in language and, therefore, in history.

It is not incidental that the death of her son crystallizes the character's long-sedimented suspicion of how language mediates and authorizes the fictitious structure of the law (Lacan 310), more precisely "the right words" of Oliveira Salazar's law.[16] Empty signifiers, pure simulacra of the world without a Real referent, language appears to her as a "deserto de palavras falsas, e então ela começou a lutar contra as palavras falsas e deixou correr a sua própria voz -" [a desert of false words, and then she began to fight against the false words, letting her own voice run free -] (Gersão 1982, 15–16).

Her refusal to represent what would pass for the postcolonial, postrevolutionary "historical reality" (which supposedly would no longer allow for the death of sons) appears to be an act of resistance that goes back to a long-standing antimimetic political stand. As a child, Hortense—this being the only moment in the text in which the protagonist's name is mentioned—"always denied everything," inattentive to composition assignments on such topics as the country, the family, and God (90); as a young woman she refuses to draw "copies" of houses, "tracing her pencil against 'them', hitting them" (81); as a wife and mother, she "attempts to create a space where his [Oliveira Salazar's] law did not have any power . . . always an open house" (69). Such refusal to reproduce what is imposed upon her as "reality" may be understood as part of her own generation's program of literary resistance—refusing to "reflect" fascist rhetoric of the "happiness of the people" (94), for example, and finding ways to reinvent "the forbidden words" (82) that would hopefully topple that rhetoric. In a political context that encourages everything to be said, such anti-mimetic gestures become one woman's mode of resisting yet another injunction to represent a political fiction that exists by virtue of the signifiers that decree it. If, at a superficial level, the text's truth claims are in tune with the belief that "we have no more than words and right" (123), it constantly erodes all illusions that another authoritarian law could not possibly authorize and work through those words and that right. After all, "um dia dirão que [O.S.] nunca existiu e ressuscitá-lo-ão noutro lugar com outro nome" [one day they will say that {Salazar} never existed and they will resuscitate him in another place with another name] (139). This is why Gersão omits any direct reference to the events that surprised the country's capital on 25 April. Instead, her protagonist evokes what seems to be an isolated "miracle" occurring in an unknown beach town, during a procession in honor of the Lord of the Sea. Although the holy image suddenly falls on its own, people think that it was their own long-standing revolt against the colonial/fascist regime that caused the icon of repression to fall (110–13). Notwithstanding, in the end, the "representational" verve of this historical allegory, it does pinpoint the mystifying implications that any attempt to represent the revolution as a narrative of "popular" victory must face. To do so would amount to ignoring what Gersão's "private" and yet "public" historical documentary forcefully impresses: "não é só fora de nós que é preciso mudar o universo, é também dentro de nós que está a tentação do caminho mais fácil, a voz da resignação, do desespero e da morte, e essa é também a voz de O.S. . . ." [it is not only outside of us that the universe needs to be changed, also inside of us is the temptation of the easy way out, the voice of resignation, of desperation and of death, and that is also the voice of O.S. . . .] (146).

Complementing the previous text's strategically unitary, "intimate" perspective, *Ora esguardae* by Olga Gonçalves, also published in 1982, presents itself, instead, as a polyphonic "mural" of the postrevolutionary society searching the past for explanations of the historical deadlock that assails its present. The novel's opening lines cannot be clearer as to how its text emerges from, and yet resists, the compulsion to represent the heroic Feast of Carnations: "Falaria do júbilo, do frenesim, da glória e da coragem do acontecer. Mas calo-me. Antes olhai. Pois que tudo aconteceu tão pleno, o quê? ah sim, era ainda Abril . . ." [I would speak of the jubilation, of the frenzy, of the glory and the courage of the happening. But I'll be quiet. Instead, look. Since everything happened so fully, what? oh yes, it was still April . . .] (1987, 230). Two interdependent strategic moves are here visible. In a gesture of negation, typical of other women's fictions of the revolution, the speaker refuses to represent the narrative of historical progress encapsulated in the overtextualized memory of a joyous April. Yet rather than resorting to silence and self-effacement, a position that would only help support the continuing oppression by what may be perhaps another male-made ruse of history, the fictional author brings together a multitude of divergent voices—slogans, newspaper reports, anonymous comments, and fragments of conversations, as well as a series of first-person accounts indirectly evoking the period before and after the revolution, including the plight of the colonized.

Such voices neither converge into an encompassing linear narrative, nor do they seem to be mediated by the scriptural "I," who is just one voice among many. Such an orchestration of mutually unintelligible, only superficially "free" voices dramatizes (as in a dramatic performance) a basic lack of social and interpersonal communication, of common understanding and purpose, between people who appear to have only "words and right" (to use once again Gersão's formulation). While it does re-present the deep structural impasse that accounts for the revolutionary deadlock, it also unveils how a basically authoritarian, patriarchal law still lives on in such voices. Interestingly enough, this law is shown to be as related to Salazar's regime as it is related to the medieval law of chivalry, epitomized in the intertext serving as the generic and semantic backbone of Olga Gonçalves's "mural"—Fernão Lopes' chronicle of the 1384 siege of Lisbon by the Castilians.

It is by way of this medieval historiographical intertext that Gonçalves succeeds in displacing authoritarian conventions typical of the genre in later periods. By framing her documentary within a theatrical, "as if" mode—*Ora esguardae* is a direct quote from the beginning of Lopes's chronicle—she calls attention to herself as author and storyteller, as the one who selects, reinvents and arranges the scenes that make up her "mural." Since these may be said to tell many stories—and all the while no story at all—the narrative of a presumed emancipatory history is thereby halted. Most importantly, however, the text's own ultimate claims to explanatory truth and representational presence are therefore suspended.[29]

In *O dia dos prodígios*, published in 1979, Lídia Jorge had already experimented with a similar antirepresentational, "performative" strategy as a way to take on a historically revisionist project without falling prey to either a subjective, necessarily limiting testimony or to the temptation of "saying it all" in a pseudo-objective, "neutral" documentary.

By framing her text within a theatrical, fictional setting avowedly geared to fulfill the preestablished plan of an authorial, gender-neuter "I," Jorge cannot but warn the reader against taking the potential "reality" of her book too seriously, that is, too representationally:

Um personagem levantou-se e disse. Isto é uma história. E eu disse. Sim.
É uma história. . . . Outro ainda disse. E falamos todos ao mesmo tempo.
E eu disse. Seria bom para que ficasse bem claro o desentendimento. Mas
será mais eloquente. Para os que crêem nas palavras. Que se entenda o
que cada um diz. Entrem devagar. Enquanto um pensa, fala e se move,
aguardem os outros a sua vez. O breve tempo de uma demonstração.

[A character got up and said. This is a story. And I said. Yes. It is a story.
. . . Another one still said. And we all spoke at the same time. And I said.
It would be good to make the misunderstanding very clear. But it will be
more eloquent. For those who believe in words. So that what each one
says is understood. Come in slowly. While one thinks, speaks and moves
about, let the others wait for their turn. The brief period of a demonstration.] (1979, 13)

The plurivalent word "demonstration" is well calculated. As Olga
Gonçalves would also later do, Lídia Jorge privileges the act of showing
(rather than telling) in order to make an ironic statement on traditional
historiographical writing as well as on the making of history itself. It performs, while simultaneously eroding, the illusion that historical characters
are preexistent to and autonomous from the authors who construct them.
The image of people speaking—some more, others less, but with no one
really hearing, let alone comprehending, any other—invites, in itself, a
historical reading. Yet the novel evades the possibility of being read as a
simple allegory for what can be called—if only too naively—"historical
reality."

Exploiting the referential ambiguity of the magic-realist mode, *O dia
dos prodígios* stages the communication gap affecting a group of semiliter-
ate peasants first visited by the supernatural omen of a flying reptile and,
one year later, by military heroes proclaiming the strange word *re-vo-lu-
ção* and announcing that they have brought the villagers freedom, justice,
and equality (152–54). This basic plot, structured by a number of parallel
narratives focusing on the everyday lives of antagonistic neighbors, ex-
plodes politicians' rhetorical investment with the idea of popular unity in
and for democratic change, emblematized in the revolution's famous motto
O povo unido jamais será vencido (A united people will never be van-
quished). In addition, the weblike structure of the stories that unfold from
the vision of the "prodigy" reveals how the failure of the revolution to
effectively transform relations of power can be genealogically traced to the
representational/reproductive trap set in the home through the cultural
mediating function of women, particularly women as mothers.

Inasmuch as women, following a Lacanian argument, can be considered the guardians of the symbolic order in their roles as "phallic mother[s]" (Lacan 1985, 76) the possibility of instilling a rupture or breaking free from this order seems to be curtailed. But this may not necessarily be true: at least, Lídia Jorge's literary "demonstration" so suggests, especially through the treatment of the symptomatically named character of Branca.[18] Just as her husband's work mule flees from him one day, leaving him angry and perplexed, so too Branca is bound to break free from Pássaro's possession.

The flying reptile, which some women of the community reportedly see and interpret as an omen for an unforeseeable future, may be thought of as that minute, apparently insignificant but potentially disruptive force that exists within each villager's home in the form of female work beasts, be they mules or wives/mothers. In fact, Lídia Jorge's exploitation of the derogatory colloquial term for women's supposedly deceitful and inconstant nature—*mula*—is supported by the implicit association between women, work mules, and reptiles. Shortly before the appearance of the military "saviors," the village's bard, Macário, improvises a significant song that is clear in this respect: "Que essa magana do pasto. Da espessura dum tostão. Morava em todas as casas. À espera de ocasião" [That lascivious snake of the wild grass. As thick as a penny. Was living in every house. Waiting for the right moment] (152). Evidently relying on the biblical notion that there is a devilish Eve behind every Virgin Mary, the idea that wives can turn out to be snakes, free and lascivious she-devils, is nothing short of provocative. It summons forth Hélène Cixous's (and Claudine Hermann's) poetic-theoretical hypothesis of women's ability to "steal and fly away," that is, to appropriate for an ulterior liberating use the cultural images that act as forms of physical and spiritual containment for females at large.

After years of silence and submission, Branca is empowered to speak and be heard thanks to the truly female art of embroidering—a bedspread, of all things. But what she embroiders, day after day, is not a typical flowers-and-hearts pattern; it is, on the contrary, a strangely threatening dragonlike creature. Once her embroidery work is over, Pássaro's wife gains the attributes of such a non-referential creature by refusing to go on representing for her husband, and then for her would-be lover, the established cultural roles of wife-mother or whore (a *mula de carga* or a sly *mula/magana*). This refusal to repeat a preexisting story masked as a "natural," universal given is accompanied by Branca's ability to tell stories for which there are no concrete, historical referents. Like a mythical female prophetess, Branca gains the ability to read people's thoughts and to predict their future, thereby gaining control over the construction of (their) historical reality.

Yet, what Lídia Jorge's exemplary female character does might not be so unique after all. As early as 1959, Agustina Bessa Luís's *Sibila* already presented the idea that women's tangential position in the cultural order can turn out to be the single most important source for reinvention of self and the world. The potential for developing an antipatriarchal, antirepresentational use of language seems therefore to be the single most important means of political/historical resistance that women have at their disposal, even if this resistance is taken to be nothing more than a result of unrequited love *(Retrato)*, of motherly pain *(Paisagem)*, of madness (the fictional writer of *Ora esguardae*), or of witchcraft *(O dia dos prodígios)*—in short, of inconsequential "feminine" imaginings.[19] On the other hand, such a tangential position is precisely what enables these female characters to posit alternative models for conceiving the speaking subject as a subject-in-community.

Literally staging a failure of communication, a *desentendimento* (to use Lídia Jorge's term) that cuts across political, social, and psychosexual modes of relation, the novels under study invite the rethinking of the dynamic relationship between the public and the private, in order to confront the simultaneously personal, interpersonal, and collective ramifications of the traditional model of community. If at the "intimate" level of human contact, founded on shared emotions, interests, and mutual conveniences or, as is often the case, on a binding contract, there are soliloquies instead of dialogues, isolated desiring souls playing power games and never reaching communion, it is hardly likely that a collectivity can merge on a Kantian *sensus communis* simply because, one spring morning, some military officials decree that it be so.

From this perspective, it becomes more difficult to determine up to what an extent the captains of April, "the Party men" (Gonçalves 1975, 123), or men in general, command the role of the oppressors, and up to what an extent an undifferentiated, feminized "people" remain their silent, defenseless objects. In fact, no clear-cut homogeneous categories—be they defined in socioeconomic, regional, political, or gender terms—make any sense at all when the impossibility of revolution is conceived as the very ontological impossibility of each and every humanist belief whereupon rests the notion of a unitary subject, first and foremost, as well as the belief in language as a neutral, transparent vehicle of self-representation, communication, and social communion.

Although this line of theoretical speculation is raised by all the fictional rewritings of the revolution discussed here, it is particularly emphasized by Maria Velho da Costa's *Lúcialima* (1983). The novel articulates a rather complex, genealogical inquiry into the status of the revolution as a rhetorical site and a figure of wholeness and consensus that exist by virtue of their representation as such.

Divided into six sections corresponding to the temporal progression of one day—dawn, morning, midday, afternoon, dusk, and night—the novel presents a chronologically random series of scenes depicting various moments in the lives of five main characters between the late thirties or early forties and the year of 1973. Although these characters are involved in relationships with other characters, they never meet each other nor seem to have anything in common except, of course, the time frames in which they appear in the novel. The first section, "Dawn," apparently fulfills a prefatorial function by setting up the historical horizon against which the remaining sections are to be read. As the city slowly awakes to the military coup, the cast of characters is introduced as set cultural types: the Poet, the Crazy Woman, the Woman, the Man, and the Child. The latter, who becomes blind even before she learns how to speak, seems to be the key metaphor for the entire text, representing the darkness, the isolation, and loneliness in which every character is helplessly plunged.

On account of this perhaps too obvious fictional setup, the text's "message" appears to be straightforward, comfortably drawing upon some of the most cherished metaphors of the "old generation" of literary resistance (the neorealists). As Isabel Allegro de Magalhães notes, "the people"— "um povo afinal de 'ausentes'"—were not prepared to come together as a collective presence under the "light" of the new dawn (1987, 297–98). The lack of communication in which the characters live as if suspended in a time outside of historical time—the so-called long night of fascism—would prevent people from coming together under revolutionary action.

Incidentally, the author herself describes the text as not only a "book of reconciliation," which, of course, positions it beyond the merely denunciatory critique, but also, along with other contemporary works, as "a meditation upon the loss" (Passos 1983, 6; my translation). If such a loss refers specifically to how "the disaster" did away with the fundamental beliefs guiding a long tradition of literary resistance, it is, in fact, a much broader loss, namely, that of the belief in community.[20]

If the impossibility of the Portuguese revolution is related to the failure of language as a vehicle of thought and as a medium of communication between self-identical, unitary subjects, then it becomes necessary to conceive of nonrepresentational, nonhomogenizing forms of togetherness for politically transformative purposes. For this reason, the book's main focus is perhaps not "the people" as such but, rather, what the author describes as "the mini-nuclei of power" (7) that prevented the emergence of a revolutionary community following 25 April.

Three basic types of traditional, failed communities, corresponding to distinct yet inherently related spheres of human relations, are dramatized in the text: the social group, the heterosexual couple, and the self-identified subject. Each of these unitary formations exists by virtue of the linguistic authority that supports it, according to a preset model of "commonness" that necessarily suppresses all differences (not only between individuals but also within each person). The psychiatric female ward of a medical establishment may be pointed out as an example of the generalized hysteria resulting from the imposition, by a powerful few, of the conventions governing the first type of community; Maria Eduarda and Eduardo, the blind child's parents, are a good illustration of the devastating effects of the conjugal mandate that two-become-one; Ramos, the Poet, represents perhaps better than any other character the alienation, the emptiness, ensuing from a virtually lifelong resistance against seeing the Other in himself— the other social class, the other ideological allegiance, the other race, and subsuming all otherness, the other gender. Hence the leitmotif that is repeatedly invoked throughout the text—"Ninguém se encontra"—suggesting how the heterogenous elements cannot coalesce and "meet" in a predetermined way, moving toward a predetermined goal.

The gloomy perspective for community, emblematized in the phrase "Ninguém se encontra," is primarily articulated by those who perceive their own conflicting otherness as always ready to disrupt the fictitious wholeness of social, sexual, and psychological entities. Female characters like Maria Eduarda herself, the schizophrenic Mariana, the doctor Maria Isaura, the rich, angry, drug-addicted housewife Iza, and the homosexual Fred all repeat variations of the same phrase, as if their recognition of being "strange" not only to others but, first and foremost, to themselves made it impossible for them to be a part of any one community.

Despite Maria Velho da Costa's grim outlook on the fate of the unitary categories presupposed by the known, sanctioned models of sociopolitical and intimate "togetherness," *Lúcialima* does, however, posit other forms of grouping, other ways of relating and of conceiving the self that may bring about an effective, structural transformation of, in this case, Portuguese society. Lima, the confused yet eager soldier, and Judith, the foreigner par excellence (as Brazilian, Jewish, feminist, and a seminomadic intellectual), are able to come together momentarily because they neither have to, nor do they attempt to, erase their condition of alterity, their noncoincidental desires, their only superficially common language. And it is only as radical "others" that they find themselves to be able to inhabit a temporarily common space: "o amor . . . um compadecimento sem remédio, uma devoção a um lugar de ser, achado involuntário, um país" [love . . . a suffering without appeasement, a devotion to a place of being, involuntarily found, a country] (312). A similar form of improvised community is suggested in the playful, purely imaginary, and gratuitous relationship between the blind child, Lucinha, and the Cape Verdean boy, Chiquinho, whose fantastic flight through an undetermined open space, without either a plan or words spoken, constitutes the book's rather hopeful finale.

Such new forms of community may be thought of as, to follow Jean-Luc Nancy's suggestion, "what happens" to people once they forgo the illusions of communion, immanence and transparency, opting instead for relations of togetherness posited upon otherness and alterity without a preset unifying project or political goal (Carroll 1993, 183). In what appears to be an almost obsessional thematization of the *desencontro* or the *desentendimento* (not necessarily originating in but, more precisely, crystallized and staged by the revolutionary demand for a community), women's fictions of the revolution enact *as literature* positive models of "unworkness" that resist every unitary, hegemonic, "devastating" myth (185). Pointing to the difference, the marginality, but also stressing, all along, the cultural and ideological overdetermination of their own voice, such texts are nonetheless dialogical gestures toward communities-to-be, which amounts to saying toward the reinvention of the revolution: revolution not as a (linguistic, performative) call to order but as transformative "happening" of the necessarily unrepresentable, unsymbolized real.

For this reason, although the texts discussed here demonstrate the "gift" of free speech supposedly bestowed upon the silenced and oppressed by the military coup, they cannot but erode the myth that language is in itself a medium of self-representation, of social communion, and of political emancipation. In this scenario, women characters (though certainly not all) are shown to be culturally equipped by their very tangential position in the symbolic order to question the meanings, the political function and value of its language, thereby opening breaches in that order, which is shown to be as tyrannical and patriarchal in postrevolutionary times as it had been in the past. Sedimented in a body whose essential movements toward the reproduction of life are silent—hence Dionísio's astute remark "I do not speak to you of love," or Gonçalves's "Falaria do júbilo. . . . Mas calo-me"—this language is not based on the symbolic economy of exchange founded upon the absence of woman and of the real, but, on the contrary, it is based on what could perhaps be conceived of as a new literalism.[21]

The almost Orphic renaming of the world from a woman's point of view, be it in Dionísio's "love letter," in Gersão's empowering recollection, in Gonçalves's "mural," in Jorge's ironic "demonstration," or in Costa's "book of reconciliation," temporarily suspends the image-reproducing process called "Revolução dos Cravos," inviting further and further reinventions of both past and contemporary "historical reality." If, indeed, a coherent political program for an alternative revolution could be deduced from such scriptural acts of resistance, these present themselves to be as suspicious of the authoritarian, exclusionary consequences of their own potentially representational claims as they are suspicious of the claims made by the officially recognized history makers. Hence the (Derridean) "dance" that these texts seem to perform before our eyes, a dance whose steps must necessarily escape any choreographer's good—or bad—intentions of pinning them down to a preconceived script.

Notes

1. For a theoretical discussion of the Lacanian notion of the "feminine act" as absolute break with the symbolic order, see Zizek, 1992, esp. 44–55.

2. In "The Subject of the Political Unconscious," Gabrielle Schwab departs from Fredric Jameson's suggestive theoretical model, arguing for the need to think of politics and the psychosexual in terms of dynamic relations of interaction and overdetermination rather than simply of self-enclosed and mutually reflective homologies.

3. See the appendix for a selective list of corresponding titles and bibliographic information. Natália Correia's diary of the revolution *(Não Percas a Rosa)* as well as Agustina Bessa Luís' novels will be omitted from the present discussion since these works do not appear to foreground the problematics of representation (linguistic *and* political) of community, women and sexuality that characterizes the remaining texts.

4. Ronald Sousa's brief theoretical essay on the topic rests upon a critique of Lourenço's thesis that the revolution had been consistently hypothesized by the prerevolutionary culture. According to Sousa, it was not "the act of revolution. . . . but rather the realization of its effects" (1984/85, 355) what held sway in politically committed cultural productions before the revolution. The "inchoateness" of such effects, a result of an "inevitable lack of a governing collective praxis" (356), is what would have demanded that writers, artists, and intellectuals "explain" the events of 25 April.

5. Santos's essay, which, deliberately or not, fails to mention previous studies on the subject, is intended for an English-speaking public. One of its merits is to contextualize the novels discussed—none of which was written by a woman—within the broader tradition of political resistance in twentieth century Portuguese literature, particularly with regard to the diverse late off-shoots of neorealism.

6. For forceful arguments suggesting that "the crisis of revolution" (Oliveira) can might be correlated to the contradictions and, in the end, conservative consequences of its mainly discursive or rhetorical character (largely sustained by the media), see the essays by Riegelhaupt, Pimlott and Seaton, and Lomax included in Graham and Wheeler 1983.

7. I refer the reader to Darlene Sadlier's overview of key novels published by Portuguese women writers from 1972 to 1981.

8. Besides the self-avowed "passionate" account *As Mulheres Portuguesas e o 25 de Abril* (1976), by Beatrice D'Arthuys, and Abílio José Salgado's very accessible *A Situação da*

Mulher na Sociedade Portuguesa Actual (1978), see also, among others, Carrilho, Romão, Silva, and Viegas for relevant information on the long-running problems associated with women's oppression, particularly in the public sector. For semiethnographic accounts of women's participation in the political movements of resistance, see Freitas 1975 and Melo 1975.

9. See, for example, the interdisciplinary collections of essays edited by Graham and Wheeler; by Ferreira and Opello Jr.; by Maxwell and Haltzel; and by Herr. Despite the conservative perspective that informs Robert Harvey's *Portugal: The Birth of a Democracy*, he at least does note that after the revolution, "[w]omen in business, much less in politics, were still a rarity: doors were still opened for men first, women second" (135).

10. This and all subsequent translations of quoted materials are mine.

11. It could be argued that the texts under discussion all explode, though in different ways, the mass-media images that led some early observers to believe that "the silent minorities, when prodded too far, can become vocal" (Harvey 1978, 2).

12. I am alluding here to Cixous's provocative metaphor in "The Laugh of the Medusa": "Flying is woman's gesture—flying in language and making language fly. . . . What woman hasn't flown/stolen? Who hasn't felt, dreamt, performed the gesture that jams sociality?" (1980, 258). Claudine Herrman's collection of essays *Les Voleuses de Langue* is inspired by this famous Cixousian passage.

13. See also, among others, Cixous, Kristeva and Bonnet. Feminist historian Joan Kelly-Gadol makes a convincing case for the possibility that major historical changes may not be perceived as such by women (in Nicholson 105).

14. In her book, *O tempo das mulheres*, Isabel Allegro de Magalhães has demonstrated that, in general, contemporary women's novels in Portugal tend to abide to a circular rather than a linear conception of time.

15. Seeing a pregnant woman while on her way to Clara's house (made pregnant by her dead son), the protagonist "tells" her silently that she too is guilty, that all the mothers are guilty for allowing their sons to go to the colonial war: ". . . e sobretudo não se finja inocente nem se arme em vítima porque também é culpada, somos todos culpados e não adianta fingir mais tempo, . . . é tempo de gritar a verdade de uma vez por todas, gritar que pactuamos contra os filhos porque nenhuma de nós disse: 'não vá' e é inútil fingir que não se é culpada. . . ." [. . . and above all don't pretend to be innocent and don't pose as a victim, because you too are guilty, we're all guilty, there's no point in denying it any longer, . . . the time has come to shout out the truth once and for all, to shout that we have conspired against our sons, because not a single one among us said "don't go," and it is useless to pretend you're not guilty. . . .] (1982, 55).

16. A graphic illustration of this Lacanian notion appears in the fragments that evoke the protagonist's experiences in grade school. The teacher, clearly described as a phallic Mother ("O.S. [Oliveira Salazar] was her mystic husband" [1982, 85]), finds it necessary to "furnish children with the right words and keep them from the false ones" (86).

17. For a more detailed analysis of Gonçalves' book, specifically as a woman- centered, revisionary historical project, see Ferreira 1989.

18. It may be noted that the name, literally meaning "white," suggests in itself the character's ability to disengage herself from the cultural myths that bind her as a woman, a wife and a mother, ironically in opposition to Pássaro ("bird"), her husband, who turns out to be a victim of his "macho" role.

19. Besides those perused thus far, other female characters who might be mentioned here are the little girl who refuses to speak while insisting on crossing over her father's

property, in Olga Gonçalves's *A floresta em Bremerhaven* (1975); and, to be discussed below, the notable case of the blind little girl in Maria Velho da Costa's *Lúcialima* (1983), who is able to visualize a very different, still unrepresentable reality, in contrast to the old, male, disillusioned poet, paragon of the so-called generation of resistance.

20. For relevant theoretical discussions on how the philosophical *and* historical condition of postmodernity has brought about the need to re-think the ideal of community see, among others, David Carroll and Iris Marion Young.

21. Margaret Homans argues that women, contrary to men, not only retain but privilege the literal or presymbolic language of the maternal (1986, esp. 12–14), an idea that—though certainly debatable from a theoretical perspective—simultaneously biologizes and genders Kristeva's notion of a disruptive "feminine language" tied to the semiotic *chora*.

Appendix

Correia, Natália. 1976. *Não percas a rosa*. Lisboa: Publicações Dom Quixote.

da Costa, Maria Velho. 1976. *Cravo*. Lisboa: Moraes Editores.

———. 1983. *Lúcialima*. 2d ed. Lisboa: O Jornal.

Dionísio, Eduarda. 1979. *Retrato dum amigo enquanto falo*. Lisboa: O Armazém das Letras.

Gersão, Teolinda. 1982. *Paisagem com a mulher e mar no fundo*. Lisboa: O Jornal.

Gonçalves, Olga. 1980. *A floresta em Bremerhaven*. 2d ed. Lisboa: Bertrand.

———. 1985. *Ora esguardae*. 2d ed. Lisboa: Bertrand.

Maria Teresa Horta. 1977. *Mulheres de Abril*. Lisboa: Editorial Caminho.

Jorge, Lídia. 1990. *O dia dos prodígios*. 6d ed. Lisboa: Publicações Europa-América.

Luís, Agustina Bessa. 1983. *Os meninos de oiro*. Lisboa: Guimarães Editores.

References

d'Arthuys, Beatrice. 1976. *As Mulheres Portuguesas e o 25 de Abril*. Porto: Afrontamento.

Bonnet, Marie-Jo. 1984. "Adieux à l'histoire." In *Strategies des Femmes,* edited by Mieke Aerts et al., 363–72. Paris: Tierce.

Carrilho, Maria José. 1975. *Alguns Dados Estatísticos Sobre a Mulher*. Lisboa: Instituto Nacional de Estatística.

Carroll, David. 1993. "Community After Devastation." In *Politics, Theory, and Contemporary Culture,* edited by Mark Poster, 159–96. New York: Columbia University Press.

Cixous, Hélène. 1980. "The Laugh of the Medusa." Translated by Keith Cohen and Paula Cohen. In *New French Feminisms: An Anthology,* edited by Elaine Marks and Isabelle de Courtivron, 245–64. Amherst: University of Massachusetts Press. Originally published in 1975.

Derrida, Jacques, and Christine V. Mcdonald. 1982. "Choreographies." *Diacritics* 12 (summer): 66–76.

Dos Santos, João Camilo. 1992. "Belles Lettres, Revolutionary Promise, and Reality." In *The New Portugal: Democracy and Europe,* edited by Richard Herr, 163–80. Research

Series No. 86. Berkeley: University of California at Berkeley International and Area Studies.

Ferreira, Ana Paula. 1989. "Para uma História-Mulher: *Ora esguardae* de Olga Gonçalves." *Luso-Brazilian Review* 26 (winter): 11–23.

Ferreira, Eduardo de Sousa, and Walter C. Opello Jr., eds. 1985. *Conflict and Change in Portugal, 1974–1984/Conflitos e Mudanças em Portugal, 1974–1984.* Third International Meeting on Modern Portugal, Durham, New Hampshire. Lisbon: Editorial Teorema.

Forrester, Viviane. 1979. "Le Truc de l'Histoire." *Tel Quel* 80 (Été): 84–90.

Freitas, Gina. 1975. *A Força Ignorada das Companheiras (Diálogos).* Lisboa: Planalto Editora.

Graham, Lawrence S., and Douglas L. Wheeler, eds. 1983. *In Search of Modern Portugal: The Revolution and Its Consequences.* Madison: The University of Wisconsin Press.

Harvey, Robert. 1978. *Portugal: The Birth of a Democracy.* London and Basingstoke: Macmillan.

Hermann, Claudine. 1976. *Les voleuses de langue.* Paris: des femmes.

Herr, Richard, ed. 1992. *The New Portugal: Democracy and Europe.* Research Series Number 86. Berkeley: University of California at Berkeley International and Area Studies.

Homans, Margaret. 1986. *Bearing the Word: Language and Female Experience in Nineteenth-Century Women's Writing.* Chicago: The University of Chicago Press.

Kristeva, Julia. 1986. "Women's Time." Translated by Alice Jardine and Harry Blake. In *The Kristeva Reader,* edited by Toril Moi, 187–213. New York: Columbia University Press.

Lacan, Jacques. 1977. *Écrits: A Selection.* Translated by Alan Sheridan. New York: Norton.

———. 1985. "The Meaning of the Phallus." In *Feminine Sexuality: Jacques Lacan and the '"École Freudienne,"* edited by Juliet Mitchell and Jacqueline Rose, 74–85. New York: Norton.

Lourenço, Eduardo. 1984. "Literatura e Revolução." *Colóquio/Letras* 78 (Março): 7–16.

Magalhães, Isabel Allegro de. 1987. *O Tempo das Mulheres: A Dimensão Temporal na Escrita Feminina Contemporânea.* Lisboa: Imprensa Nacional - Casa da Moeda.

———. 1992. "Os Véus de Artemis: Alguns Traços da Ficção Narrativa de Autoria Feminina." *Colóquio/Letras* 125–26 (Julho–Dezembro): 151–68.

Mailer, Phil. 1977. *Portugal: The Impossible Revolution?.* London: Solidarity.

Maxwell, Kenneth, and Michael H. Haltzel. 1990. *Portugal: Ancient Country, Young Democracy.* Washington, D.C.: The Wilson Center Press.

Melo, Rose Marie Nobre de. 1975. *Mulheres Portuguesas na Resistência.* Lisboa: Seara Nova.

Nicholson, Linda. 1986. *Gender and History.* New York: Columbia University Press.

Oliveira, César, et al. 1976. *A Crise da Revolução: Para uma Análise do Concreto da Revolução Portuguesa.* Lisboa: Iniciativas Editoriais.

Passos, Maria Armanda. 1983. "Maria Velho da Costa sobre *Lúcialima*: 'Este é o livro da reconciliação'." *Jornal de Letras* 58 (7–16 Maio): 6–8.

Riegelhaupt, Joyce Firstenberg. 1983. Introduction to *In Search of Modern Portugal: The Revolution and Its Consequences,* edited by Lawrence S. Graham and Douglas L. Wheeler, 3–13. Madison: The University of Wisconsin Press.

Romão, Isabel. 1977. *Discriminações Salariais Contra as Trabalhadoras Portuguesas e Remunerações Praticadas*. Lisboa: Comissão da Condição Feminina.

Sadlier, Darlene J. 1989. *The Question of How: Women Writers and the New Portuguese Literature*. Contribution in Women's Studies No. 109. New York and Westport: Greenwood Press.

Salgado, Abílio José. 1978. *A Situação da Mulher na Sociedade Portuguesa Actual: Os Preconceitos e a Luta pela Emancipação*. Lisboa: Iniciativas Editoriais.

Schwab, Gabrielle. 1993. "The Subject of the Political Unconscious." In *Politics, Theory, and Contemporary Culture,* edited by Mark Poster, 83–110. New York: Columbia University Press.

Silva, Manuela. 1984. *The Employment of Women in Portugal: Report*. Luxembourg: Commission of the European Economic Communities; Washington, D.C.: European Community Information Service.

Sousa, Ronald W. 1984/85. "Literature and the Revolution of 1974: General Directions for the Study of Contemporary Portugal." *Journal of the Society for the Study of Contemporary Hispanic and Lusophone Revolutionary Literatures* 1:353–60.

Viegas, Lia. 1977. *A Constituição e a Condição da Mulher*. Lisboa: Diabril.

Winders, James. 1991. *Theory, Gender and the Canon*. Madison: The University of Wisconsin Press.

Young, Iris Marion. 1990. "The Ideal of Community and the Politics of Difference." In *Feminism/Postmodernism,* edited by Linda J. Nicholson, 300–323. New York and London: Routledge.

Zizek, Slavoj. "Why is 'Woman' a Symptom of Man?" In *Enjoy Your Symptom! Jacques Lacan in Hollywood and Out,* 31–67. New York: Routledge, 1992.

Notes on Contributors

BOAVENTURA DE SOUSA SANTOS is a professor in the Department of Economy at the University of Coimbra, Portugal, and director of the Center for Social Studies (Centro de Estudos Sociais). He is the author of numerous books and articles published internationally. Among them are *Toward a New Common Sense: Law, Science and Politics in the Paradigmatic Transition* (1994), *Pela Mão de Alice, O Social e o Político na Pós-Modernidade* (1994), *Portugal—um Retrato Singular* (1933), *Estado, Derecho y Luchas Sociales* (1991), and *Introdução a uma Ciência Pós-Moderna* (1989).

FERNANDO J. B. MARTINHO teaches literary theory in the Department of Romance Languages at the University of Lisbon. He is the author of two books of poetry—*Resposta a Rorschach* (1970) and *Razão Sombria* (1980)—as well as several books on literary history and criticism: *Pessoa e a Moderna Poesia Portuguesa* (1983), *Pessoa e os Surrealistas* (1988), and *Mário de Sá-Carneiro e o(s) Outro(s)* (1990). He is also a contributing author for the literary journal *Colóquio/Letras*.

JOSÉ OLIVEIRA BARATA is a professor of Portuguese literature at the University of Coimbra, Portugal, where he directs the study of Portuguese theater and Portuguese baroque literature. His most recent book, *História do Teatro Português* (1992) has been preceded by various publications about theater: *Didáctica do teatro* (1979), *Estética Teatral* (1981), *Para uma Leitura de O Judeu de Bernardo Santareno* (1983), and *António José da Silva: Criação e Realidade* (1985), as well as by numerous articles, translations, and critical editions of Portuguese dramatic works.

ONÉSIMO T. ALMEIDA is chairman of the Department of Portuguese and Brazilian Studies at Brown University. Author of various books on Portuguese cultural and literary history, he has won a prize for his *Mensagem—Uma*

Tentativa de Reinterpretação (1987). A columnist for *Jornal de Letras,* Lisbon, he has also written *(Sapa)teia Americana* (1983), a book of short stories. His most recent book is a play, *No seio Desse Amargo Mar* (1992).

JOSÉ ORNELAS is a professor in the Department of Spanish and Portuguese at the University of Massachusetts-Amherst. He has published numerous articles on Portuguese contemporary fiction as well as on nineteenth-century and Lusophone African narrative. He recently co-edited *Jorge de Sena: O Homem que Sempre Foi* with Francisco C. Fagundes. He has in preparation a co-edition on contemporary women writers and a book on the fiction of the contemporary Portuguese author José Cardoso Pires.

ELLEN W. SAPEGA is an associate professor of Portuguese at the University of Wisconsin-Madison. In addition to a book-length study on the modernist prose of José de Almada Negreiros *(Ficções Modernistas: Um estudo sobre a prosa de José de Almada Negreiros, 1915–1925,* 1992), she organized and wrote the preface for the third volume of Almada Negreiros's *Obras Completas (Artigos no "Diário de Lisboa")*. She has published various articles on Portuguese modernism and on the contemporary Portuguese novel in such journals as *Colóquio/Letras, Luso-Brazilian Review,* and *Discursos.*

PHYLLIS PERES teaches Portuguese and Brazilian-African relations at the University of Maryland in College Park. Her articles have appeared in such publications as *Luso-Brazilian Review, Ideologies and Literatures, Modern Fiction Studies,* and *Calalloo.* Her book *Narrating Nation, Imagining Angola* is forthcoming from University Presses of Florida.

ISABEL ALLEGRO DE MAGALHÃES is an associate professor at the Universidade Nova in Lisbon, and currently teaches in the Department of Portuguese Studies. She is the author of *O Tempo das Mulheres: A Dimensão Temporal na Escrita Feminina Contemporânea* (1987) and numerous essays and articles published in Portuguese and international literary journals.

ANNA PAULA FERREIRA is an associate professor of Portuguese and Brazilian literatures at the University of California, Irvine. She has published a book and numerous articles on the Portuguese neorealist novel. Her latest research focuses primarily on the representation of history and sexuality in contemporary Portuguese women writers.

Index